How to
Beat the Russians

How to
Beat the Russians

by

Edmar Mednis
International Master

David McKay Company, Inc.
NEW YORK

LIBRARY OF CONGRESS CATALOGING IN PUBLICATION DATA

Mednis, Edmar, 1937–
   How to beat the Russians.

   Includes index.
   1. Chess. 2. Chess—Collections of games. I. Title.
GV1445.M35   794.1′2   78–15977
ISBN 0–679–13376–3

1 2 3 4 5 6 7 8 9 10

Manufactured in the United States of America

To my mother

Preface

Without question, the leading chess nation since the end of World War II has been the Soviet Union. Not surprisingly, many books have detailed reasons for their success; yet, nowhere have studies appeared on any weak spots the Soviets may have. They can be beaten—as Robert J. Fischer demonstrated in his 1971–72 sweep of Taimanov, Petrosian, and Spassky.

My three objectives in writing this book have been to entertain, instruct, and provide reasonably scientific information on the weak chinks in the Soviet armor. Since there is always pleasure in seeing how the mighty can be made to fall, the entertainment is obvious. Throughout the book, I have tried to present the major principles of opening, middlegame, and endgame play clearly and consistently. Since I have emphasized and explained principles and avoided the routine presentation of long complicated variations, the amateur should find the book not only entertaining and understandable, but also helpful in furthering his chess knowledge.

To give any study scientific validity, conclusions must be based on broad samplings. A detailed presentation of Soviet losses over a number of years is one approach. However, publishing costs being what they are, such a study is simply impractical. Therefore, I used all games lost by Soviet international grandmasters against foreigners in 1973. This technique yields a total of sixty-eight games, which is ample number and runs alphabetically the gamut of grandmasters from Antoshin to Vasiukov.

Besides the meaningful sample size, 1973 has other desirable characteristics. As you may recall, it was at the end of the summer in 1972 that Fischer dethroned Spassky. The Soviet functionaries took this defeat exceptionally hard and embarked on an aggressive program to reestablish Soviet chess supremacy. This meant greater opportunities, incentives, and responsibilities for the Soviet players in international competition. Thus, 1973 offered an opportunity to study Soviet grandmasters at their most serious and best.

So each player's strength could be objectively analyzed, an international (FIDE) rating system was developed. Under this system, if a player wins, he gains rating points; if he loses, he loses rating points. The brief table below gives the relative meaning of various ratings:

FIDE Rating	*Comment*
2200	Master
2450	International Master (if peak results over 24 games)
2550	International Grandmaster (if peak results over 24 games)
2600	High-quality grandmaster
2690	Karpov in 1977
2780	Fischer after 1972 Spassky match

For each player in this book, I have given the latest FIDE rating. It should be pointed out that Fischer's rating is the highest of all time. By comparison, the best 25-year averages for three other world champions are Capablanca 2685, Emanuel Lasker 2690, Botvinnik 2690.

I readily admit that the book title "How to Beat the Russians" involves the use of authorial license (e.g., Petrosian considers himself a "true Armenian," as does Vaganian; Tal is Latvian; Keres, Estonian; Tukmakov and Kuzmin, Ukrainian). Thus, a less striking, but more accurate title would have used the word "Soviets." It is quite proper, however, to consider all players as part of a collective system since—with the exception of Keres who had reached world-class status in pre–World War II Estonia—the others are very much the product of the "Soviet Chess System."

Evaluating moves by question and exclamation marks is becoming standard in chess literature. However, to ensure that the reader and author are on the same wavelength, these are the presently accepted meanings:

  ! = a strong move
  !! = a very strong move; a fantastic move
  ? = a bad move; a weak move
  ?? = a horrible move; a blunder
  !? = an enterprising move; a move worthy of consideration
  ?! = a dubious move, for theoretical or practical reasons

In compiling information for this book, these standard sources were used: personal knowledge, personal contacts, and leading chess books and periodicals. When appropriate, direct credit is given in the text. I do want to acknowledge the assistance of Mr. V. Baturinsky, Director of the Central Chess Club of the U.S.S.R., who provided some of the biographical information. As always, my deepest gratitude goes to my wonderful blonde wife, Baiba, not only for typing the entire manuscript but for never-ending physical and moral support.

In an undertaking of such scope, some errors of fact and interpretation are almost inevitable. The author accepts responsibility for all of these. Your assistance in bringing them to my attention will be appreciated.

New York, 1977 EDMAR MEDNIS

Contents

xiv   *Contents*

How to
Beat the Russians

Chapter 1

How to Beat the Russians: Statistics, Reasons, Explanations

Well, how can we beat the Russians? In my extensive study of Russian games, the Russians were found to have these strengths and weaknesses:

1. The Russians, although far from invincible with White, are more likely to lose with Black.

Of the 68 lost games in this book, 39 (57 percent) were lost with Black. That the Russians—like everyone else—are more likely to lose with Black is not surprising. What is surprising is the relatively high number of losses with White. This unusual ratio results from a Soviet policy which dictates that one should try to win with White, whereas with Black a draw is fine. This strategy is used in team tournaments and matches, major activities of Soviet chess life. Given the high number of White losses, however, this strategy seems less successful in practice than in theory.

Therefore, don't think your chances of winning with Black are zilch—they are considerable.

2. The Russians lose relatively few games as a direct result of opening errors.

In only 13 of the games (that is, 19 percent) was opening play directly responsible for the Russian losses. As serious professionals, the Soviets are well versed in modern opening theory, and it is unrealistic to expect them to be easily outplayed in this phase. If they stick to good lines, they handle them well. Their weakest spot in this phase is a tendency to indulge in unjustified opening experiments. In 12 (18 percent) of the games, this tendency was directly or partially responsible for losses. Opening novelties did, however, account for 14 (21 percent) of their opponents' wins.

1

Overall, don't count on a Russian to misplay a known opening. Opening successes depend on your original discoveries or on your opponent's unjustified and unexpected experiments.

3. The choice of an opening system is basically unimportant, though with White closed openings offer somewhat better prospects.

Since the Soviets are well prepared for all opening systems, it hardly matters which one you choose. When choices are available, a closed opening for White is usually somewhat more effective than a KP opening. Of the 39 games won by White, 22 (56 percent) were closed openings and 17 (44 percent) were KP. These statistics correlate well with the middlegame finding that strategic motifs trouble the Soviets more than tactical threats. Conversely, it makes little difference where Black steers the opening. In 15 (52 percent) of the games, Black defended against the KP (9 of the 15 were Sicilians) and won; and 14 (48 percent) of the wins were scored against closed systems.

4. The chances of beating the Russians in the endgame are slight.

Only 11 (16 percent) of the games were lost because of endgame errors, and two of these (Games 12, 13) were time-control flukes. Thus, the chances of outplaying a Soviet in an even or theoretically drawn endgame are poor. Again, this is because the Russians are serious professionals who spend much time studying the technical aspects of endgame positions and play. In addition, they are experienced, practical players who have encountered many, many endgame positions in their tournament careers. Endgame principles are less prone to exceptions than those for the middlegame. Thus the practical Russian player knows best those principles that change least.

The above situation does not mean you should be reluctant to enter into a superior endgame against a Soviet. Superior endgames are always delightful because they offer fine winning chances with minimum risk of losing.

5. The primary arena for beating the Russians is the middlegame.

Nearly two-thirds (44 out of 68 games or 65 percent) of the Soviet losses came in the middlegame. Unquestionably, this is the area in which they are most vulnerable. In the middlegame, deep strategic concepts, creativity, and original thought assume the greatest importance, and general technical knowledge and experience diminish in importance. And so it is in the middlegame that the talented and less experienced nonSoviet can compete effectively with his professional Soviet counterpart.

6. The Russians are more likely to err in strategic than tactical positions.

Although combinational motifs are an integral part of any game, tactics often recur. As practical players the Soviets are very strong in tactics. In only 25 of 66 applicable games (38 percent) were errors in tactics responsible for the loss. Again, it was in positional judgment that most of the errors occurred.

7. The Russians are much more likely to make errors in defending than in attacking.

Only in 13 out of 55 cases (24 percent) did the Soviets misplay an attack seriously enough to lose the game. This is not surprising given their strong points: solid opening knowledge, which enables them to attack right out of the opening, tactical ability, and practical experience (attacking motifs generally recur more often than defensive strategies). Losses from defensive errors are more than three times (76 percent vs. 24 percent) higher.

8. The Russians suffer somewhat from time pressure.

Considering their great technical knowledge and extensive experience, you would not expect the Soviets to have trouble with time pressure. Nonetheless, in slightly more than one-fourth (18 of 68 = 26 percent) of the losses, time pressure was a significant factor. Thus, in strategically unfamiliar situations, the Soviet player must think as much as anyone else.

9. The surest way to beat the Russians is to play better; by hoping for a lucky break you have little chance of success.

As excellent practical players, the Soviets rarely beat themselves. Only 11 (16 percent) of the games were lost by carelessness (i.e., blunders) and only 6 (9 percent) by trying too hard to win. In most of the games, 51 of 68 (75 percent), their opponents simply outplayed them.

10. Psychological factors influenced the results of a moderate number of games.

The Soviets are generally calm, knowledgeable, and practical. They are very much human, however, and in 14 games (21 percent) psychological factors were a major factor in these losses.

11. The strongest players have the best chance of defeating the Russians.

Grandmasters have a much better chance (49 of 68 for 72 percent) of defeating the Soviets than other competitors (19 of 68 for 28 percent). However, since nongrandmasters scored more than one-fourth of the successes, there is no reason to approach a game against a Soviet grandmaster with undue awe.

More informative than the overall numbers are individual results. The most successful "Russian killers" are grandmasters Lajos Portisch of Hungary and Jan Smejkal of Czechoslovakia, both having defeated five. Both are well known as meticulous students of openings and as sensible strategists. Tied for 3rd and 4th place, with three wins each, are grandmasters Vlastimil Hort of Czechoslovakia and Wolfgang Uhlmann of East Germany. Again, both are basically strategists. By contrast combinational/tactical adherents fared poorly; for instance, Larsen had only two wins, Ljubojevic only one.

To summarize the above analysis: avoid the Soviet strengths; that is, their great theoretical knowledge of both openings and endgames, their experience, continuous practice, and fine tactical ability.

The keys to beating the Russians are:

• Select a healthy sensible opening. If you have made a significant discovery, fine, but don't expect to put something over in a known position.

• Emphasize a thoughtful strategic approach in the middlegame.

• Avoid all unnecessary complications once you have an advantage.

• Play the whole game with confidence.

The Russians can be beaten!

Chapter 2

Antoshin, Vladimir

Not every grandmaster can be front-line and Vladimir Antoshin—a grandmaster since 1964—is not. Antoshin has participated in five U.S.S.R. Championships and been a member of two winning U.S.S.R. student teams; his FIDE rating of 2475, although perfectly respectable, is the lowest in this book. Among his best international results are first place at Zinnowitz 1966 and second place at Ve ice 1966. At Budapest 1973, he tied for 7th–8th with an 8–7 score; at Reykjavik 1976, he scored 9–6 and tied for 5th–6th.

Antoshin was born in Moscow on May 14, 1929. He now works as an administrator for the Soviet Chess Federation, with the official title of "trainer."

GAME 1

White: V. Hort
    (Czechoslovakia)

Black: V. Antoshin
    (U.S.S.R.)

Played at Budapest (Hungary) International Tournament, February 21, 1973, Round 8.

Reti Opening

The Czech grandmaster plans to go for a win by setting up a strategically sound but unbalanced position. Here, just a bit of carelessness allows Black to make a creative and vicious attack, and he gains a sound extra pawn in an endgame. The practical cost, however, is a huge expenditure of time, resulting in severe time pressure. To take advantage of this, White plays for complications by attacking Black's King, even though little material remains on the board. White's strong nerves carry the day when Black panics, blunders, and suddenly finds himself facing an unstoppable mate threat. A gutsy win by White; a very unlucky loss by Black.

1. P–QB4   N–KB3
2. P–KN3   P–B3
3. N–KB3   P–Q4
4. P–N3

Hort plans to go for the win by establishing a sound, unbalanced, strategic, full-play middlegame. He sees no need to play 4. B–N2!?, which could allow Black to win and retain the QBP after 4. . . . PxP!?.

4. . . .   B–N5

Black chooses the most active and modern continuation. With this move, Black shows his readiness to exchange his QB for White's KN at the proper moment. This reduces White's control over the key Q4 and especially the K5 central squares. Other theoretically sound approaches for Black are 4. . . . B–B4 and 4. . . . P–KN3 followed by 5. . . . B–N2.

5. B–KN2   QN–Q2
6. B–N2   P–K3

A logical central and developmental move. There is also the opportunity for a sharper approach: 6. . . . BxN!? 7. BxB P–K4! 8. P–Q3 B–B4 9. P–K3 Q–K2 10. O–O P–K5, with Black having full and sound equality in Andersson–Vaganian, Hastings 1974/75, which was drawn in 29.

7. O–O   B–Q3
8. P–Q4

8. P–Q3 followed by 9. QN–Q2 seems logical to keep the central diagonal open for the QB and to reinforce White's K4-square. With the immediate 8. . . . BxN! 9. BxB O–O Black can prevent White from gaining anything, since after 10. N–Q2 P–QR4 the passive location of White's QN does not allow much opportunity for action. This point was well demonstrated in Ribli–Geller, Round 13 (Black's KB was on K2 and White had not played P–QB4); Black easily equalized and drew in 31 moves.

8. . . .   O–O
9. QN–Q2   Q–K2

A dual-purpose move: preparing a potential central advance by means of . . . P–K4 and enabling . . . B–QR6 to exchange White's QB.

10. P–QR3

Preventing the second of Black's plans. At the start of this round, both Hort and Antoshin have 4–3 scores and are anxious to improve their tournament standing. After the text move, the middlegame offers more strategic play than would follow after the exchange of the dark-square Bishops. The disadvantage is that White gives up a full tempo for development, and this is just sufficient for Black to equalize. According to theory, White's most accurate continuation is 10. R–K1, after

10. . . . B–QR6 11. Q–B1!
BxB 12. QxB White has a slight
advantage because of his greater
central space.

10. . . .   P–K4!

This liberating advance establishes approximate equality.

11. BPxP   BPxP

Black must retain central influence. 11. . . . NxP? 12. P–
K4! N–B3 13. Q–B2 with White
better is therefore inferior.

12. PxP   NxP

Black's active piece placement compensates for his isolated QP. White's safest approach is 13. NxN BxN 14. BxB
QxB 15. N–B3. But this offers
little in the way of winning
chances, so White plays . . .

13. N–Q4?!

Hort does not overlook the
rejoinder but judges it harmless.
It turns out to be anything but
that.

13. . . .   N–Q6!
14. B–QB3?!

Continuing to rate Black's
13th as harmless. After the safe
14. Q–B2! Black's advantage,
if any, is minute.

14. . . .   QR–B1
15. Q–B2

What now, Knight?

15. . . .   NxP!!

A most brilliant, creative,
sound sacrifice, whose deep
point appears as late as move
22. The practical difficulty is
that the preparation and execution of such sacrifices requires
time-consuming thought. Too
often serious time trouble results, which then spoils everything that has been achieved.

16 KxN

The King ventures out be-
cause 16. RxN fails to 16. . . .
Q–K6 17. R–QB1 BxRP and
Black regains, with interest, his
sacrificed material.

16. . . .   KR–K1!

The quiet first point. The obvious threat is 17. . . . Q–

K6ch, and White's response is
the only reasonable one.

17. Q–Q3   BxKP!!

A second brilliant sacrifice
whose primary purpose is to
gain time for . . . N–N5 *check.*

18. NxB

18. QxB allows the same
move, 18. . . . N–N5ch!, and
after 19. K–N1 (19. QxN? Q–
K6 mate) QxQ 20. NxQ RxN
White's position is so awkward
that he loses back even more
material than he gained.

18. . . .   N–N5ch
19. K–N1

19. K–K1? is punished by 19.
. . . RxB! 20. QxR QxN mate
and 19. K–B3? by 19. . . .
RxB! 20. NxR (20. QxR QxN
mate) 20. . . . NxPch 21. K–
B2 B–B4ch followed by mate.

19. . . .   QxN
20. R–B3?!

At first glance, this is a satisfactory answer; however, Black
sees far more deeply than
White. It may be more difficult
for Black to handle the sharp 20.
QxQP!?, after which the position remains exceedingly complicated. For instance, Black can
win back most of the sacrificed
material with 20. . . . B–B4ch
21. K–R1 N–B7ch 22. RxN
BxR! and still maintain a strong
attacking formation. The situation is unclear, however. Clearly

unsatisfactory for White is 20.
QxQ?, which transposes into the
note after White's 18th move.

20. . . .   QxQ
21. RxQ   RxB!!

The third brilliant sacrifice of
the game.

22. RxR   B–K4!

This elegant followup is the
ultimate point of Black's play.
Any attempt to save the Rook
allows 23. . . . B–Q5ch, so . . .

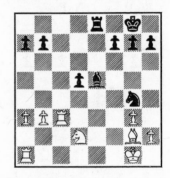

23. R–Q3?!

White has had enough of the
complications and is satisfied
to enter a pawn-down, opposite-
color Bishops endgame. This
gives White fair drawing
chances. Even so, the complicated 23. R/3–QB1! (but not
23. R/1–QB1? B–Q5ch 24. K–
R1 N–B7ch 25. K–N1 N–K5ch
26. K–R1 NxR) seems like the
right move. Black does have a
perpetual check in hand after
23. . . . B–Q5ch 24. K–R1
(24. K–B1?? NxP mate) N–
B7ch 25. K–N1 N–K5ch 26.

K–R1!, but attempts for more give no clear advantage.

23. . . .   BxR
24. RxP   N–K6

Starting here, Black, despite (or possibly because of) great time pressure, ignores the safety of his King. He has clearly won the battle, but ultimately he loses the war. A nice safe move here is 24. . . . N–B3!, which keeps White's Rook away from the seventh rank. Black does not need to rush matters—the important thing is to get safely to move 40.

25. R–Q7   NxB
26. KxN   P–KN3

Objectively this is playable, but it needlessly weakens the KR3- and KB3-squares. This proves decisive at the end. The good, safe move is 26. . . . P–KR3!.

27. N–B4

27. RxNP?? R–K7ch and Black wins the Knight.

27. . . .   P–QN4
28. N–Q6   R–K6
29. NxBP?!

White, speculating on Black's time pressure, plays for an attack against Black's King. The move carries definite hazards for White but in the end leads to a win. The sound way to go for a draw is to exchange all Queenside pawns starting with 29.

NxNP!. The resulting position, in which Black has a 3P vs. 2P advantage on the Kingside, is a theoretical draw.

29. . . .   RxP
30. RxP   B–Q5!
31. N–R6ch   K–R1

Again playable but dangerous. Much safer *and* stronger is 31. . . . K–B1!. Then after 32. RxP RxRP! Black's QNP is a very dangerous threat.

32. R–Q7   B–K6?

Attributable to time pressure. Obviously correct is 32. . . . B–N7!, which not only keeps the KB3-square protected but also ensures winning the QNP.

33. N–N4   B–B8??

Protecting against a nonexistent threat (34. NxB) and ignoring the real one (34. N–B6). 33. . . . B–N4 may not be fully satisfactory after 34. P–KR4 P–R4 35. N–K5 followed by 36. NxPch, but Black can still keep equality after 33. . . . K–N1! 34. N–B6ch K–B1 35. NxPch K–K1. Then, because of the threat to the QRP, White seems to have nothing better than to take the perpetual check after 36. N–B6ch, etc.

34. N–B6

And so the combination of the King in the corner and the weakness of Black's KB3 leads to an unstoppable mate on KR7. Tragic!

| 34. | . . . | R–N7ch |
| 35. | K–R3 | **Black resigns** |

GAME 2

White: V. Antoshin
        (U.S.S.R.)

Black: G. Sax
        (Hungary)

Played at Budapest (Hungary) International Tournament, March 1, 1973, Round 14.

Grünfeld Defense

White uses a rather obscure opening system and emerges with a clear spatial and developmental advantage. But by being too greedy, he throws away his pluses to gain a rather inconsequential pawn. As compensation, Black gets good squares for his pieces. Soon a position results in which White can do nothing with his extra pawn. The position remains in balance, until White plays to win with a ridiculous Queen retreat, instead of accepting the draw by repetition of moves, and soon suffers a painful loss. Black storms in with his pieces and opens lines in front of White's King; suddenly there is no defense to mate.

This game demonstrates excellent practical middlegame play by the youthful Sax, who deservedly punishes White for trying to win with stupid moves.

1. P–Q4

Antoshin, a strategist, generally opens with the strategic QP.

1.	. . .	N–KB3
2.	P–QB4	P–KN3
3.	P–KN3	

The KB fianchetto is a popular, sound, flexible approach. The centrally sharpest move is 3. N–QB3.

| 3. | . . . | B–N2 |
| 4. | B–N2 | P–Q4 |

With this move, Black establishes the Grünfeld Defense, named after Austrian Grandmaster Ernst Grünfeld, who demonstrated its playability in the early 1920s. The Grünfeld, Black's most unbalancing response to the QP, is a popular weapon when Black is playing for a win. In this defense, Black invariably allows White to build a strong center, hoping eventually to attack and annihilate it. If this does not turn out successfully, Black may be smothered.

Instead of the text move, Black can also choose 4. . . . P–Q3, leading to the King's Indian Defense, or 4. . . . P–B4, which often leads to the Benoni Defense or the Yugoslav Variation of the King's Indian. An interesting example of what can happen when both sides are satisfied with a draw occurred in Round 1, Antoshin–Adorjan (after 4. . . . P–B4): 5. N–KB3 Q–R4ch 6. B–Q2 Q–N3 7. N–B3 PxP 8. N–QR4 Q–Q3 9. B–B4 Q–N5ch 10. B–Q2 Q–Q3 11. B–B4 Q–N5ch 12. B–Q2 draw!, because of the three-fold repetition of position.

5. PxP   NxP
6. P–K4

This continuation has gone out of style because such sharp advances have been shown to be too early for White to adopt. The normal and popular approach now is 6. N–KB3 followed by 7. O–O.

6. . . .   N–N5!

Sharpness is required to take advantage of White's incomplete development. Black's move has two tactical points: (1) 7. N–K2? loses a pawn after 7. . . . BxP! 8. NxB QxN 9. QxQ N–B7ch followed by 10. . . . NxQ; and (2) 7 Q–R4ch? fails

to 7. . . . N/1–B3 8. P–Q5 N–Q6ch 9. K–B1 (or 9. K–Q2 NxNP!) NxB 10. PxN P–QN4! 11. Q–B2 BxP!!.

6. . . . N–N3 is too passive, and White gets nice if small advantage: 7. N–K2 O–O 8. O–O P–K3 9. N–R3!.

7. P–QR3

Chasing the Knight where it basically wants to go. 7. P–Q5 is more logical, but Black obtains full counterchances with 7. . . . P–QB3!.

7. . . .	N/5–B3
8. P–Q5	N–Q5
9. N–QB3	O–O
10. KN–K2	B–N5

In combination with the next move, this is a rather artificial concept which allows White to achieve a significant central superiority. The correct and book move is 10. . . . P–QB4! to fortify the powerfully placed Knight. After 11. O–O P–K4 Black's chances were at least equal in Donner–Keres, Beverwijk 1964.

11. O–O   B–B6?!

And here 11. . . . NxNch 12. NxN P–QB3 is a better approach.

12. BxB	NxBch
13. K–N2	N–K4
14. P–B4	N/4–Q2
15. B–K3	

With strong, simple moves White achieves a significant advantage in development and in central space. He stands better.

15. . . .   **P–QB3**
16. **Q–N3**   **N–N3**
17. **PxP?!**

This premature dissolution of the central tension throws away nearly all White's advantage. He does win a Queenside pawn, but Black's compensation is sufficient. The strategically correct approach is 17. KR–Q1! followed by 18. QR–B1 with a clearly superior position.

17. . . .   **NxP**
18. **KR–Q1**   **Q–B1!**
19. **BxN**

Here 19. QR–B1 has no meaning because of 19. . . . N–R4 followed by 20. . . . N/4–B5. So White takes the pawn.

19. . . .   **PxB**
20. **QxP**

Leads to nothing. The more patient 20. N–Q5! Q–K3 21.

P–K5 still allows White to retain a slight edge.

20. . . .   **N–R4!**

From now on the game becomes increasingly Black's, though White never seems to realize that things are changing. Black wins the game by patient, purposeful strategy, combining throughout attack and defense. His compensation for the pawn rests on a number of imperceptible factors: White's somewhat loose Kingside, pressure and attacking chances against White's Queenside, and a good diagonal for the KB. Equally important is that White has no opportunities either for active play or to realize his Queenside pawn advantage.

21. **Q–B2**   **Q–B5**
22. **R–Q5**   **P–K3**
23. **R–QB5**   **Q–R3**
24. **R–Q1**   **KR–Q1!**

Black is unafraid to exchange a pair of Rooks since he will obtain control of the Q-file.

25. **RxRch**   **RxR**
26. **P–K5**

To close off the Bishop's diagonal is logical. However, there is a cost attached to it: White is now weaker along his KR1–QR8 diagonal. This weakness will be decisive.

26. . . .   **B–B1**
27. **R–N5**   **N–B5**
28. **Q–B3**   **R–Q2!**

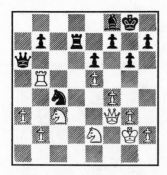

A position dynamically in balance. Black protects his QNP and threatens 29. . . . N–Q7 30. Q–K3 Q–B3ch.

29. K–R3!

Looks awkward but is required to prevent Black's Queen from getting to its QB3 with check.

29. . . .   B–K2!

An excellent practical move. Black improves the position of his Bishop and awaits further developments. Now 29. . . . N–Q7 30. Q–K3 Q–B3 can be parried by 31. N–Q4!.

30. P–R4

Neither important nor harmful.

30. . . .   K–N2!

One more excellent waiting move, forcing White to decide what to do. Such a tactic is very annoying when the opponent (such as White here) is in time pressure.

31. Q–K4

White has no way to strengthen his position, so he correctly threatens to chase away the Knight.

31. . . .   N–Q7
32. Q–K3   N–B5

Black also has nothing better than to repeat the position since 32. . . . Q–B3?! is again met by 33. N–Q4.

33. Q–K4   N–Q7
34. Q–R1??

An act of sheer madness: in order to play for a win White puts his Queen on the worst square of the board and thereby allows Black's pieces to achieve total domination. Such action is explainable partially by White's time pressure but mainly by psychological factors. At the start of this round Antoshin had a respectable 7–6 score and, with White, was looking forward to improving it at the expense of young Sax, who at that moment was in last place. Sax is now a grandmaster, but at the time of the game he had just become an international master. Nevertheless, he calmly and logically demonstrates the folly of White's approach. This game illustrates what happens when obviously stupid moves are played in an attempt to win.

34. . . .   P–R4!!

Opening the KR-file is deadly.

35. P–N3?

35. Q–N2 has to be better, and after 35. . . . P–R5 36. PxP R–Q6ch 37. N–N3. Black's strongest after 35. Q–N2 is 35. . . . Q–R1! preparing for play on the KR-file.

35. . . .   P–R5!
36 Q–KN1?!

36. PxP fails to 36. . . . R–Q6ch, since 37. N–N3 leaves the other Knight hanging. 36. Q–N2 still has to be better.

36. . . .   Q–B3!

Thank you for the diagonal!

37. Q–N2   N–B6
38. Q–B2

38. K–N4 allows 38. . . . NxKPch!.

38. . . .   PxP
39. PxP   R–Q1!

On the way to the open KR-file.

40. K–N4   N–Q7!
White resigns

White is still up the Queenside pawn but has no defense to Black's threat of 41. . . . Q–R8! followed by 42. . . . Q–R4 mate. If 41. Q–K1 or 41. Q–N1 Black mates with 41. . . . Q–B6ch 42. K–R3 R–KR1.

Chapter 3

Balashov, Yuri

Yuri Balashov was born on March 12, 1949, in Shadrinsk and now lives in Moscow. Although he caught the eye of Mikhail Botvinnik early, his great leap forward came in 1973 when he became an international grandmaster. By profession a teacher, he has always "worked" as a professional chess master. His best international results include 2nd at Wijk aan Zee 1973, 2nd–3rd at Cienfuegos 1975, and winner at Halle 1976. At the 1976 Manila Interzonal, he finished a respectable 7th–9th with a 10½–8½ result.

Balashov has participated in seven U.S.S.R. Championships. His second-place finish (behind Karpov) in the strong 1976 championship was his best result. His greatest capitalistic achievement was his tie for first place at Lone Pine (U.S.A.) 1977, which was good for $5,750.

Balashov's 1977 FIDE rating is an excellent 2565.

GAME 3

White: A. Planinc
    (Yugoslavia)

Black: Y. Balashov
    (U.S.S.R.)

Played at Wijk aan Zee (Netherlands) International Tournament, January 1973, Round 13.

Ruy Lopez (Steinitz Deferred Variation)

Satisfied with his tournament standing and facing an impulsive attacking player, Balashov elects to defend a strategically cramping variation. The decision proves quite incorrect. Rather than engage in premature attacking sorties, White follows a strategy of playing clearly, simply, and well. Black is ground down without opportunities for counterplay.

1. P–K4   P–K4
2. N–KB3   N–QB3
3. B–N5

The world famous Ruy Lopez—a deadly weapon in the hands of a Fischer or Karpov. Who hasn't heard of it and what more is to be said about it? Just one brief comment may be in order, though. Despite first appearances, the "Ruy" is much more of a strategic opening than a tactical one. The Bishop move puts clear pressure on Black's K4 square and in particular on the King pawn. However, the threat is not immediate; e.g., 3. . . . P–QR3 4. BxN QPxB 5. NxP?! Q–Q5 and Black wins back the pawn and has an excellent position. Yet on a longer range basis, the Ruy Lopez is a most effective "Black center threatening" opening.

3. . . .   P–QR3
4. B–R4   P–Q3

The most common move of course is 4. . . . N–B3 and we'll see it first in game 13. The text forms the Steinitz Deferred Variation, an improved version of the basic Steinitz (3. . . . P–Q3). The interpolation of the moves 3. . . . P–QR3 4. B–R4 gives Black considerably more defensive flexibility. An obvious illustration is the "No-

ah's Ark" trap: 5. P–Q4 P–QN4 6. B–N3 NxP 7. NxN PxN 8. QxP?? P–QB4 9. Q–Q5 B–K3 10. Q–B6ch B–Q2 11. Q–Q5 P–B5 and Black wins a piece.

5. O–O

One of Robert J. Fischer's many, many contributions to opening theory is the demonstration that the immediate castling is not only completely playable, but is in fact White's most flexible approach. Here White's most unbalancing continuation is 5. BxNch, and 5. P–B3 often leads to variations similar to 5. O–O.

5. . . .   B–Q2

The sound move. The dangerous looking 5. . . . B–N5 6. P–KR3 B–R4 (now 6. . . . P–KR4!? is more common) 7. P–B3 Q–B3?! was deflated pretty well in Fischer–Geller, Bled 1961, after 8. P–KN4! B–N3 9. P–Q4 BxP 10. QN–Q2 B–N3 11. BxNch PxB 12. PxP PxP 13. NxP! with Fischer winning in 22.

6. R–K1   KN–K2

Theoretically playable but in practice quite passive. The strategic idea is for the Knight to go to KN3 where it guards Black's K4. The practical problem is that Black will have no meaningful chances for counterplay. Somewhat more active are

6. . . . P–KN3 and 6. . . . N–B3.

7. P–Q4   N–N3
8. P–B3   B–K2
9. QN–Q2

Note White's healthy play: sound development toward the center.

9. . . .   O–O

Both Keres and Tal feel that 9. . . . P–R3 to be followed by 10. . . . B–N4 is more accurate.

10. P–KR3!

A good preemptive move to prevent a . . . B–KN5 followed by . . . N–R5.

10. . . .   R–K1

Once more protecting K4. After the game Balashov criticized this move and suggested 10. . . . B–N4 instead. Although Black's KB remains quite passive throughout the game, to exchange it off for a Knight paradoxically gives White the two-Bishop advantage to go with his greater center influence. Black's problem simply is that he has chosen a sound but very passive buildup.

11. B–N3!

Black's last has weakened his KB2; so that's where White points his KB.

11. . . .   N–R5

This exchange does not lighten Black's load. Perhaps a shade better is 11. . . . B–B3 or 11. . . . B–KB1.

12. PxP!

An opportune moment to liquidate central tension. White is sure to obtain a superior, risk-free position.

12. . . .   NxNch?!

Balashov suggests 12. . . . PxP as more accurate. If then 13. NxN BxN 14. N–B3 B–B3 and Black is a move ahead of the game continuation.

13. NxN   PxP

But not 13. . . . NxP? 14. NxN PxN 15. Q–Q5 and White wins material.

14. B–Q5!

The opening phase is over and White has emerged with basic but important advantages: the more active KB, pressure against Black's KP, and pressure against Black's KB2. On the other hand Black can do nothing to White. Some pluses, no minuses: White has an ideal *practical* situation.

14. . . . B–B3
15. Q–N3

The attack against the KBP is real, whereas that against the QNP is not. Thus it is useful to precede the text move with 15. P–QN4!, thereby expanding White's space on the Queenside.

15. . . . Q–K2
16. B–K3

The Queen is trapped after 16. QxP?? KR–N1 17. QxBP R–R2.

16. . . . QR–N1

Black has no meaningful way to improve his position; e.g., after 16. . . . N–Q1 White expands on the Queenside with 17. P–QR4, and 16. . . . N–R4 allows White a favorable endgame after 17. Q–N4! QxQ 18. PxQ N–B3 19. P–R3!.

17. Q–B4 P–QN4
18. Q–K2 N–Q1
19. P–QN4! B–K3
20. B–B5 Q–Q2
21. KR–Q1!

GM Planinc gives a perfect demonstration—the first one in this book—of "how to beat the Russians": play strategically clear, healthy moves. Such an approach is doubly useful for practical play since the chances for winning are excellent, and

the dangers of losing minimal. After the text move White commands the Q-file.

21. . . . BxB
22. RxB Q–B3
23. R–QB1!

Again crystal-clear strategy: with Black's Queen on the QB-file, White prepares to open that file for his other Rook with P–QB4; he will then have strong pressure against Black's backward QBP.

23. . . . N–N2

23. . . . N–K3 is no improvement: after 24. P–N3! (not 24. NxP? N–B5!) NxB 25. RxN White will soon have doubled Rooks on the QB-file.

24. P–B4!

After careful preparation, White executes his first sharp advance in the game. Even so it comes only on the Queenside, is purely strategic, and does not threaten Black's King. Nevertheless, Black's position is nearly critical.

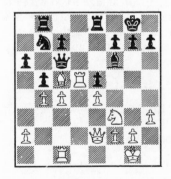

24. . . .   QR–Q1?

Now Black's position becomes critical. 24. . . . PxP 25. RxBP Q–K3 offers slender chances for defense.

25. B–K3!

Clears the QB-file for the QR and thereby threatens 26. PxP. Thus Black must capture something.

25. . . .   PxP

Will lose quickly. No better, however, is 25. . . . RxR 26. BPxR Q–Q2 27. R–B6! R–R1 28. Q–B2 B–Q1 29. NxP.

26. RxBP   Q–R5
27. RxBP

The first well-deserved fruit.

27. . . .   QxNP

No matter what Black does he will be down at least a pawn. For instance, 27. . . . N–Q3 28. B–B5 or 27. . . . RxR 28. PxR P–K5 29. RxN PxN 30. QxBP.

28. QxP   QxKP?!

Leads to the loss of the Knight. Also of little long-term use is 28. . . . N–Q3 29. B–Q2! Q–N8ch 30. R–B1 Q–N1 31. B–R5, etc.

29. R–Q2!!

If now 29. . . . RxR 30. NxR followed by capture of the stranded Knight. Thus Black must protect it.

29. . . .   R–N1

With the slender hope of 30. B–R7? N–B4!! 31. BxN? (31. Q–B1 is about even) R–N8ch 32. K–R2 Q–B5ch 33. P–N3 QxN and it is Black who wins.

30. R–N2!   Black resigns

The thematic piling up on the Knight wins it for nothing. Pointless is 30. . . . N–B4 31. RxR! RxR 32. RxN (or 32. R–B8ch or 32. Q–B8ch), etc. If 30. . . . R–K2 White has the tactical 31. QxN! QxQ 32. R/2xQ!. Black would not have needed to fear these variations if he had played 9. . . . P–KR3!?.

GAME 4

White: Y. Balashov
    (U.S.S.R.)

Black: A. Saidy
    (U.S.A.)

Played at Tallinn (Estonia) International Tournament, February 27, 1973, Round 6.

Sicilian Defense
(Closed Variation)

The American international master completely outplays his opponent in a strategic masterpiece. Whereas White can't decide what to do on the Kingside, Black very thematically gets his play going on the Queenside. He opens the QN-file and penetrates with his major pieces. The exchange of Queens is of no help to White and soon Black starts to win material. The rest is an efficient mop-up operation.

1. P–K4   P–QB4

The first of many, many—a total of twenty—Sicilians in this book. The Sicilian is by far the most unbalancing of Black's replies to 1. P–K4. In effect, Black ignores White's sharp, active first move in order to start fashioning his own play on the Queenside. Such an approach is double edged because Black runs the risk of being mated before he can accomplish anything on the Queenside. Nevertheless, the Sicilian is Black's primary weapon when he must win. In the latter stages of his 1972 match against Fischer, Spassky selected it exclusively. Generally play is tactical, the major consideration being the speed of either side's attack. In this game, however, strategic considerations soon dominate.

Overall the Sicilian is a successful defense for Black in this book: of the twenty decisive games Black wins nine.

2. N–KB3   P–Q3
3. N–B3

In place of the usual 3. P–Q4, but the text has little independent meaning or value.

3. . . .   P–QR3

An invitation to the Najdorf Variation after 4. P–Q4 PxP 5. NxP N–KB3. 3. . . . N–KB3 is also good.

4. P–KN3

A strategic decision more logical in the abstract than in practice. White enters a closed variation in which he expects Black's 3. . . . P–QR3 to be a waste of time. However, the position is not very useful for White either since the early development of the Knights has robbed the BPs of a central role. In addition, Black's third move will prove to be quite helpful later on.

4. . . .   N–QB3
5. B–N2   B–N5!?

Introduced into modern tournament practice by Fischer, which already makes it worth a closer look. The strategic idea has two points: to clear the

Queenside for quick action and to establish control of Black's key central square Q5. Black does have to allow White the two-Bishop advantage, but the closed nature of the position makes this relatively unimportant.

6. P–KR3   BxN
7. QxB

Hort–Fischer, Palma de Majorca Interzonal 1970, continued 7. BxB P–KN3 8. P–Q3 B–N2 9. P–QR4 P–K3 10. B–N2 KN–K2 11. O–O O–O 12. B–K3 Q–R4 with full equality for Black, who went on to win in 72. Balashov's move is of equivalent value.

7. . . .   P–KN3
8. P–Q3   B–N2
9. O–O   N–B3

With 9. . . . P–K3 and 10. . . . KN–K2 Black could follow in Fischer's footsteps. His move is also O.K.

10. P–KN4

White quite correctly starts activity on the Kingside, which is where his opportunities lie.

10. . . .   R–QB1

Black must exhibit necessary precaution. The immediate 10. . . . P–QN4?? is a losing blunder because of 11. P–K5!.

11. N–K2   P–QN4
12. B–Q2   N–Q2!

Both sides have completed their initial development. Black has not yet castled, but since White has no immediate threats against Black's King, Black can do so at his convenience. With the text move, Black opens the diagonal to his Bishop and establishes firm control of his Q5- and K4-squares. Chances are in balance.

13. P–B3?

But this unbalances things in Black's favor by giving him a readily attackable object. Correct is the nonweakening 13. QR–N1.

13. . . .   P–N5!

Black knows where his chances lie: along the to-be-opened QN-file and against the Queenside pawns. His execution of the strategic objectives is very impressive.

14. Q–N3   Q–N3
15. P–KB4

White's last attacking move in the game.

15. . . .	O-O
16. K-R1	PxP!
17. PxP	R-N1!

QN-file, here I come!

18. Q-K1?!

The critical moment in the game. Basically White had two choices: to go ahead with his Kingside attack, thereby handing over the Queenside to Black, or to try to minimize the danger there by adding defensive power, as he does with the text move. The tournament standings significantly influenced the course and result of this game. At the moment Balashov was undefeated and had a good 3–2 score, whereas Saidy had only one win in five decisive games. Thus Black is quite ready to play chess, that is, to find out what the position offers, whereas White prefers not to take undue chances and risk a loss. Returning the Queen, however, simply ensures that White will have *no winning* chances; the difficulties of defense remain. Such a passive approach invariably gives poor results.

Saidy correctly suggests that White should try to work up an attack with 18. P-KR4, 19. B-KR3, 20. P-N5, etc. Black is better, of course, but at least White has some chances. In the game he has none.

18. . . .	Q-N4!
19. Q-N1	Q-N7!

So that when White exchanges, Black's Rook gets to the seventh.

20. Q-B1   KR-B1

Protecting the Knight and thereby negating the threat of 21. P-K5. Throughout, Black's play is careful and incisive.

21. R-Q1	R-N3
22. B-B1	R/1-N1

QN-file, here we come!

23. QxQ

What else?

23. . . .   RxQ

The exchange of Queens has not lightened White's task. Black's Rooks control the open file; one Rook is even on the seventh. Black's Bishop and Knights have excellent objects to attack on the Queenside. In theory, White's position may be barely tenable, but in practice such joyless positions almost always are lost.

24. B-K1	R-B7!
25. R/Q-B1	

Doubling on the seventh must be prevented.

25. . . .	RxR
26. RxR	R-N7

Exchanging a pair of Rooks has not helped White much. Black's Rook towers over White's, and Black's Knights are ready to move in for the kill. Note the impotence of White's Bishop pair.

| 27. | R–R1 | N–N3 |
| 28. | P–QR4 | |

Otherwise after 28. . . . N–R5 and 29. . . . R–B7 the QBP is lost. However, Black immediately takes advantage of the weakened QN3-square.

28.	. . .	N–R4!
29.	K–N1	N–N6
30.	R–R3	P–QR4!

Not giving White the chance for a bit of air after 31. P–R5. Despite severe time pressure, Black's strategy and execution are impeccable.

31. B–B2?!

Allowing further Knight penetration. 31. K–B2 is better.

| 31. | . . . | N–Q7 |
| 32. | R–R1? | |

Leads by force to loss of material. Therefore 32. B–K1 has to be better.

| 32. | . . . | R–N8! |

The beginning of the end. After the forced exchange of Rooks, one of White's Queenside pawns will be lost. Thus the weaknesses in White's Queenside, created as a result of 13. P–B3?, will have had their effect.

33.	RxR	NxR
34.	P–Q4	NxRP
35.	P–K5	P–B5!

Fixing White's QBP and thereby accentuating its weakness.

| 36. | PxP | PxP |
| 37. | P–Q5 | |

Otherwise Black plays 37. . . . P–Q4 and protects his QBP.

| 37. | . . . | N–Q7! |

After 37. . . . N(either)xP 38. NxN NxN White has 39. BxP. Therefore, Black plans to exchange White's KB first and then go after the QBP.

38. B–N2

Desperation. There is nothing left for White.

38.	. . .	NxP
39.	N–B1	N/7–K5
40.	B–K1	B–Q5ch
41.	K–R1	B–B7
	White resigns	

Two pawns down and with more to come; e.g., 42. QBxN NxB 43. B–B1 B–B6 44. N–K2 NxP, etc. It is time to concede.

GAME 5

White: J. Timman
 (Netherlands)

Black: Y. Balashov
 (U.S.S.R.)

Played at Sochi (U.S.S.R.) International Tournament, September 1973, Round 4.

King's Indian Defense (Sämisch Variation)

White has a slight edge all the way through. The decisive strategic elements are a better Bishop and some space advantage. White builds on these until cracks appear in Black's position. With superhuman defense Black may eventually have drawn, but White's patience, perseverance, and good play bring him a deserved win.

1. P–Q4   N–KB3
2. P–QB4   P–KN3
3. N–QB3   B–N2
4. P–K4   P–Q3

Black selects the King's Indian Defense, a relatively modern concept. It came forward in full force only after World War II mainly as a result of creative contributions by Soviet analysts and practitioners. The King's Indian is another unbalancing counter to 1. P–Q4, though not so unbalancing as the Grünfeld. White has a considerable advantage in space; however, Black has a flexible, sound position and plans to undermine White's center by means of an early . . . P–QB4 or . . . P–K4. If the undermining effort is not successful, White will retain a tangible and meaningful spatial advantage. All in all, the King's Indian is a fighting defense, giving Black good winning, and excellent losing, chances.

5. P–B3

White chooses the Sämisch Variation, named for the German grandmaster who introduced it into modern tournament practice over fifty years ago. The Sämisch is at present considered to be among the very best methods against the King's Indian. Despite first appearances, the Sämisch is actually a positional, strategic variation.

White believes that, with his QBP, QP, and KP out in full, his center influence is more than sufficient, if only he takes steps to support and stabilize it. 5. P–B3 obviously supports the KP and allows 6. B–K3 without having to worry about Black's . . . N–KN5. Another popular approach for White is the so-called Normal variation starting with 5. N–B3 and 6. B–K2. (Our first example of this is Game 21, Korchnoi–Ghitescu, Bath 1973.)

5. . . .   O–O

By far the most popular and flexible move. For the unusual 5. . . . P–N3 see Game 31, Polugaevsky–Szabo, Hilversum 1973.

6. B–K3   P–K4

Historically the most common method: Black immediately and directly challenges White's QP. But as this game shows, it has the long-term strategic disadvantage of locking in Black's KB. More popular now, therefore, are systems with 6. . . . N–B3 or with 6. . . . P–N3, 7. . . . P–QR3, and then 8. . . . P–B4.

7. P–Q5

Forced and forcing. 7. PxP instead leads to an even endgame, and 7. KN–K2 blocks the KB.

7. . . .   P–B3

Attacking White's outpost is the most consistent approach, even though White is bound to retain a considerable space advantage, anyway. A reasonable alternative is Uhlmann's 7. . . . N–R4 followed by 8. . . . P–KB4.

8. Q–Q2

A good, flexible approach, once played almost exclusively. Among other plans, White gets ready for Queenside castling. Currently in fashion is the even more flexible and developmental 8. B–Q3, followed by 9. KN–K2 and 10. O–O.

8. . . .   PxP
9. BPxP

9. NxP only looks good; in reality White's center influence is lessened. After the text move, we have the basic position in this subvariation. White has a number of strategic pluses: more space, as a result particularly of his QP on the fifth rank; play against Black's Queenside, possibly along the QB-file; and the better dark-square Bishop, since Black's is hemmed in by his KP. It is usually in White's interest to exchange the light-square Bishops (Black's good Bishop) to accentuate the advantage of the one which remains. Black's counterplay is based on attacking the base of White's center pawn chain by means of a . . . P–KB4. Overall White's objective is to minimize Black's

counterplay and develop his own advantages.

9. . . .   N–R3

Aiming at QB4 without blocking the QB (as 9. . . . QN–Q2 would). The text move and 9. . . . P–QR3 are equivalent in value.

10. B–QN5!

A theoretical and strategically meaningful novelty. White develops the KB, thereby enabling further development with 11. KN–K2. White also makes it harder for Black to develop his Queenside since now 10. . . . B–Q2 leads to a Bishop exchange desirable for White. A good theoretical novelty is of extra value against the Russians for two reasons: (*1*) it tends to take away the value of their superior opening knowledge; and (*2*) by surprising them in their own backyard, it has undisputed psychological effect (Does he really know more than I?, etc.). After the known 10.

KN–K2 or 10. B–Q3 Black can equalize more easily.

10. . . .   N–R4

Here the Knight is actively but somewhat loosely placed. Better perhaps is 10. . . . N–K1!?.

11. KN–K2   P–B4
12. PxP!?

A double-edged capture which strengthens Black's center and decreases White's center influence. On the other hand, Black's forced recapture with the pawn (12. . . . BxP? or 12. . . . RxP? loses a piece after 13. P–KN4) definitely loosens Black's Kingside, and White's pieces are well situated to exploit that looseness. After 12. O–O N–B3! Black has definite pressure against White's K4 and is in a position to recapture on KB4 with his Bishop, if he so desires.

12. . . .   PxP
13. O–O   N–B2?!

The QN is not able to get to a useful spot via this route. Timman suggests 13. . . . N–B4 14. P–QN4 N–Q2 as a better approach.

14. B–QB4   N–B3
15. P–QR4!

Necessary to prevent Black's counterplay. The immediate 15. B–KN5?! allows 15. . . . P–N4! (16. NxP?? NxN 17. KBxN Q–N3ch wins a piece for Black).

15. . . .	K–R1
16. B–KN5!	

An annoying pin. If now 16.
. . . Q–K1, then Black's QN
has no place to go.

16. . . .	N/2–K1
17. N–N3!	P–B5

Handing over full control of
White's K4-square to White, but
the coming 18. B–Q3 would
force it anyway. The looseness
of Black's Kingside is quite apparent now.

18. N/N–K4	P–KR3
19. BxN!	

The Knights are of more
value here. In particular White
would willingly trade three pairs
of minor pieces in order to be
left with a Knight against
Black's locked-in KB.

19. . . .	NxB
20. B–Q3	P–R3
21. P–KN4!	

Black has not even completed
his Queenside development, but
White, with his pieces well
placed, is ready to expand his
space on the Kingside. If Black
lets the pawn be, White will play
K–R1 and then prepare to play
on the Kingside, Queenside, or
both, for he then has a clear advantage everywhere. And if
Black captures, . . .

21. . . .	PxP e.p.
22. PxP	NxN
23. NxN	B–B4!?

Playing to exchange his QB
for the Knight and thus avoid
the KB vs. Knight disadvantage.
This is Black's most logical strategic approach.

24. K–N2

Black's Queen now finds a
good location on his QN3. Unfortunately this cannot be prevented by 24. Q–K3?! because
of 24. . . . Q–R4!.

24. . . .	BxN
25. BxB	Q–N3
26. R–R1	

With the threat of 27.
RxPch!.

26. . . .	R–B3
27. QR–QB1	QR–KB1
28. R–B4	

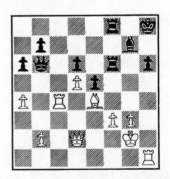

White looks better, but what
are the strategic reasons? White
obviously has the active Bishop
and chances against Black's
weakened Kingside and along
the open QB-file. On the other
hand, Black has no opportunities to attack White. This does
not mean that White's task of

realizing his advantages is easy, however. Black has quite sufficiently protected everything attackable. Sophisticated maneuvers are required to get Black to misplace his pieces, but this takes time. Thus White very practically elects to undertake nothing substantial until time control on move 40; he simply ensures that at adjournment he'll still have all the present advantages.

28. . . .	P–QR4
29. Q–B3	K–N1
30. R–R4	R/3–B2

Combinations played from a position of weakness are seldom good; here 30. . . . RxP? fails to 31. BxR P–K5 32. R–KN4! PxBch 33. K–B1.

31. P–N3	R–B3
32. Q–Q3	K–R1
33. R–R5	K–N1
34. B–R7ch	K–R1
35. B–K4	K–N1
36. B–B5	K–R1
37. R/4–R4	Q–B4
38. R–QB4	

38. B–N6 leads to nothing after 38. . . . K–N1, so White maintains the status quo.

38. . . .   Q–R6?

Black should do the same with 38. . . Q–N3!. The text is a tempting infiltration into White's position, but the Queen proves impotent as a lonely general caught behind the enemy lines. By itself the Queen can do

nothing offensively, and its absence as a defender will soon be felt.

39. P–KN4!	Q–N7ch
40. K–N3	Q–R8
41. Q–K3!	

At once preventing all checks by Black and taking up a more effective attacking location.

41. . . .	Q–Q8
42. B–K4	K–N1
43. R–R2!	R–B5
44. R/2–QB2!	

This sealed move threatens 45. R–B1! trapping Black's Queen. This gives White time to penetrate along the QB-file.

44. . . .	Q–QR8
45. R–B1	Q–N7
46. R–KR1!	

The immediate 46. R–B8 allows 46. . . . B–B3! and suddenly Black has the threat 47. . . . B–R5ch!. After the text move White has forced Black's Queen onto the seventh rank where it has much less scope than on the eighth.

46. . . .	R/1–B3
47. R–B7	R–B2
48. RxR	RxR

If 48. . . . KxR, then 49. Q–N6! is very strong.

49. B–B5	R–B3
50. R–QB1!	

The exchange of a pair of Rooks has benefited White since his remaining Rook can now develop extra power along the QB-file by going after either the seventh or eighth rank; then Q–N6 may follow.

50. . . .   P–K5!?

Positionally Black's prospects are hopelessly bleak, so he tries to get some breathing room with this sacrifice. If now 51. BxP R–B1! and Black is threatening 52. . . . B–K4ch. But White can time the capture of the KP better.

51. P–B4!   R–B1
52. R–B4!

Prepares to take off the KP efficiently and, equally important, prevents Black's . . . B–Q5.

52. . . .   P–R4
53. RxP   PxP

53. . . . P–R5ch?! just loses the pawn: 54. KxP Q–R7ch 55. Q–R3 Q–B7ch (or 55. . . . B–B3ch 56. P–N5) 56. K–N5 and it is White who is attacking!

54. BxP   B–R3?

Such an attacking move is tempting but turns out poorly. The reason in hindsight is clear: the attack doesn't amount to anything, and the Bishop will stand quite badly for defensive purposes. The only practical chance is 54. . . . Q–B6!; then after 55. QxQ BxQ Black has . . . B–QN5, which protects the QP and generally keeps the Bishop in an active spot. White's technical difficulties in achieving the win would be considerable. Things are much easier after the text move.

55. R–B4!   Q–B3
56. Q–K6ch   K–R1
57. QxQch   RxQ
58. B–K6

Note that in this endgame Black's Bishop has a significantly less useful location than above. White's active pieces, in combination with the passed KBP, must lead to a certain win. Timman's technique is very convincing.

58. . . .   R–B1
59. K–N4   K–N2
60. R–K4   K–B3
61. K–B3!

To deny Black's Bishop, after an eventual P–B5, access to White's K3-square.

61. . . .   R–K1
62. R–K2   R–K2
63. R–KR2   B–N2

64. R–QB2!   B–R3
65. R–B8

Compared to the position after White's 58th move, White's Rook is more active here, Black's less so. As a result Black has no satisfactory way to protect his QP.

65. . . .   P–N4
66. R–KR8   K–N2
67. R–N8ch

Saving time to reach the control on move 72.

67. . . .   K–B3
68. R–KR8   K–N2
69. R–Q8!

White used 30 minutes for this move in order to be completely sure of the coming complications.

69. . . .   PxP
70. PxP   R–N2
71. RxP   R–N5
72. R–Q7ch   K–N3
73. R–KB7!

Protects the KBP and clears the way for the advance of the QP. The loss of the QRP is immaterial here.

73. . . .   RxP
74. P–Q6   B–N2

Leads to a prosaic finish. The end after 74. . . . R–Q5 75. P–Q7 P–R5 76. R–B5! B–N2 (to get to KB3) 77. B–Q5!! is prettier.

75. P–B5ch   K–R3
76. P–B6   Black resigns

The Bishop is lost: 76. . . . B–R1 77. R–B8, etc. Timman considers this the best game of his life.

GAME 6

White: J. Smejkal
   (Czechoslovakia)

Black: Y. Balashov
   (U.S.S.R.)

Played at Sochi (U.S.S.R.) International Tournament, September 1973, Round 14.

English Opening

Black mixes several strategic ideas in the opening and gets a fair amount of indigestion. White saddles Black with a number of uncompensated positional weaknesses. While under an unpleasant squeeze, Black makes a middlegame error and the strategic pressure becomes unbearable. Soon White wins material, and Black resigns when he must give up even more. A clear, logical, strategic, no-risk effort by White—excellent for "beating the Russians."

1. P–QB4   P–K4
2. N–QB3   P–Q3

Theoretically a playable move but not too popular in practice. The reason is that Black sets his central pawn formation very early and thus deprives himself of flexibility in this regard. More common is to develop a Knight with 2. . . . N–KB3 or 2. . . . N–QB3.

3. P–KN3

A quiet, sound approach. Centrally more active is 3. N–B3, which we'll see in Game 27, Uhlmann–Lutikov, Leipzig 1973. The sharpest is 3. P–Q4!?, made possible by the passive nature of Black's second move. After 3. . . . PxP 4. QxP N–QB3 5. Q–Q2 White follows up with 6. P–QN3 and 7. B–N2 and has a slight central advantage.

3. . . .   B–N5?!

Unquestionably a novelty, but it does not have a sound strategic basis. Such experimentation hardly ever gives positive results. The Bishop's position on KN5 has a number of deficiencies, and what does it accomplish here? Black should imitate White by playing 3. . . . P–KN3, with an eventual . . . P–KB4 in mind. Such an approach would give meaning to

the deferral of the KN's development.

4. B–N2

Gains a tempo by attacking the QNP—the first minus of Black's third move.

4. . . .   P–QB3
5. N–B3   N–B3
6. O–O   QN–Q2
7. P–Q4!

White's nice, harmonious centrally developed position confers a small but safe edge.

7. . . .   B–K2

Black adds an element of the Old Indian to his pawn formation. Because of 4. . . . P–QB3, 7. . . . P–KN3 followed by 8. . . . B–N2 is now disadvantageous since Black's QP may be weak. The position after Black's 7th move reveals that he's mixed several opening systems. This will make it very difficult for him to come up with a meaningful plan.

8. P–KR3

What now, Bishop?

8. . . .   B–R4?!

The retreat does not work out well. Therefore 8. . . . BxN is best, even though White is left with a sound two-Bishop game.

9. N–KR4!

A creative method of taking advantage of the newly created

weakening of Black's KB4. Black should now further retreat the Bishop to KN3.

9. . . .	O–O?!
10. N–B5	R–K1?!

Too mechanical. Still best is 10. . . . B–N3 to force the Knight to declare its plans.

11. P–Q5!

White's pieces are well posted for this central advance, which ensures White new gains.

11. . . .	PxP?!

Leads to new weaknesses, for which nothing is gained in exchange. 11. . . . Q–B2 is also faulty because of 12. PxP PxP 13. NxBch RxN 14. N–N5! and Black's QP is gone. The minor evil is 11. . . . P–B4. After 12. Q–Q3, followed by 13. P–K4, White has a significant space advantage in the center. However, the closed nature of the position does not allow this to be immediately realized.

12. QNxP	NxN
13. BxN	

In strategic terms this position is very favorable to White. White's KB has a marvelous central diagonal, whereas Black's KB is tied to protecting Black's backward and weak QP. In addition Black's Q4-square has been chronically weakened. White has gained much and given nothing.

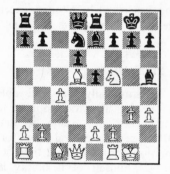

13. . . .	Q–B2
14. P–N3	B–B1
15. B–KN2	QR–Q1
16. B–N2	

The Bishop has no future here. As Smejkal points out the immediate 16. B–R3! would save White a move.

16. . . .	N–B4
17. Q–Q2	P–B3
18. KR–Q1	

Applying pressure to the backward QP.

18. . . .	B–B2
19. B–R3!	

And now the QB, too, is pointing in the right direction.

19. . . .	Q–B1
20. N–K3!	

Black's last chased the Knight where it wanted to go anyway. White's control over his Q5-square is now absolute. Black is completely without play, whereas White can further strengthen his position before undertaking definitive action.

20. . . .	P–QN3
21. QR–B1	P–B4

Unquestionably weakens the Kingside. It can hardly be criticized, however, since Black needs room to breathe.

22. N–Q5	P–KR3
23. K–R2	R–K3?

Black's position though rather without prospects is possibly tenable. But the text allows tactics that produce a strategically devastating exchange. The best way to keep the status quo is 23. . . . N–K3.

24. BxN!!

Exchanging Black's best minor piece so that all of Black's strategic deficiencies remain. The problem with 23. . . . R–K3? is that the "logical" 24. . . . QPxB fails to 25. N–B6ch and White wins the Exchange.

24. . . .   NPxB

Equivalent to 24. . . . QxB.

25. P–K4!

With no danger of a Black Knight's getting to White's Q4, White can readily weaken that square to launch an attack against Black's Kingside, particularly the light squares.

25. . . .   P–N3?!

25. . . . R/3–K1 has to be a shade better than this new weakening.

26. Q–B2!	PxP
27. BxP	K–N2
28. R–Q3!	

Going immediately for Black's chronic weakness, the QP. Throughout the game, White's general approach consists of crystal-clear strategy. About the only overt tactical possibility occurred in the note to White's 24th move, and that was the moment at which White's permanent strategic superiority was ensured.

28. . . .	B–K2
29. R/1–Q1	B–B3?!

The Bishop stands awkwardly here. The abject 29. . . . B–B1 is better.

30. N–B3!

Threatening 31. B–Q5 to exchange Black's good Bishop and make White's Knight the much superior minor piece. At the moment that threat also includes winning the QP, and Black's reply does nothing about it. Black could prolong resistance only with 30. . . . Q–N1.

30. . . .	B–K2?!
31. B–Q5	R–B3
32. N–K4	R–B4
33. BxB	RxB
34. NxQP!	

The Knight is beautiful, but a pawn is a pawn, especially here where the QP serves to support both the QBP and KP.

34. . . .	BxN
35. RxB	RxR
36. RxR	

With an attack on the KNP, thereby forcing Black's reply.

36. . . .	R–B3
37. RxR!	KxR
38. Q–Q2	**Black resigns**

White threatens both 39. QxP and 39. Q–Q6 (ch). Black resigns because he must lose additional material; e.g., 38. . . . Q–B4 39. Q–Q6ch K–N2 40. QxBP, etc.

GAME 7

White: R. Knaak
(East Germany)

Black: Y. Balashov
(U.S.S.R.)

Played at Leipzig (East Germany) International Tournament, October 1973.

Modern Benoni Defense

The characteristic situation in this opening is that White has superiority in the center while Black's chances lie on the Queenside. Some carelessness on Black's part allows White's QR to penetrate Black's Queenside, and this means that White's chances are superior across the board. When out of frustration Black weakens his Kingside, White uses sharp play to establish a very convincing attack against Black's King. To stem the tide Black acquiesces to some material inferiority, but White is not to be denied. He executes the technical part faultlessly and demonstrates that Black's last twenty moves are in vain. Overall the course of the game is an excellent illustration of the value and logic of playing a good, healthy opening system with which one is familiar. That official theory does not give its highest rating to this system is of secondary practical importance.

1. P–QB4	P–KN3
2. P–Q4	B–N2
3. N–QB3	

Now after 3. . . . P–Q3 we could anticipate the King's Indian and after 3. . . . N–KB3 either the King's Indian or Grünfeld. But with his next move Black shows that he has something else in mind.

3. . . .	P–QB4

This flank counter signifies the onset of the Benoni (the usual move order is 1. P–Q4 N–KB3 2. P–QB4 P–B4 3. P–Q5), for White's next is pretty much forced because 4. N–B3?! PxP 5. NxP N–QB3 leads to an excellent position for Black.

4. P–Q5	P–Q3
5. P–K4	N–KB3
6. B–Q3	

This and the following form a rather unusual but fully playable setup against the Benoni. It is a method which Knaak knows, likes, and has succeeded with. These considerations are more important than theory's ruling that White's most promising approach is 6. N–B3.

6. . . .	O–O
7. KN–K2	

Here, too, 7. N–B3 is possible.

7. . . .	P–K3
8. O–O	PxP
9. BPxP	

After 9. KPxP the pawn formation is rather symmetrical, the chances rather even. After the text we get the characteristically unbalanced pawn formation of the Modern Benoni. White will seek to take advantage of his extra pawn in the center by trying to get in the central advance P–K5. Black, on the other hand, has a Queenside extra pawn and will aim for a pawn advance there. The White KN is theoretically misplaced because it will not be able to directly assist in the P–K5 advance. But the Knight will find a useful spot on KN3, where it will efficiently protect the KP and thus minimize Black's counterplay against that important point.

9. . . .	QN–Q2

Obviously to overguard Black's K4. There also are other logical moves. An immediate 9. . . . P–QR3 generally leads to play similar to that in this game. In Beyen–Tal, 1972 Skopje Olympiad, Tal was successful with 9. . . . P–N3!? followed by . . . B–QR3. 9. . . . N–R3 seems somewhat less useful. In Knaak–Cobo, Camaguey 1974, White achieved a slight advantage with 10. P–KR3 N–B2 11. P–QR4 P–N3 12. B–KN5 Q–K1 13. P–B4.

10. P–KR3	R–K1
11. N–N3	P–QR3
12. P–QR4	R–N1

13. P–B4	Q–B2
14. B–K3	P–B5
15. B–QB2	

The previous moves were easy to follow. White started his play in the center, and Black took steps to contain White's central activities, while starting to fashion his own play on the Queenside. The chances are *dynamically* roughly balanced; however each side must play almost perfectly to retain this balance.

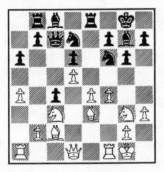

15. . . .   P–QN4?

In strategic terms this is already the losing move. To get in . . . P–QN4 is of course logical, but as played Black allows White's QR to penetrate Black's Queenside devastatingly. White's QB must be cut off from Black's Queenside, as Timman–Ljubojevic, Amsterdam (IBM) 1975 demonstrated: 15. . . . N–B4!, and now after either the game's 16. B–Q4?! or the more accurate 16. Q–B3, Black achieves full counterplay with 16. . . . P–QN4.

16. PxP	PxP
17. R–R7	

Since 17. . . . R–N2? now fails to 18. NxP, White's Rook dominates both the Queenside and part of the seventh rank.

17. . . .	Q–Q1
18. Q–Q2	P–N5
19. N–R4	

Note how useful White's KN is now on KN3 where it protects the KP.

19. . . .	B–N2
20. B–B2	B–QR1
21. B–N1!	

An excellent nothing move. White ensures that Black cannot play . . . P–N6 with a gain of time and says to Black, "Can you come up with a reasonable move now?" In cramped, lifeless positions—like Black's here—it is most difficult to play when no direct threats are involved. Black needs a "pass" move which is at least semiuseful. Something like 21. . . . R–K2 may fit the bill here. Instead . . .

21. . . .   P–R4?

At least partly out of frustration, Black feels that he must do something here and threatens 22. . . . P–R5. But the move just seriously weakens the Kingside. Note that White's previous move set it up. Today Rainer Knaak is a grandmaster, but at the time of this game he was

still a 20-year-old youngster.
Nevertheless, he handled the position like a real trooper.

22. P–K5!

From now on he plays the
position with all his youthful
vigor and energy.

22. . . . PxP
23. P–B5!

The clear weakness of Black's
KN3, as a consequence of
Black's 21. . . . P–R4? is the
rationale behind White's central break, culminating in a
pawn sacrifice.

23. . . . P–K5

The White KB's diagonal
must be shortened.

24. PxP PxP
25. B–Q4!

Except for the QN, nearly all
White's pieces are trained in the
direction of the Black King.
White threatens 26. Q–N5 since
then 26. . . . K–R2 is refuted
by 27. BxN BxB 28. RxB.
Black has no satisfactory defense. If now 25. . . . NxP
simplest is 26. BxP. Black's try
is neither better nor worse.

25. . . . BxP
26. R/7xN!

The active location of the QR
enables this fairly routine combination, whereby White wins
two pieces for a Rook.

26. . . . QxR

Or 26. . . . NxR 27. BxB
KxB 28. QxB.

27. BxN P–K6
28. Q–QB2

Black's KN3 is obviously
weak. Another advantage of 21.
B–N1! is that the Queen can
be placed on the Bishop's diagonal.

28. . . . B–B2

The weak spot must be pro-
tected. There is no time for 28.
. . . P–K7 29. NxKP RxN 30.
QxR QxN because of 31. Q–
K5! and Black will not be able
to protect all of his weak spots.

29. BxB

And now 29. . . . KxB? is
refuted by 30. NxPch! PxN 31.
Q–R7ch K–B1 32. B–N6 so
that in order to deflect the KN
Black must throw away his
passed KP.

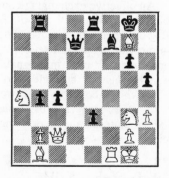

29. . . . P–K7
30. NxKP KxB
31. N–B4

White has the clear material advantage of two Knights for a Rook and pawn and again menaces Black's KN3. There is no direct defense, and 31. . . . P–N6 leads to a mating attack by White after 32. Q–B3ch. Thus Black settles for a lost endgame—no bargain either.

31. . . .	R–N4
32. NxP	Q–Q5ch
33. K–R1	P–N6
34. Q–B3	QxQ
35. NxQ	R–N3
36. N–KR4	

Now White has two Knights for a Rook. Black does have some chances in his extra Queenside pawn, but with sufficient care on White's part nothing should come of that. And White is very careful.

36. . . .	R/3–K3
37. K–R2	R–K8
38. RxBch!	

An effective exchanging combination. White gets rid of the Bishops because his has little immediate scope and sets up an endgame of two impregnable Knights against a single Rook. The whole concept goes well with the general principle: "when material ahead, exchange pieces."

38. . . .	KxR
39. B–N6ch	K–B1
40. BxR	KxB
41. N–B3	R–QB8
42. N–Q2	

Wins the QBP and destroys any hope Black may have. Even so the care with which White handles the remainder of the game is impressive. First he makes the position of his Knights and QNP impregnable and then maneuvers his Knights step by step to more active locations, without neglecting the defense of his QNP.

42. . . .	R–B7
43. NxBP	P–R5
44. N–K4!	K–K2

44. . . . RxN? 45. N–Q6ch and 46. NxR. Thus with the help of tactics White stabilizes his Knights.

45. N/K–Q2!	K–B3
46. K–N1	K–N4
47. K–B1	R–B8ch
48. K–B2	R–B7
49. K–B3	R–B8
50. N–K3	R–B1
51. N–K4ch	

After 51. NxP?! R–QN1 Black wins back the QNP. White has absolutely no rea-

son to allow such an exchange. The corollary to "when material ahead, exchange pieces" is "when material ahead, do *not* allow the *routine* exchange of pawns." The hope in superior endgames is to queen a pawn; the more pawns there are, the easier it is to do.

51.	. . .	K–N3
52.	N–Q5!	R–B7
53.	N–B4ch	K–B4
54.	N–Q3	R–B3
55.	N/4–B5	R–Q3
56.	N–B1	R–Q7
57.	N/1–Q3!	K–N3
58.	K–K3!	R–QB7
59.	NxP	K–N4

Obviously 59. . . . RxKNP? drops the Rook to 60. N–B4ch.

60.	N–Q2	**Black resigns**

With Black's last hope, the QNP, gone, there is nothing to do but give up.

Chapter 4

Bronstein, David

A leading member—if not *the* leading member—of the post–World War II generation of creative Soviet masters was David Bronstein. Born on February 19, 1924, in Belaya Tserkov (Ukraine), he lived his entire adult life in Moscow. In 1948 and 1949 he won the U.S.S.R. Championships, but it was his victory in the 1948 Interzonal Tournament at Saltsjobaden, Sweden, that brought him to the chess world's attention. Subsequently, in the Candidates Tournament at Budapest in 1950, he tied for first and then won the play-off match against Boleslavesky. Thus, in 1951, Bronstein was the official challenger to Botvinnik for the world championship. That match ended in a draw at 12–12, with Botvinnik retaining the title.

In the next world championship cycle, Bronstein tied for 2nd–4th (behind Smyslov) in the 1953 Candidates Tournament at Zurich. That tournament also marked the end of his quest for the highest of chess achievements. Although he remained a high quality grandmaster, he was never able to equal his results of the period from 1948 to 1953. Bronstein's latest international success was his tie for the first three places at Hastings 1975/76. His ultimate 1977 FIDE rating was 2560.

By profession a journalist, Bronstein has written a much-acclaimed book about the 1953 Zurich Candidates Tournament. His second book, *200 Open Games*, was published in 1970.

GAME 8

White: S. Kagan
(Israel)

Black: D. Bronstein
(U.S.S.R.)

Played at Petropolis (Brazil)
Interzonal Tournament, August
6, 1973, Round 10.

Sicilian Defense
(Najdorf Variation)

Bronstein unwisely plays into
a variation which is a specialty
of his opponent. After suffering
through an inferior opening and
middlegame he gets nothing
more for his efforts than an inferior endgame. Kagan plays the
endgame consistently and well;
in due course he transforms the
advantage of Queenside passed
pawns into the win. Another
good example in which a well-
prepared opening, followed by
consistent strategic play, is rewarded by a Russian scalp.

1. P–K4	P–QB4
2. N–KB3	P–Q3
3. P–Q4	PxP
4. NxP	N–KB3
5. N–QB3	P–QR3

The Najdorf Variation! Who-
ever has heard of chess has
heard of Bobby Fischer, and
nearly everyone who has heard
of Fischer has heard of the
Najdorf Variation of the Sicilian
Defense. The variation is named
after Argentine Grandmaster
Miguel (Misha) Najdorf, who
was the first top-level player to
demonstrate its playability.
Very early in his career Fischer
chose the Najdorf as his defense
to the KP, and until his 1972
match against Spassky, it remained essentially his only defense to 1. P–K4. But what is
good for Fischer is not always
good for everyone else! Black's
other popular 5th moves, 5.
. . . N–B3, 5. . . . P–K3, 5.
. . . P–KN3, can all be explained and justified by normal
opening considerations, such as
development or control of the
center. But what does 5. . . .
P–QR3 do? Well, it takes
Black's QN4 away from White's
KB and Knights and makes an
eventual . . . P–QN4 possible. Still that is very little considering how active White's position is in the Sicilian. The
point of the Najdorf is to challenge White in the strongest
manner possible to an unbalanced fight. Such an approach
fits Fischer's fight-to-the-end
style perfectly. The theoretical
justifications for the variation
derive from an apparently inex-
haustible series of tactical
counterchances unearthed by
Fischer and his legion of followers.

But the variation is not for
the amateurs, who will quickly
come to grief in its muddy
waters. One must be a hard-
studying professional. Bronstein

has a very broad opening repertoire which includes the Najdorf, but his selection of it is a serious psychological error. We'll have more on that in a moment.

6. P–KN3

Long out of fashion. In fact, at present the only steady user is the Israeli IM. The strategic point is to achieve a solid setup, somewhat similar to that reached after 6. B–K2 P–K4 7. N–N3 but with the KN placed more flexibly on K2 and the fianchettoed KB acting at long range on Black's Q4-square.

By far the most popular move is the sharp 6. B–N5, which we'll first see in Game 30, Timman–Polugaevsky, Hilversum 1973. The positionally active 6. P–B4 arises in Game 29, Sax–Polugaevsky, Hilversum 1973. Other popular moves are the sharp 6. B–QB4 and the positional 6. B–K2.

6. . . .   P–K4?!

With this Black enters the Najdorf proper. Objectively the move is fine so that the ?! marks are meant only for this specific instance. The choice is wrong because (*1*) Kagan is probably the world's leading expert on it, and so Bronstein is playing into his opponent's strength; and (*2*) even though Black was forewarned about it (for instance in Round 8 against Reshevsky Kagan had already

played thusly), he apparently had done no preparation for it, for he obtains a clearly unsatisfactory position out of the opening. What of the strategic trade-offs in 6. . . . P–K4? Black chases the Knight away from its active central location and achieves some control of White's Q4. On the other hand, Black's QP is rendered backward and Black's Q4-square is permanently weakened. In the course of this game, the disadvantages are clearly the more apparent.

Of course, Black could ignore 6. P–KN3 and continue 6. . . . N–B3 or 6. . . . P–KN3. In Kagan–Csom, Sao Paulo 1973, which followed the Interzonal, Black successfully employed a Scheveningenlike formation with 6. . . . P–K3.

7. KN–K2   QN–Q2

About equivalent is 7. . . . B–K2 8. B–N2 B–K3 9. P–QR4!, as in Kagan–Reshevsky, Round 8. A slight plus for White resulted after 7. . . . B–K3 8. B–N2 QN–Q2 9. P–QR4 B–K2 10. O–O R–B1 11. P–R3, in Holmov–Petkevich, U.S.S.R. Club Teams 1976. Premature is 7. . . . P–QN4? 8. P–QR4! P–N5 9. N–Q5! with advantage to White.

8. P–QR4!

But here it's necessary and useful to prevent Black's . . . P–QN4.

8. . . .   B–K2
9. B–N2   O–O

Can't be bad, but immediate Queenside development is Black's most promising route to equality: 9. . . . P–QN3! 10. O–O B–N2 11. N–Q5 NxN 12. PxN R–QB1!.

10. O–O   R–N1?!

The idea behind this move is strategically deficient. 10. . . . P–QN3 is correct.

11. P–R3

Prepares B–K3 and enables an eventual P–KN4. Kagan knows these types of positions well.

11. . . .   P–QN4?!
12. PxP   PxP
13. R–R7!?

Another good, and possibly better, move is 13 P–QN4! fixing Black's QNP. As in Game 7, the opening of the Queenside favors only White, for he controls the QR-file and at the mo-

ment even has a Rook on the seventh rank. In addition, Black has an isolated, weak QNP, a backward QP, a permanent weakness on his Q4, and absolutely nothing to show for these deficiencies. Overall White is clearly better and can look forward to a number of favorable fields of action: Queenside, center, Kingside. But most important is that White is familiar with and comfortable in these kind of positions. At the time of the game Kagan was in last place (he finished the tournament in a tie for last) whereas Bronstein was among the leaders. Yet the self-assurance with which White handles the game could easily indicate that the roles were reversed!

13. . . .   B–N2?!

Here and later Black plays too passively. Necessary is 13. . . . P–N5! 14. N–Q5 B–N2 (14. . . . NxN 15. QxN N–B4 also looks playable) 15. B–Q2 (15. B–K3!) NxN 16: PxN Q–N3 17. R–R4 B–R3! 18. RxP Q–B4 and Black had positional pressure for the pawn in Mestel–Balashov, European Team Championship, Moscow 1977.

14. B–K3   N–N3
15. P–N3   N–B1

Chasing the Rook away at the cost of misplacing the Knight. Moreover, Black's QNP is now awkward to defend.

16. R–R2	Q–Q2
17. Q–Q3	B–B3
18. N–Q5!	P–N5

Otherwise 19. N–N4. The pawn is even weaker on QN5, however.

| 19. Q–Q2 | B–Q1 |
| 20. P–N4! | |

Expanding his space on the Kingside and creating a useful place for the KN on KN3. White is better all across the board. Do note how patiently he plays to increase his advantage. Unless the position requires sharpness—which this obviously does not—such an approach is very practical.

| 20. . . . | Q–N2 |
| 21. N–N3 | NxN |

This does shield the QP but gives up more space and frees White's K4 for his pieces. Still, there is no constructive continuation.

| 22. PxN | B–Q2 |
| 23. KR–R1 | |

A little intermezzo on the QR-file. Nothing comes of it, but there is no harm done. Black is too passive to be able to undertake anything of value.

23. . . .	Q–B2
24. B–K4	P–N3
25. B–KR6	R–K1
26. K–R2	B–KB3
27. R–KN1	

Black has no play on the Queenside—his traditional area

in the Sicilian—and the center is semiblockaded, although White does have spatial advantage there. Thus in due course White is able to create realistic attacking chances on the Kingside, traditionally his strongest field of play. Black is sentenced to much long, unpleasant defending.

27. . . .	Q–Q1
28. R–R6	B–R1
29. N–B5!	

Obviously the Knight is inviolate (29. . . . PxN?? 30. PxPch, etc.), and so one more piece has become actively placed.

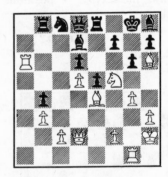

| 29. . . . | Q–B2 |
| 30. P–R4! | |

Continuing the attack.

| 30. . . . | B–N4 |
| 31. R/6–R1 | Q–B6?! |

For some reason, this move has gotten an "!" in a number of chess publications. Black, with a weak QBP and a chronically weak QP, willingly enters a much inferior ending. After the Queen exchange White's QNP becomes passed. The middlegame *is* inferior for Black, but the chances for an opponent to err in this stage are considerably higher. An inferior ending is easy to lose and offers no hope to win. A reasonable middlegame move is 31. . . . N–K2.

32.	QxQ	PxQ
33.	N–K3	B–KB3
34.	B–N5!	

White goes quickly to work on Black's weak QBP and QP. He doesn't need to worry about the resulting doubled KNPs, especially since they help to hold back Black's Kingside pawn majority.

34.	. . .	BxB
35.	PxB	N–N3
36.	N–Q1!	R/K–QB1
37.	R–N3	B–K7

The only move, otherwise Black loses the QBP for nothing. The KNP does not equal the QBP here, but it is better than nothing.

| 38. | NxP | BxP |
| 39. | N–N5 | B–B4 |

Again the only try since White was threatening both 40. NxP and 40. RxB.

40. NxP!

A play for passed pawns!

| 40. | . . . | BxB |
| 41. | NxB | |

Black can reestablish material equality in two ways, but the strategic deficiencies remain. If now 41. . . . RxP White can choose to attack with 42. N–B6ch K–N2 43. R–KB3, followed up by 44. K–N2 and 45. R–R1, or to activate his passed QP with 42. P–Q6. As played, however, Black allows White to retain connected passed pawns on the Queenside.

| 41. | . . . | NxP |
| 42. | P–QB4 | N–B5? |

The Knight is too far from the scene of action—the Queenside here. Only with the blockading 42. . . . N–N5! are there some chances for successful resistance.

43. R–R7!

It's obviously quite useful to have command of the seventh rank.

43.	. . .	R–N3
44.	R–QB3	P–R3
45.	P–B5	R–K3
46.	P–N4!	

Passed pawns must be pushed! White consistently follows this sound endgame principle. Foolish instead is 46. PxP because of 46. . . . P–N4! when Black's Kingside pawns are mobilized and his Rook is able to bother White's King.

46. . . .   PxP
47. R/3–QR3

There is more than one way to play such a position, while still keeping in mind the strategic requirements. 47. NxP is O.K. With the next move White tries to hasten his passed pawns by enchanging one defending Rook.

47. . . .   K–N2
48. R–R8   R/3–K1
49. RxR   RxR
50. P–N5!

Passed pawns must be pushed!

50. . . .   N–K3
51. P–B6   R–QN1
52. N–Q6   P–K5
53. R–R7   K–B3
54. P–B7

Wins the Knight all right but leads to considerable technical difficulties since White's pieces become awkwardly placed. IM Kaplan gives 54. R–N7! R–Q1 55. NxBP followed by an early P–N6 as a considerably simpler and surer win.

54. . . .   NxP
55. RxN   K–K3
56. N–N7   P–B4

57. P–N6   K–Q4
58. K–N2

White is a Knight and passed QNP ahead, but it is difficult to do anything with them. Black has to move his King very carefully so that White gets no opportunity for a Knight fork. Correct therefore is 58. . . . K–K3! 59. R–B6ch (59. N–B5ch K–Q3 60. N–Q7? fails to 60. . . . RxP) 59. . . . K–Q4! 60. R–Q6ch K–K4 61. R–Q7 K–B5!, and it is not really clear how or whether White can extricate his Knight without losing the QNP.

58. . . .   K–Q5?!
59. R–Q7ch   K–B6?

59. . . . K–K4? also fails because of 60. N–Q6!: 60. . . . RxP? 61. N–B4ch. However, 59. . . . K–B5! still leaves some drawing chances after 60. N–Q6ch K–B4 61. N–B7 RxP!.

60. N–B5!   K–B5

Too late now. Of course 60. . . . RxP? allows 61. N–R4ch.

61. R–QB7!   K–N4

Or 61. . . . RxP 62. N–Q7ch.

62. N–Q7

Winning easily. If the Rook moves away, the QNP moves forward. Even so it is impossible to explain why Black does not resign. White is short of time, but not *that short*.

62.	. . .	RxP
63.	NxR	KxN
64.	R–N7	K–B4
65.	RxP	K–Q5
66.	RxP	P–K6
67.	PxPch	KxP
68.	RxP	Black resigns

GAME 9

White: V. Hort
(Czechoslovakia)

Black: D. Bronstein
(U.S.S.R.)

Played at Petropolis (Brazil) Interzonal Tournament, August 12, 1973, Round 14.

Queen's Gambit Declined, Slav Defense

Hort decides on a sly method of countering Bronstein's own special variation: he's willing to give up a tempo to get the game into the normal variation. The choice turns out to be excellent since Bronstein is not at all comfortable in the normal waters. First White achieves a nice central superiority, then the two Bishops, then the Q5-square, and then a pawn. The material advantage gets exploited in an instructive passed-pawn endgame. The game is an excellent example of the effectiveness of playing away from a Russian's strength.

1.	P–Q4	P–Q4
2.	P–QB4	P–QB3

This, one of the two sound ways to reinforce Black's Q4, is called the Slav Defense. The more common method, 2. . . . P–K3, leads to various positions in the Orthodox Defense, and we'll see a number of them in this book later on. Theoretically playable, but currently unpopular, is to accept the Gambit with 2. . . . PxP.

3.	N–QB3	N–B3
4.	N–B3	PxP

Giving up of the center here leads to the variations of the Slav proper. The playability of the Slav rests on the point that the recovery of the gambit pawn by White entails certain slight disadvantages. If Black doesn't want to give up the center he can play 4. . . . P–K3, which usually leads to various Meran positions. Our first example here will be Game 20, Rukavina–Korchnoi, Leningrad 1973.

5. P–QR4

The only meaningful way to recover the pawn. However, the positional cost is a slight weakening of the Queenside and the loss of a tempo for development. But there is nothing else. 5. P–K4?! leads to a dubious gambit after 5. . . . P–QN4 6. P–K5 N–Q4, and 5. P–K3 P–QN4 6. P–QR4 does allow the eventual recovery of the pawn but under circumstances where there is no advantage.

5. . . . B–N5!?

One of a number of Bronstein's creative innovations. The usual theoretical move is 5. . . . B–B4 to directly hinder White from getting in the central advance P–K4. That is how Hort defended as Black against Portisch in round 11, and there he drew in 27. What is the point of Bronstein's move? To gain counterplay as a result of the pin on the Knight or, if the Knight moves away, on the KP. The move came as no surprise to Hort since Bronstein had been employing it successfully for years. Indeed in round 4 Bronstein had obtained a 24-move draw against Keres with it.

6. P–K3!?

But this move surely surprised Bronstein! The normal theoretical continuation is 6. N–K5 B–R4 and then either the positional 7. P–KN3, as Keres played, or the sharp 7. P–B3. With the text move, however,

Hort voluntarily allows the pin and ignores, in general, Black's possibilities. He aims for the usual Slav positions fully realizing that he may arrive a tempo down. He hopes that Bronstein will be ill at ease in them.

6. . . .	P–K3
7. BxP	QN–Q2
8. P–R3	B–R4
9. Q–K2	B–QN5

A standard maneuver in the Slav. The Bishop finds a secure home here and seeks to prevent or minimize indirectly the effect of White's P–K4.

10. O–O   Q–K2

Black aims for . . . P–K4 as quickly as possible.

**11. P–K4   P–K4
12. P–Q5**

To break the pin with 12. P–N4?! is too dangerous because of 12. . . . NxNP! 13. PxN BxP when Black has two pawns and excellent attacking chances for the sacrificed piece. Thus White must push on by.

12. . . .   P–R4?!

Bronstein has a penchant for this move in "his variation," but here it seems rather pointless. Correct is 12. . . . P–KR3!, to give the QB a convenient retreat square at KR2 and prevent a potential B–KN5 by White.

13. R–Q1!

White logically and consistently strives to support his strong point, the passed QP.

13. . . .   O–O?!

Too routine or careless. This was the last chance for 13. . . . P–R3!.

14. P–N4!

But unlike the position after Black's 11th move, here this is safe enough since White is a couple of defensive moves ahead.

14. . . .   B–N3
15. N–R4!

The correct way to play the position. After exchanging Black's QB, White will have a clear spatial advantage, a strong point on Q5, and the two Bishops, whereas Black will have nothing to counter these pluses. Faulty instead is 15. B–KN5?! P–R3 16. B–R4 B–R2! with Black having at least full equality.

15. . . .   PxP?!

As a general principle, central tension should not be resolved unless something is gained in exchange. Here Black permanently hands over control of his Q4 to White without any countergain. Black's position is somewhat lifeless, but a normal move like 15. . . . KR–Q1 to keep the status quo (suggested by GM Gheorghiu) is in order.

16. NxB   BPxN?!

Bronstein would be the first to realize that the capture toward the center is positionally correct: 16. . . . RPxN. Then after 17. NxP White has a small but safe and enduring advantage. To allow this doesn't seem practically advisable to Bronstein, so he tries to mix things up by opening the KB-file. Strategically, however, this is unsound, and it is he who gets mixed.

17. BxPch!   K–R1

In line with his previous move. After 17. . . . NxB 18. NxN White has a colossal Knight on Q5.

18. BxP!

White has to take what Black is forced to give; otherwise Black will be all right.

18. . . .   QR–N1
19. B–Q5

White has a sound pawn, and it is up to Black to demonstrate what he has for it.

19. . . .   N–B4
20. B–N5!

Developing while attacking.

20. . . .   P–R3
21. B–R4   N–K3
22. KBxN   QxB?

After this Black's cause becomes hopeless. The zwischenzug 22. . . . BxN is imperative since then after 23. PxB QxB Black doesn't have to worry about a White Knight arriving on its Q5. Black then has reasonable chances to hold a draw since White has a number of weaknesses in his position, and this makes the realization of the pawn advantage technically very demanding.

23. N–Q5!   B–B4

23. . . . NxN 24. RxN! is no better.

24. BxN!

Closing off the KB-file, establishing the Knight on Q5, and winning another pawn. Black is theoretically lost. However, the consistent accuracy of White's play is very impressive.

24. . . .   PxB
25. Q–Q2   K–N2
26. QxP

Why not? White now has two Queenside passed pawns.

26. . . .   B–Q5
27. Q–B7ch   K–R1
28. QR–B1!

With Black in severe time pressure, Hort sees that active play is the best method to underscore the many weaknesses in Black's position. If Black now plays the normal 28. . . . RxP, White has 29. R–B6 Q–B2 30. Q–Q6! followed by 31. R–B7 and the attack must be decisive. Therefore Black searches for salvation in a lost endgame, but this is hardly to be recommended.

28. . . .   KR–B1?!
29. Q–K7!   QxQ
30. RxRch   RxR
31. NxQ   R–B7
32. P–N4!

White's pride obviously is the connected passed pawns, and they must be retained. By comparison, White's KBP and Black's KNP are, at the moment, of little significance.

32. . . .   K–N2

Of course 32. . . . RxP?? is met by 33. RxB!.

33. P–N5!

Passed pawns must be pushed!

33. . . .   R-R7
34. N-Q5   RxRP
35. P-N6!

Black has recovered the QRP, but White is still ahead a strong, advanced passed QNP.

35. . . .   R-R7
36. R-N1!

Rooks belong *behind* passed pawns. After this move it is clear that White's QNP will cost Black his Bishop.

36. . . .   RxP
37. K-R1   R-B6
38. P-N7   B-R2
39. K-N2

An immediate 39. P-N8=Q BxQ 40. R-N7ch! is equally winning.

39. . . .   R-B7ch
40. K-N3   R-K7
41. P-N8=Q   BxQ
42. R-N7ch!

By taking the Bishop off with check White is able to save his KP.

42. . . .   K-B1
43. RxBch   K-B2
44. R-N7ch   **Black resigns**

Chapter 5

Furman, Semyon

Though a solid grandmaster himself, Semyon Furman is more familiar to the rest of the world as the trainer of World Champion Anatoly Karpov. Karpov has always credited much of his success to the fruitful relationship with his trainer. Furman is a teacher by profession, and this no doubt has helped in his coaching and training work. For this work he has received the title "Merited Trainer of the U.S.S.R."

Furman was born on December 1, 1920, in Gomel (White Russia) and like Karpov lives now in Leningrad. (As a matter of fact Karpov moved from Moscow to Leningrad to be near his trainer.) Furman became a grandmaster fairly late in life—in 1966. Even though he has taken part in fourteen U.S.S.R. Championships, he has never come close to winning. His best international results include first places at Kharkov 1966 and Polanica Zdroj 1967 and third at Madrid 1973 and at Bad Lauterberg 1977. Furman's 1977 FIDE rating is a good 2535.

GAME 10

White: S. Furman
(U.S.S.R.)

Black: R. Calvo
(Spain)

Played at Madrid (Spain) International Tournament, December 13, 1973, Round 14.

Catalan Opening

By playing accurately and actively, Black emerges from the opening with ready equality. When White hesitates in the center, Black quickly establishes clear superiority over both the center and Queenside. The superiority gained as a result of

strategic play is transformed
into a full point by means of
sharp tactics against White's
weakened Kingside. A perfect
blend of strategy and tactics, in
which the former is used to set
up the decisive combinational
motifs.

1. N–KB3   P–Q4
2. P–Q4

Despite starting off with the
Reti, White quickly jumps at
the opportunity to establish a
Queen's Gambit Declined, a
rather safe opening. In the previous round, Furman gained an
important victory against Uhlmann in a long tough endgame
and in this, the next to last
round, is tied for first place with
his "pupil" Anatoly Karpov. He
evidently isn't in the mood for
a tough fight, however, and this
psychological factor is significant.

2. . . .   N–KB3
3. P–B4   P–K3
4. P–KN3

Instead 4. N–B3 enters the
normal channels of the QGD.
With the text move White opts
for the Catalan, a sound opening but against which Black has
known methods for equalization, especially if White has already played P–Q4.

4. . . .   QN–Q2!?

Black selects an interesting
and an effective order of moves.
The conventional continuations

are 4. . . . B–K2 and 4. . . .
PxP.

5. B–N2   PxP
6. O–O

Safe and routine. The active
6. Q–R4, leading to play similar to the main variations, is
preferable.

6. . . .   P–B4!

Because White ignores
Black's Queenside, Black is able
to initiate freeing activity there.

7. N–R3

Again quite harmless. More
active is 7. Q–R4 or 7. PxP.

7. . . .   N–N3!
8. NxP   NxN
9. Q–R4ch   B–Q2
10. QxN   P–QN4!

Looks weakening, but Black
correctly sees that with Black's
development of the Queenside
essentially complete, White has
no way to take advantge; moreover, Black obtains a definite
spatial advantage on the Queenside.

11. Q–Q3

Tempting the QBP forward
turns out quite fine for Black.
Perhaps 11. Q–B2 is sounder.

11. . . .   P–B5!
12. Q–B2   B–B3

Black has established a sound
3P vs. 2P majority on the
Queenside, and White has an

extra pawn in the center. To obtain prospects for meaningful play, White must be able to make use of his central pawns. His next move, contesting the K4-square, is good.

13. B–N5　　B–K2
14. P–QR4?!

The accurate move order is 14. BxN! BxB 15. P–K4.

14. . . .　　P–QR3?!

With the immediate 14. . . . B–K5! Black could transpose into the text game. After Black's 14th, the chances are dynamically balanced. Black has his Queenside majority; White, if he plays resolutely, has an opportunity for an active pawn majority in the center.

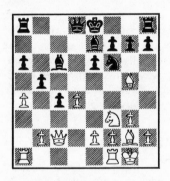

15. KR–Q1?

This routine move does nothing for the needs of the position. The only logical approach is to give up the two Bishops with 15. BxN! BxB 16. P–K4. White then has a good central

presence and chances for a full-play middlegame.

15. . . .　　B–K5!

Yes! Black now has advantages both in the center and Queenside, whereas White has nothing.

16. Q–B1　　O–O

Castling is one of the objectives of opening play. Of course, another saying goes "castle only when you have nothing better to do." Black castles ten moves later than White, only after achieving his strategic goals. On the other hand, White castled on move 6 and achieved nothing.

17. N–K5

What else?

17. . . .　　BxB
18. KxB　　P–R3
19. B–B4?!

In cramped positions, the defensive side benefits by an exchange of pieces. The right approach, therefore, is 19. BxN!. Apparently White is not aware of his position's deficiencies.

19. . . .　　R–B1
20. P–B3?!

Hoping to get in P–K4, but the move turns out to be nothing but a Kingside weakness. Opening the QR-file with 20. PxP is absolutely required to gain some breathing room for the QR.

20. . . .   N–Q4!
21. B–Q2?!

Last chance for 21. PxP!.

21. . . .   P–N5!

The first use of tactics to further a strategic aim: to advance
the Queenside pawns.

22. B–K1?!

Such passivity is doomed to
fail. White had to try the gutsy
22. NxQBP!?. Calvo gives then
22. . . . P–N6 23. P–K4 N–N3
24. B–R5 RxN 25. BxN Q–B1
26. Q–K3 R–B7ch 27. R–Q2
B–N5 "with advantage to
Black"; even so White is in better shape here than in the game.

22. . . .   P–B6!
23. P–N3?!

There really is nothing good
to suggest, but giving Black a
protected passed QBP can't be
right.

23. . . .   P–B4!
24. B–B2   B–N4
25. P–K3?!

Now the floodgates will burst.
25. P–B4 is a must. White didn't
want to weaken his K4, but the
King is more important than a
central square . . .

25. . . .   P–B7!!

Black has used fine strategy
to outplay his opponent and
achieve a marvelous position.
Starting here he shows admirable tactical sharpness and
transforms his superiority into
a win. Positionally speaking,
the text move looks quite risky
since the safe protected passed
pawn becomes a far-advanced
passed pawn with uncertain future. However, it is the start of
a devastating Kingside attack.

26. R–Q3   P–B5!!

Continuing to strike while the
iron is hot. If now 27. NPxP
BxP 28. PxB NxPch 29. K–N1
NxR 30. NxN RxP and White
is in shambles. So . . .

27. N–B4   PxKP
28. BxP   NxBch
29. NxN   P–K4!
30. P–R4   Q–B3!

Every Black move contains a
threat. There is no defense; e.g.,
31. PxB QxBPch 32. K–R3
RPxP! followed by 33. . . . R–
KB3 (or 33. . . . R–QB3) and
then 34. . . . R–R3ch. And

after 31. P–B4 annihilation follows by means of 31. . . . BxBP 32. PxB QxBP. White's text move at least leads to a unique position!

31. N–Q5   Q–B2
32. PxB   QxN
33. NPxP

There is nothing. If 33. Q–K3 RxP! 34. QxR P–K5, etc.

33. . . .   P–K5!

One more active shot—the last one required.

34. RPxP   PxR
35. PxR=
   Qch   RxQ

What an unusual sight! White is even a pawn ahead, but the unsafe King and Black's far-advanced passed pawns obviously guarantee Black a win. The passed pawns are decisive in the variation after 36. Q–K3

QxPch 37. QxQ RxQ 38. KxR P–Q7.

36. Q–R6   QxPch
37. K–R2   R–B3

Obviously the end is very, very near.

38. Q–R4   K–N2

Or 38. . . . P–Q7! 39. Q–N5ch K–R2 40. QxP R–R3ch.

39. R–K1   Q–B7ch
40. K–R3   QxR
   White resigns

Chapter 6

Geller, Yefim

For about twenty-five years now, Yefim Geller has been among the strongest grandmasters in the world. Born in Odessa (Ukraine) on March 8, 1925, he became an international grandmaster in 1952. He has participated in seventeen U.S.S.R. Championships (winning in 1955), been on six winning U.S.S.R. Olympiad teams, and has taken part in six Candidates events. His international successes are much too numerous to be listed here; among the most important recent results are first at Budapest 1973 (ahead of Karpov), first at Teesside 1975 and first at the very strong grandmaster tournament at Moscow 1975. Geller was a member of the U.S.S.R. team that played against the U.S.A. in dual matches at New York in 1954 and at Moscow in 1955. He has the best record of all top players against Robert Fischer, having defeated him five times.

Since becoming a strong master in the late 1940s he has been living in Moscow. Geller wrote *Over the Chessboard* in 1962, and his recent autobiography, entitled *Grandmaster Geller*, was published in 1976. Geller's 1977 FIDE rating is 2590.

GAME 11

White: L. Szabo
    (Hungary)

Black: Y. Geller
    (U.S.S.R.)

Played at Hilversum (Netherlands) International Tournament, June 12, 1973, Round 1.

Sicilian Defense (Dragon Variation)

The Hungarian GM demonstrates an excellent practical choice of opening variations. Rather than indulge in sharp unclear tactics—something his opponent apparently counted on—he prefers a strategically clear position in which White can count on a minute advantage. White ultimately gets an advantage of a two-to-one Queenside pawn majority. It should not be enough to win, but Black's defensive task is unpleasant and he fails to do his best. As a result White gets a passed pawn and a demonstrable technical win. The game further exemplifies the logic behind the "much to gain, little to lose" approach.

1.	P–K4	P–QB4
2.	N–KB3	P–Q3
3.	P–Q4	PxP
4.	NxP	N–KB3
5.	N–QB3	P–KN3

With this move Black establishes the Dragon Variation, a strategically sound, logical opening. The fianchettoed KB will bear down effectively on his central diagonal and the King will be ready to castle. The only very slight theoretical minus is that . . . P–KN3 weakens the Kingside and gives White's KRP an attackable object after P–KR4 and P–R5. This is exactly the factor that White tries to exploit in the most modern and popular subvariations.

Even though the Dragon is not Geller's primary weapon, he is a recognized authority on it. As a matter of fact, he was *the* author of the section on the Dragon in the *Encyclopedia of Chess Openings*.

6.	B–K3	B–N2
7.	B–K2!?	

Forty years ago everybody played thusly, but over the last twenty or so years *the method* has become the Yugoslav Attack with 7. P–B3, 8. Q–Q2, 9. B–QB4, followed by O–O–O and a Kingside pawn storm. The variations here have become very long (easily twenty moves and more), complicated, and ever-changing. Geller can be expected to be thoroughly up-to-date. Therefore Szabo prefers a change of pace. He steers the game into the "old" variation, whose major benchmarks are strategic rather than obscurely tactical. In this way he risks considerably less against a theoretically well-prepared opponent. The "old" variation may not even be inferior to the Yugoslav Attack.

7.	. . .	N–B3
8.	O–O	O–O

White has a slight central superiority because his KP is on the fourth rank, whereas Black's QP is only on the third. Theoretically speaking, if Black can get in . . . P–Q4 without incurring disadvantages he is sure of full equality. He does "threaten" 9. . . . P–Q4 now, to which White's most analyzed response is 9. N–N3. However, after 9. . . . B–K3 Black gets good development and White's chances for an advantage are quite problematical. Therefore White tries . . .

9. Q–Q2

Not as "bookish" as 9. N–N3 but at least as good.

9. . . .   P–Q4

And so Black gets in this freeing push with good chances for theoretical equality. In practice, however, the resulting positions are rather lifeless for Black and offer scant hope for anything more than a laborious draw. Theoretically no worse and practically more promising are 9. . . . B–Q2 and 9. . . . N–KN5.

10. PxP   NxP
11. KNxN   PxN
12. QR–Q1!

In conjunction with the following move, this strengthens White's play significantly. White stands clearly superior after 12. KR–Q1 B–K3 13. B–Q4 NxN? 14. QxN BxB 15. RxB Q–N3 16. R–QN4 Q–R4 17. R–QB4!, as in Mednis–Drakert, 1955 New York State Championship. However, Black saves a full tempo and obtains approximate equality with the correct 13. . . . BxB! 14. QxB NxN! 15. QxN Q–N3, as in Mednis–O'Keefe, 1956 U.S. Open Championship.

12. . . .   B–K3

By far the soundest response. After 12. . . . BxN?! 13. PxB Black's Kingside will miss the KB; after 12. . . . B–B4?! White

has 13. NxN! with greater power than in the game (Smyslov–Denker, Groningen 1946); after 12. . . . Q–B2 13. B–Q4 P–K4 14. B–B5 R–Q1 15. N–K4 B–K3 16. Q–N5 (analysis by Gufeld) White is also better.

13. NxN!

This paradoxical capture allows White to retain a slight edge. Black's center appears to be strengthened, but this will be true only momentarily. Instead, the routine 13. B–Q4 can be met by the maneuver from the Mednis–O'Keefe game, 13. . . . BxB! 14. QxB NxN 15. QxN Q–N3, and Black's good development gives him equality.

13. . . .   PxN

After 13. . . . QxN 14. P–QB4! White has the advantage of the superior Queenside pawn formation.

14. B–B3   Q–B2

The QP can't be protected, so Black must counter against White's pawns. 14. . . . BxP? is faulty because of 15. P–B4! and 16. PxP with a big plus for White.

15. BxQP   BxB
16. QxB   QxP

This is better than 16. . . . BxP?! 17. P–QB4, when after 18. P–B5 White will have a sound passed QBP. In the game White has a harder time establishing a passed pawn.

17. R–Q2

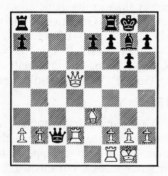

The opening phase has been completed, and White has the tangible advantage of the Queenside pawn majority. Black's extra Kingside pawn cannot forcibly be made passed, whereas White has realistic chances to do so on the Queenside. Overall, of course, White does not have all that much since Black's position is unquestionably defensible. But in a practical game White's "something" is worth a lot more than Black's "nothing."

17. . . .   Q–B2
18. P–QN4!

To be of any benefit, the majority must be mobilized.

18. . . .   QR–Q1
19. Q–K4   RxR
20. BxR   Q–Q2
21. B–K3   R–B1
22. P–QR4!

Continuing, with the help of tactics, to mobilize the pawn majority. After 22. . . . QxP?! 23. Q–N7! White will win

Black's QRP and obtain a passed QNP. Black's response is quite correct.

22. . . .   P–QR3!
23. P–R5   P–K3
24. B–B5   Q–N4!
25. P–R3!

Up to here both sides have played excellent chess, from both theoretical and practical points of view. Black has stopped, for the foreseeable future, the further advance of White's Queenside pawns. On the other hand, White does still have his majority and a position generally without risk. With the sound practical text White gives his King an escape hatch so that he won't ever have to worry about back-rank mates. White is not going to force or over-extend anything; he'll play good moves and if Black defends perfectly the game will end a draw.

25. . . .   R–Q1?!

Black takes a clear step in the wrong direction. Control of the Q–file is not at issue since Black can undertake nothing there. It is time to try to break White's Queenside formation with 25. . . . B–B1!. But Black is so transfixed by the beauty of his Bishop on the "Dragon diagonal" that he doesn't want to part with it. Yet the beautiful Bishop has nothing to do on his diagonal.

26. R–B1!   P–R4?

Now things get serious since White gets the QB-file for his Rook. It is imperative to return the Rook: 26. . . . R-QB1!.

27. B-N6!   R-Q4
28. K-R2

A move that comes in fantastically handy at the end!

28. . . .   B-B3?!

By now Geller is in time pressure, and good moves are hard to find under such circumstances. The text makes matters worse by allowing White a favorable Rook exchange. Perhaps 28. . . . B-K4ch 29. P-B4 B-Q3 is a better defense. In any case, Black's position is nearly critical.

29. R-B5!

The exchange of the Rooks breaks the blockade of White's QN5-square and thus enables White to get his Queenside pawns going. Szabo plays the resulting endgame with great energy and accuracy.

29. . . .   Q-Q2

This way Black at least gets a passed pawn. 29. . . . RxR? 30. PxR! is completely hopeless.

30. RxR   PxR
31. Q-KB4   B-K2
32. B-Q4!   B-Q3

The threat was 33. Q-R6!, and 32. . . . Q-Q3 is met by 33. B-K5 QxNP 34. Q-R6!.

33. B-K5   BxB
34. QxB   P-Q5

Allows an immediate advance of White's QNP. But even after the preferable 34. . . . Q-N4 comes 35. Q-Q6! threatening 36. Q-N6! and Black is lost.

35. P-N5!!

A beautiful tactical way to reach the strategic objective of a passed Queenside pawn. Now 35. . . . QxP? allows 36. QxQ PxQ 37. P-R6 and White queens with *check*. And little better is 35. . . . PxP 36. P-R6 P-Q6 (or 36. . . . Q-R2 37. QxNP followed by 38. Q-N7, etc.) 37. Q-N8ch K-N2 38. P-R7 P-Q7 39. P-R8=Q P-Q8=Q 40. Q-R8 mate! So Black pushes on . . .

35. . . .   P-Q6
36. PxP   P-Q7
37. Q-N8ch   K-N2
38. P-R7   P-Q8=Q
39. P-R8=Q

Four Queens make this situation unusual. White again threatens the same mate as given in the previous note, so Black must exchange a pair of Queens.

39. . . .   Q/2–Q3ch
40. P–B4   Black resigns

Actually Black was unable to complete his 40th move before his flag dropped and he lost on time. This was a humane ending to the game since after the forced 40. . . . QxQ 41. QxQ White's extra passed QRP promises a theoretical win which is not that difficult for a grandmaster to demonstrate.

GAME 12

White: P. Biyiasas
(Canada)

Black: Y. Geller
(U.S.S.R.)

Played at Petropolis (Brazil) Interzonal Tournament, August 6, 1973, Round 10.

Sicilian Defense

Geller does well enough against an unusual setup by White and has at least full equality as the middlegame is reached. However, White defends well to hold the game in balance, and Black must accept an approximately even double-Rook endgame. Searching for winning attempts, Geller gets into serious time pressure and compounds his difficulty by choosing a rather complicated variation. With three moves to go both sides have horrible hallucinations, and Black oversteps the time limit on move 40. A loss caused by being over-eager to win an even position.

1. P–K4   P–QB4
2. N–KB3   P–Q3
3. B–N5ch

Formerly thought to be a harmless amateur check, this move acquired a solid reputation in tournament practice in the 1970s. From a developmental point of view White quickly clears the Kingside for castling and is then ready for rapid central action. And there is a logical strategic point also. After the exchange of Bishops White can get a Maroczy type of pawn formation (P–QB4 and P–K4), thereby limiting Black's potential counterplay from either . . . P–QN4 or . . . P–Q4. Note that as a result of exchanging his KB, White doesn't have to worry about having a bad Bishop in the Maroczy formation.

3. . . . B–Q2

The normal response. There is no reason to allow a pin with 3. . . . N–QB3, and 3. . . . N–Q2 is a bit unsound, though well suited to a risky attempt at winning.

4. BxBch QxB
5. O–O

The immediate 5. P–B4 is most common here, though the text is perfectly O.K.

5. . . . N–QB3

Or 5. . . . N–KB3.

6. P–QN3?!

The IM and Canadian Champion is a resourceful player who does not, however, pay much attention to opening theory. The fianchetto of the QB has nothing to do with either the strategic or developmental requirements of the position, and it allows Black to effortlessly get at least equality. The modern approach is 6. P–B4! with a nice slight plus for White.

6. . . . N–B3
7. R–K1 P–KN3

O.K., but since Black will soon play . . . P–K4, the Bishop will be rather dead here. More effective is 7. . . . P–K4! 8. P–B3 B–K2 9. P–Q4 O–O 10. PxBP PxP 11. QxQ NxQ as in Suba–Ghitescu, 1973 Rumanian Championship (by transposition), with some endgame advantage for Black who is better developed.

8. B–N2 B–N2
9. P–B4

So White does set up a Maroczy pawn formation but loses considerable time in misplacing the QB. A more logical followup to White's 6th is 9. P–Q4 with approximate equality.

9. . . . P–K4!

Prevents any play White could have in the center, and deadens White's Bishop. Black now has a slight edge because he will be able to develop some play on the Kingside, whereas White is ill-placed to do anything on the Queenside. This is just the reverse of the situation usually true in the Sicilian, but the blocked center changes the scene drastically. White's central bastion K4 is to be attacked by Black's . . . P–KB4, whereas Black's . . . P–QB4 should be attacked by White's P–QN4. Black is closer to realizing his plan than White is.

10. N–B3 O–O
11. P–Q3 N–KR4

Black is obviously ready for play along the KB-file with . . . P–KB4, whereas White has prepared nothing on the Queenside. Black's a shade better, but White's position is quite defensible. From now up to move 38 White plays perfect chess, doing whatever the position requires.

12. N–Q5!   N–K2!

The dominating Knight must be eliminated. 12. . . . P–B4?! is premature because of 13. PxP, and the centrally desirable 13. . . . PxP? fails to 14. NxP!. After 13. . . . RxP 14. N–Q2! White has full control of the important K4-square.

13. B–B1!

White realizes which is the proper diagonal for this Bishop. Somewhat late, but not too late!

13. . . .	**NxN**
14. BPxN	**N–B5**
15. BxN	**PxB**
16. R–QB1	**QR–K1**
17. Q–Q2	**P–B4**

Black gets in this thematic advance and stands slightly better.

18. N–N5!

The threat of 19. N–K6 forces the following exchange, whereby White's pawn formation is improved.

18. . . .	**PxP**
19. PxP	

After 19. N–K6?, very strong is 19. . . . P–B6!.

19. . . .	**Q–N5**
20. N–B3	

Forced, since 20. N–K6? again allows 20. . . . P–B6. After the text move Black still stands a shade better because of his Kingside chances. Most exact now is 20. . . . B–K4!, which would blockade White's KP and prepare a pawn advance on the Kingside.

20. . . .   Q–R4?!

The Queen gets in the way of its own pawns here. The correct approach is still 20. . . . B–K4!, and if 21. P–KR3 Q–Q2! (22. N–N5? P–B6!).

21. P–KR3	**P–N3**
22. P–QN4!	

So White starts his thematic Queenside play—late, but not too late!

22. . . .   B–K4

A required blockading move. After the immediate 22. . . .

P–KN4?! White establishes strong counterplay with 23. PxP NPxP 24. P–K5!.

23. P–QR4!   P–KN4!

More thematic play by both sides.

24. NxB   RxN
25. P–B3   Q–N3
26. K–B2!

White gets his King out of the way of Black's coming pawn storm. White is able to neutralize Black's threats on the Kingside and create some play on the Queenside. The position remains in dynamic balance.

26. . . .   P–KR4
27. R–KR1   Q–N2

27. . . . P–N5!? 28. RPxP RPxP 29. QR–KN1 is double-edged, but if Black is hell bent to win, that is a logical approach. It is surely more effective than Black's try later on in the Rook endgame.

28. PxP   NPxP
29. Q–B3   R–N1
30. R–QN1!

White is ready to obtain an advantage on the Queenside, so Black must acquiesce to an even double-Rook endgame.

30. . . .   R/4–K1
31. QxQch   KxQ
32. K–K2

Both sides correctly centralize their Kings.

32. . . .   K–B3
33. K–Q3   K–K4
34. K–B4   R–KR1

The endgame is even, and considering his time shortage, Black's soundest approach is to offer a draw. At the moment Geller was only a half point out of first place and a draw with Black would not really be unsatisfactory. Nevertheless, he had decided that a win against the youthful Canadian was a must. The result was a very unpleasant loss caused by seriously overestimating the condition of his own nerves.

35. P–R5!

What now, Black?

35. . . .   KR–QB1

Preparing the following unclear sacrifice. A safety-first move is 35. . . . P–R3, and after 36. R–N6 RxR 37. PxR R–QN1 38. R–QN1 R–N2 we have a successful double blockade for a draw.

36. KR–N1!

Accurately anticipating Black's plan, White protects his KNP, which Black could possibly be attacking with an eventual . . . R–QB7.

36. . . .   R–N5ch?!

Objectively the move is O.K., but it leads to no advantage, and it is quite foolish, almost madness, to make it in time pressure. A waiting move or maneuver such as 36. . . . R–Q1, following by . . . R–K1, . . . R–KB1, etc., is in order to reach the safety of the time control on move 40.

37. RxR   PxRch
38. K–N5??

Completely overlooked by Black in his calculations. Instead Black anticipated 38. KxP R–QN1ch 39. K–R3 R–N4 40. K–R4 R–N7, and he has reached the time control. Even so, the chances here are also about even. Black has compensation for the pawn but no more.

The text, though unexpected, is based on a hallucination which gripped both players not only during the game but apparently thereafter.

38. . . .   K–Q5??

Black is too unnerved to think clearly. Correct is the obvious 38. . . . P–N6! and White is lost. White no doubt intended 39. K–R6 P–N7 40. R–N1, but

overlooked the devastating strength of 40. . . . R–QN1!! 41. KxP R–N5. White's King is a captive on the edge of the board, his Rook can't move, and Black wins easily by infiltrating with his King; e.g., 42. P–R6 K–Q5 43. K–R8 K–B6 44. P–K5 PxP 45. P–Q6 K–B7 46. RxPch KxR 47. P–Q7 R–Q5, etc. In his notes to the game Geller gives 39. K–N4! as drawing against 38. . . . P–N6, but that must also be based on some hallucination. Obviously after 39. . . . P–N7 40. R–N1 R–B7 White's position is hopeless after either 41. K–N5 RxP or 41. K–N3 RxP.

39. K–R6!

Going after QRP is very strong in this position.

39. . . .   P–N6
40. R–Q1ch!

Black overstepped the time limit and lost.

White's last move also came as a surprise to Black, and as

he was searching for a reply, his flag fell. The proper response is the retreat 40. . . . K–K4!. Then after 41. KxP R–B5! (given by Geller in his notes to the game) 42. K–N6 R–N5ch White is somewhat better, but Black's active Rook placement should allow him to hold the draw.

GAME 13

White: Y. Geller
(U.S.S.R.)

Black: L. Portisch
(Hungary)

Played at Portoroz (Yugoslavia) Playoff Match Tournament to select qualifiers for Candidates matches, September 10, 1973, Round 5.

Ruy Lopez (Breyer Variation)

A game Geller loses rather than Portisch wins. Employing a theoretical opening novelty, White enters the middlegame with a slight but clear advantage. Continuing resolutely he wins a pawn by move 26. For the next 60 moves he remains a pawn ahead. However, because of time pressure he does not play most accurately in the first session and the material advantage subsequently turns out to be insufficient to win. But Geller refuses to accept the ob-

vious and drives himself so hard that he loses control of the situation, unexpectedly oversteps the time limit, and loses. A tragic example of self-pressure. Portisch delivers an excellent demonstration of how to hold an inferior position for a draw, but the other half point is a gift from Caissa.

1.	P–K4	P–K4
2.	N–KB3	N–QB3
3.	B–N5	P–QR3
4.	B–R4	N–B3
5.	O–O	B–K2

Entering the labyrinth of the "closed" variation. The "closed" is by far the most modern way of defending the Ruy. Black prepares to castle and will then try to defend his K4 central post. The other main variation is the "open" with 5. . . . NxP and we'll see that in game 22. It is not at all clear that Black has an easier time defending in the former than in the latter. The reason for the popularity of the closed variation is simply that when Black currently allows the Ruy, he looks forward to a slow, strategic, maneuvering game rather than a sharp tactical one. The closed variation offers this; the open does not.

6.	R–K1	P–QN4
7.	B–N3	P–Q3
8.	P–B3	O–O
9.	P–KR3	

An immediate 9. P–Q4, though playable, allows the pin 9. . . . B–N5. The text move prevents the pin—at the cost of a tempo—and ensures that White will be able to proceed with the P–Q4 central advance without being bothered by Black. What can Black do about White's coming 10. P–Q4, which will put pressure on Black's KP and establish a central superiority for White? Well, there is no way to prevent White's P–Q4, so Black should satisfy himself with setting up the most useful formation to minimize the strength of the advance.

9. . . .   N–N1

What kind of a move is this? When the young and talented Hungarian Master Breyer suggested this retreat in the 1920s, his "reward" was long derisive laughter. How can such a retreat be logical? But there are two sound reasons behind it. First, the current position of the QN prevents the QBP from being used centrally. When the Knight goes to Q2 (the QN is required to protect the KP after White's P–Q4), the QBP is ready to advance. Second, the Black QB has little to do on its present diagonal and also would have little scope on QN2 with the QN on QB3. But with the QN on Q2 the fianchettoed Bishop has a nice central diagonal. Are there any disadvantages to Black's plan? Yes, the obvious: the maneuver costs two tempos.

The Tchigorin Variation, 9. . . . N–QR4 10. B–B2 P–B4, has been Black's most popular defense since the early 1900s, but it has the strategic drawback of leaving the QN out of play on the edge of the board. Other reasonable moves for Black are 9. . . . P–KR3, 9. . . . B–K3, and 9. . . . N–Q2.

10. P–Q4   QN–Q2
11. P–B4

When the Breyer became popular in the mid-1960s, this was White's main weapon. Actual practice over the last ten years has shown that Black's position is too sound to be stormed successfully by such positionally brutal means. Even so, Geller has remained partially true to this move. White's strongest continuation is the logical developmental 11. QN–Q2!. The second time Geller was White against Portisch in this play-off he did play thus, obtained a won position, but then allowed Portisch to escape with a draw. We'll see 11. QN–Q2! in Game 61, R. Byrne–Tukmakov, Leningrad 1973.

11. . . .   P–B3!

Note how well the QBP now helps Black's position on both Queenside and center.

12. Q–B2?!

Geller's novelty, a successful one in this game. Objectively speaking, however, it is difficult to see the point of placing the Queen here. The main line long, long ago (i.e., 1960s!) was the sharp 12. P–B5 Q–B2! 13. BPxP BxP 14. B–N5 PxP! 15. BxN PxB (15. . . . NxB?? 16. P–K5 wins material for White), and now after either 16. NxP N–B4, as in Gligoric–Petrosian, Los Angeles 1963, or 16. QxP N–K4, as in Fischer–Portisch, Santa Monica 1966, Black's active pieces and the two Bishops are sufficient compensation for the weakened Kingside. Such a conclusion is not obvious, but extensive master practice has shown it to be so. Nevertheless, White has nothing better than 12. P–B5. The problem is simply that 11. P–B4 is too prematurely sharp to pose objective problems for Black.

12. . . . P–QR4?!

A brave but positionally unmotivated sortie. In Tal–Timman, Sochi 1973, contested a few days after this game, Black played the sound developmental 12. . . . B–N2! and after 13. N–B3 P–N5 14. N–K2 PxP! 15. N/2xP P–N3! 16. N–K2 N–B4 already had a slight advantage (the game was drawn in 68).

13. P–QR4

This, too, is overeager. White obtains better opportunities to take advantage of Black's weakened Queenside with 13. P–R3!.

13. . . .   PxBP
14. BxP   P–Q4!
15. B–Q3

In his analysis Geller rates Black's position as equal after move 14. Even so, to spend over an hour on the text move is excessive. Clearly, after 15. KPxP BPxP 16. PxP PxB 17. PxN NxP (of 17. . . . BxP) 18. QxBP, Black's two Bishops and White's weakened Queenside give Black full compensation for the pawn. So what else does White have but the text? The time wasted here will be worth a lot later on.

15. . . .   QPxP
16. BxP   NxB
17. QxN   B–N5?!

Geller criticizes this and instead recommends 17. . . . N–B3! 18. QxKP B–Q3 feeling that Black's Bishops and open lines compensate fully for the pawn.

18. B–Q2   BxB?

This move, which furthers White's development and leaves Black with weak Queenside pawns, is the real reason for Black's coming difficulties. Szabo has correctly pointed out that after the correct 18. . . . PxP! White's advantage is quite minor.

19. QNxB   PxP
20. QxQP!

But here White's advantage is major: he is ahead in development, has a well-placed Queen, and will be ready to start menacing Black's isolated QRP and QBP.

20. . . .   N–B3
21. QR–QB1 B–Q2

The exchange of Queens loses the QBP by force.

22. N–B4

Perfectly O.K., though 22. N–K5!? to prevent Black's next may be a shade better.

22. . . .   P–B4!?

Correctly exchanging one of his weak pawns.

23. QxP   BxQRP
24. N/3–K5!

24. N–N6?! N–Q2! leads to nothing. Now, however, 25. N–N6 is the threat.

24. . . .   R–N1

Leads to the loss of the QRP,

but there is nothing good to recommend. If 24. . . . N–Q2 25. NxN BxN 26. KR–Q1 and Black is stuck in a most unpleasant pin.

25. Q–R3!   B–N4

Instead 25. . . . R–N5? is refuted by 26. NxRP! QxN 27. N–B6!.

26. NxRP

And so White has won Black's remaining Queenside pawn, is a sound pawn ahead, and will remain at least a pawn ahead for the rest of the game. But for the missing pawn, Black's position is satisfactory, so his practical chances for a draw are reasonable. Nevertheless, with accurate, matter-of-technique play, White should be able to win. However, a shortage of time, caused by thinking excessively in the opening phase, begins to rear its unwelcome head.

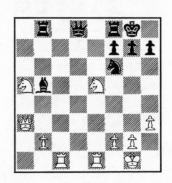

26. . . .   Q–N3
27. P–QN4   KR–K1

28. Q–QB3!	R–K3
29. N/K–B6	QR–K1
30. RxR	RxR
31. Q–B5?!	

Exchanging Queens is logical both from the standpoint of the position and White's time pressure, but this is not an accurate way to accomplish it because Black's Rook can reach an active behind-the-pawn location. Correct is 31. N–Q4! R–K1 32. Q–B5!, and after 32. . . . QxQ 33. PxQ White's Rook is well placed behind his passed pawn.

31. . . .	QxQ
32. RxQ	

Here 32. PxQ?? loses a Knight.

32. . . .	R–K8ch
33. K–R2	B–R5
34. P–N5?!	

A logical move in time pressure, but the pawn is rather exposed here. To prevent Black's coming KRP advance with 34. P–B3! P–R4 35. P–R4! is better. White should then still win in due course.

34. . . .	R–QN8!

Black's Rook is ideally placed *behind* the passed pawn. This allows Black to watch both the QNP and White's King.

35. N–Q4	P–R4
36. R–B8ch	K–R2
37. R–QN8	P–R5!

The pawn severely limits the White King's activity and even gives Black certain chances for a mating attack.

38. R–N7	K–N3?!

The King is awkwardly placed here. Correct is the active 38. . . . N–K5! 39. RxP N–Q7!, and the threat of 40. . . . N–B8ch forces White to allow the drawish position after 40. P–N3 PxPch 41. PxP BxP, etc.

39. N/5–B6!	N–K5
40. N–K5ch	K–B3
41. N–N4ch	

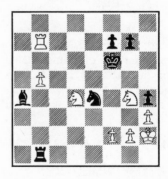

The game was adjourned here, with Geller sealing his 41st move. It was resumed two days later so the players (and their seconds!) had enough time to analyze. After the match tournament, Portisch stated that he was sure of having qualified for the Candidates matches when he couldn't find a win for White in this position. Black has a sufficient bind on White's Kingside, and so White is eventually forced to exchange his QNP for Black's KRP.

41. . . .   K–N3
42. N–K5ch

Black can defend against this. After the game Geller suggested 42. P–N6!? as worth trying.

42. . . .   K–B3
43. P–B4

White now threatens 44. RxP mate, so Black has no time for 43. . . . N–N6??.

43. . . .   B–N6!
44. N/5–B3!

The KRP must be eliminated; otherwise White is in great danger of being mated. For instance, 44 NxB? N–N6 and the best White can hope for is a draw after 45 N–N4ch and 46. N–B2.

44. . . .   P–N3!

Taking White's KB5 away from White's Knights.

45. NxP   B–Q4
46. R–B7

As frustrating as it is, there is no way for White to prevent his QNP from eventually being lost. Thus if 46. R–N6ch K–K2 47. N/R–B3 N–B6!, and now 48. N–K5 is foiled by 48. . . . R–N7!.

46. . . .   R–Q8

Satisfactory, but even more exact is 46. . . . R–N5! 47. N/R–B3 N–Q7!.

47. N–B2   R–QN8
48. N–K3

The QNP cannot be saved.

48. . . .   RxP
49. N–B3   B–K3
50. N–Q4

White's chances to win in this ending are scant, but Geller is nonetheless determined. Such impractical determination is psychologically motivated. He began the play-off disastrously, having lost twice to Polugaevsky and drawn once with Portisch. Having had a "won" game from early on, Geller couldn't accept any other result. Under such unhealthy pressure strange things can happen.

50. . . .   R–N5
51. NxB   KxN
52. R–B4

The exchange of Rooks can't be the way to success. But Black's R and N are placed quite well, so keeping Rooks on also offers no real hope. The problem simply is that the position is too dry for a win.

52. . . .   RxR
53. NxR

The pawn formation is rather symmetrical, except that Black is missing his KRP. Otherwise Black stands well, and with accurate and logical play Portisch is able to hold the position for a draw. However, something unbelievable happens at the very end!

53. . . .   K–B4

But not 53. . . . P–N4? 54. PxP and White has a passed RP and fantastic winning chances. Black does want to exchange pawns but only on *his terms*. This means a symmetrical exchange, such as KBP for KBP, Black's NP for White's RP, or Black's KBP for White's NP. The last thing that Black wants to allow is a passed pawn.

54. P–N3   N–B4
55. K–N2   N–Q6
56. K–B3   N–B4
57. N–Q6ch

As the course of the game shows, it is insufficient for White to play with only his King and Knight. To begin to use the

pawn majority with 57. P–N4ch! is necessary and correct. This gains space for White, and an eventual . . . P–B4 can be met by P–N5!; Black's NP may then become a real weakness.

57. . . .   K–K3
58. N–K4   N–Q2!

A good defensive spot for the Knight. At the moment there is nothing to attack in White's camp; thus "attacking" Knight moves such as . . . N–Q6 or . . . N–N6 serve no purpose. Exchanging Knights leads to a normal lost K + P endgame.

59. K–K3

Black's reply cannot be prevented since 59. P–N4 is also met by 59. . . . P–B4! with an attack on the Knight.

59. . . .   P–B4!

This paralyzes White's pawn majority since a later P–N4 can be easily parried by the symmetrical pawn exchange, and all that White has achieved is a symmetrical and drawn N + 2P vs. N + P endgame. As it turns out, this is the last pawn move in the game. The game was again adjourned with Black having sealed this move. After a four-hour break it was resumed for another two sessions of play.

60. N–N5ch   K–B3

Black's King is going to stay near the weakened KNP. There

is little point in the aggressive
60. . . . K–Q4.

61. K–Q4   K–N2!
62. N–K6ch

62. K–Q5?! leads nowhere:
62. . . . N–B3ch 63. K–K6? N–
R4 and White's NP is lost.

62. . . .   K–B2
63. N–B7   N–B3
64. N–Q5   N–Q2!

Black has achieved what to
him looks like an impregnable
defensive formation, and he is
not about to depart from it except for the best of reasons.
Thus he eschews 64. . . . N–
K5?! 65. P–N4! N–B7 66. P–
N5! NxP 67. K–K3! and Black's
Knight is trapped and may well
go lost.

65. N–B7   N–B3
66. N–Q5   N–Q2
67. N–B3   N–B3
68. K–K5   N–R4!

Note how the lack of White's
P–KN4 gives Black's Knight
more scope.

69. N–K2   K–K2!
70. K–Q5   N–B3ch
71. K–K5   N–R4
72. K–Q4   N–B3
73. K–K3   N–Q4ch
74. K–B3   K–B2!
75. N–B1   K–N2!

Black is more than happy to
keep the status quo.

76. N–Q3   K–B2
77. K–B2   K–N2

78. N–K5   N–B3
79. K–K3   K–R2
80. N–Q3

Over the last twenty moves
White has not made any progress. He again refrains from 80.
P–N4 because of 80. . . . N–
Q4ch 81. K–B3 PxPch, etc. He
can't get himself to concede the
draw.

80. . . .   K–R3
81. N–K5   K–N2
82. N–B4   K–B2
83. K–B3   N–Q4
84. K–K2   K–N2
85. K–Q3   N–B3
86. K–K3   K–B2

**White overstepped the
time limit and lost!**

As White was playing 87. K–
B3 his flag fell, and he had to
be forfeited. How could such a
thing happen in such an easy
position? The explanation is almost unbelievable. As a result
of a massive block—induced no
doubt by nervous overexertion
—Geller had marked move *84*
(instead of the correct *88*) on

his score sheet as the end of the time control. Thus with the "time control" over, he paid no attention to the clock until he was forfeited. Tragically, this very half point prevented Geller from reaching the 1974 Candidates matches.

Chapter 7

Holmov, Ratmir

Ratmir Holmov, though little known in the West because he hasn't played here, is a very strong grandmaster. Born in Archangelsk on May 13, 1925, he has lived in the Moscow area since 1967. Holmov was a relative latecomer to tournament chess. When in October 1943 he spent a month at Portland, Oregon, as a young sailor on a Soviet ship, he was only of First Category (about our Class A) strength. But with his sailing days over, his interest and successes in chess increased significantly: master in 1947, international master in 1954, international grandmaster in 1960.

Holmov has taken part in sixteen U.S.S.R. Championships, finishing in a triple tie for first in 1963. He has won six international tournaments outright and tied for first in four others, the latest being Budapest 1976. At Havana 1965 he beat Fischer in an excellent game on the Black side of a Ruy Lopez.

His book *Selected Games* was published in 1958. Holmov is proud that he had an opportunity to present a copy to Fischer, who is reported to have found it "very interesting." Holmov's FIDE rating is 2555.

GAME 14

White: J. Smejkal
 (Czechoslovakia)

Black: R. Holmov
 (U.S.S.R.)

Played at Luhacovice (Czechoslovakia) International Tournament, May 1873.

English Opening

White comes out of the strategic opening with a freer position, having a space advantage on the Queenside and with no weaknesses whatever. In trying to build on these, he chooses a double-edged pawn advance on the Kingside. This creates a dynamically balanced situation, and when Black doesn't respond with sufficient energy, White achieves a clear superiority in space and position. Though in considerable time pressure, Smejkal maneuvers purposefully and by adjournment is ready to penetrate Black's camp. Some pretty motifs with passed pawns seal Black's fate.

1. P–QB4	N–KB3
2. P–KN3	P–K4
3. B–N2	P–B4

A controversial decision. Black establishes a strong central position with a particular grip on White's Q4-square. The cost, however, is a permanent weakening of Black's Q4. Normal moves here include 3. . . . N–B3 and 3. . . . P–KN3.

4. N–QB3	N–B3
5. N–B3	

White plans to complete his Kingside development before thinking about anything else. More incisive is 5. P–Q3! P–KR3 (otherwise 6. B–N5 puts great pressure on Black's Q4) 6. P–QR3! followed by 7. R–N1 aiming for an early P–QN4. In this way White should be able to retain the first-move advantage.

5. . . .	P–Q3
6. O–O	B–K3
7. P–Q3	P–KR3

Again 8. B–N5 must be prevented.

8. P–QR3   P–Q4?!

In trying to eliminate the hole on Q4 even before he has completed his Kingside development, Black is clearly over-eager. White is now able to take advantage of Black's uncastled King to obtain a solid initiative on the Queenside. The patient 8. . . . B–K2 is in order and only after 9. R–N1 P–Q4!. Then Black is O.K.

9. Q–R4!

With the threat of 10. NxKP, 9. . . . P–Q5? is refuted by 10. NxKP! PxN 11. NxN Q–Q2 12. Q–N5!. Thus Black must protect the KP.

9. . . .   **B–Q3**
10. **P–QN4!**   **O–O**

All captures are worse; e.g.,
10. . . . PxNP?! 11. PxNP BxP?!
12. NxQP NxN 13. PxN BxP
14. P–K4 B–K3 15. NxP!, or
10. . . . PxBP 11. NPxP! (11.
. . . BxP?! 12 NxP).

11. **P–N5**   **N–K2**
12. **PxP**   **N/2xP**
13. **B–N2**   **N–N3**

13. . . . NxN just makes it
easier for White to apply pressure: 14. BxN N–Q2 15. N–
Q2! N–N3 16. Q–B2 Q–K2 17.
P–QR4.

14. **Q–B2**   **R–B1**

If 14. . . . P–B5?!, 15. P–
Q4! with substantial advantage
for White (Minev).

15. **N–Q2!**

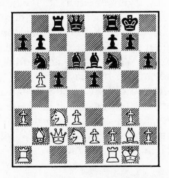

The opening phase has ended
and White has space advantage
on the Queenside, a fantastic
diagonal for his KB, and good
potential for his QB on the central diagonal. Black's KP is
awkward to protect. Overall
White has a safe and comfortable plus.

15. . . .   **Q–K2**
16. **N–R4!**

Gaining more space on the
Queenside and opening the
QB's diagonal. 16. P–QR4? is
faulty because of 16. . . . N/
N–Q4! and the Knight gets the
important QN5-square.

16. . . .   **NxN**

Now after 16. . . .N/N–Q4
17. N–B4! Black has problems
keeping both his KP and QNP
protected.

17. **QxN**   **B–N1**
18. **N–B4**   **B–Q4**
19. **P–K4!**

A major and correct posi-
tional decision. White locks in
his KB and weakens his QP and
Q4-square. His compensation is
the two Bishops and a significant space advantage. The following exchange is forced since
19. . . . B–K3? drops the KP.

19. . . .   **BxN**
20. **QxB**   **QR–Q1**
21. **B–R3?!**

White is already in incipient
time pressure. The Bishop is
not safe here and the move just
wastes time. White has two
logical methods to capitalize on
his greater space. The first, suggested by Smejkal, is to improve
the location of the Kingside

pieces with 21. KR–Q1, 22. P–KR4, 23. B–KR3, and then to continue the Queenside expansion with P–QR4, P–QR5, etc. This is slow, but Black is very cramped and has no meaningful counterplay. The other, sharper approach is to play on the Kingside and center with 21. QR–K1 and 22. P–B4, as the Bulgarian IM Minev suggested.

21. . . .   N–R2!
22. B–N2

A correct retreat. Of practical value is the ability to recognize one's own errors quickly; there is then often still enough time to minimize potential damage. That's quite true here.

22. . . .   N–N4
23. P–B4!?

A brave, double-edged advance, especially in time pressure. Even so Smejkal feels that the positional 23. KR–Q1! is sounder.

23. . . .   PxP!?

Black is also quite brave, for this capture opens the position and increases White's central strength. Black counts on having sufficient play against White's somewhat loose position. This evaluation is correct but his coming play insufficiently energetic. Safe, sound, and good enough for equality is 23. . . . N–K3! and after 24. P–B5 N–Q5.

24.	PxP	N–K3
25.	P–K5!	N–Q5
26.	QR–K1	K–R1
27.	P–QR4	P–QN3
28.	K–R1	P–B3!
29.	P–K6	KR–K1?

This move costs valuable time, which White can use to consolidate his position. Moreover, the Rook will be chased back with additional loss of time. The attack against the KP turns out to be a sham. The moment is ripe here for 29. . . . P–N4!, especially because White has no time for 30. P–B5?? in view of 30. . . . Q–Q3. After 29. . . . P–N4! Smejkal considers 30. B–B1 the only correct move and rates the chances as dynamically equal.

30. R–B2!

But now Black is in trouble. It's too late for 30. . . . P–N4? because with his KR2 protected White has 31. P–B5 Q–Q3 32. B–K4. White now threatens 31. P–B5 transforming the KP into a *protected* passed pawn. Black feels constrained to prevent this but incurs the disadvantage of weakening his Kingside and of increasing the potential of White's QB.

30. . . .   P–B4
31. B–B6!!

An elegant way to take advantage of Black's last move. After 31. . . . NxB 32. PxN White doubles Rooks on the KN-file and Black's KNP is indefensible. However, the alternative—allowing White's KB to reach Q7—results in Black's being tied in knots.

31. . . .   R–KB1
32. R–KN1!

The careless 32. B–Q7?? allows 32. . . . RxB.

32. . . .   K–R2
33. B–Q7   R–B3
34. BxN!

An attractive, practical time-pressure move; Black is now completely without counter-chances, and White runs no risk of time pressure errors. The key advantages of space and passed KP remain.

34. . . .   PxB
35. Q–Q5!

Of course not 35. QxP? RxP! and an even endgame after 36. RxPch QxR 37. QxQch KxQ 38. BxR RxP, etc. White will take off the QP when it's safe to do so!

35. . . .   B–Q3
36. R/2–KN2

And here 36. QxQP? allows 36. . . . B–B4.

36. . . .   P–N3
37. R–KB2   K–N2
38. R–QB1!   B–B4
39. P–R5!

White pays attention to the whole board; Queenside, center, Kingside. Such an approach makes it almost impossible for a cramped defender to parry all threats.

39. . . .   K–R2
40. R–K2   B–Q3?!

Allows White a risk-free win. There is nothing better than 40. . . . K–N2, even though 41. RxB! PxR 42. P–N6 does lead to a winning breakthrough.

41. PxP   BxP

Allowing White a passed pawn on QN7 is equivalent to suicide. However, Black's days are also numbered after 41. . . . PxP 42. QxQP.

42. R–KB1   B–N1
43. P–N7!

White now infiltrates with heavy artillery along the QB-file, and then something must break in Black's position. White's Kingside does look semibarren, but he is quite safe because Black has no attacking power to swing over there.

43. . . .	**P–KR4**
44. R–B1	**P–B5**
45. Q–B3	**K–R3**
46. R–B8	**R/3–B1**
47. R/2–QB2!	**P–N4**
48. RxR	**RxR**
49. R–B8	

White's infiltration route is clear and potent. As soon as the Queen joins in, the end will be near.

49. . . .	**B–Q3**
50. Q–B6	**R–B1**
51. P–N8=Q!	

"In won positions there is more than one way to skin the *King*." Equally winning is 51. RxR QxR 52. P–N8=Q! QxQ (52. . . . BxQ 53. P–K7ch) 53. P–K7.

51. . . .	**BxQ**
52. RxR	**P–N5**

If 52. . . . QxR 53. P–K7ch. Black could resign.

53. R–B7	**Q–N5**
54. P–K7ch	**B–Q3**
55. Q–B1	

Or 55. QxBch QxQ 56. P–K8=Q.

55. . . .	**BxP**
56. QxPch	**B–N4**
57. R–B6ch	**K–R2**
58. Q–B5ch	**Black resigns**

GAME 15

White: R. Holmov
(U.S.S.R.)

Black: V. Jansa
(Czechoslovakia)

Played at Luhacovice (Czechoslovakia) International Tournament, May 1973.

English Opening

Using an interesting Queen maneuver, Black brings about

an early endgame, in which he has virtual equality. In the ensuing play, Black consistently prepares and executes his thematic pawn advance on the Queenside and obtains full equality. At the critical moment White undertakes an unmotivated, reckless central pawn push and quickly begins to suffer from it. Black's pieces spring to life, and White has all he can do to protect the resulting weak spots. Although little material remains, Black's Rook and two Bishops accomplish a mating attack, and White is done in on move 37.

1. N-KB3

A Reti or King's Indian Reversed?

1. . . .   P-QB4

Offering a Sicilian after 2. P-K4.

2. P-B4

White prefers an English Opening.

2. . . .	N-QB3
3. N-B3	**N-B3**
4. P-Q4	**PxP**
5. NxP	**P-KN3**
6. P-KN3	

Sticking to the English. With 6. P-K4 he could establish the Accelerated Dragon Variation of the Sicilian Defense.

6. . . .	**B-N2**
7. B-N2	**O-O**
8. N-B2	

White has a slight central superiority and feels that the best way to keep Black cramped is to prevent the exchange of Knights. This seems logical, but the Knight is not usefully placed on QB2 and the text move has little theoretical import. It's O.K., but that's all. The normal way to handle this English/King's Indian position is 8. O-O NxN 9. QxN P-Q3, as we'll see in Tal-Torre, Leningrad 1973, Game 52.

| 8. . . . | **P-Q3** |
| **9. O-O** | **Q-R4!** |

A creative idea. Black, taking advantage of the passively placed White KN, shifts his Queen to the Kingside for action there.

| 10. B-Q2 | **Q-R4** |
| **11. P-K4** | |

Black was planning 11. . . . B-R6 to exchange Bishops and thus weaken White's King position. White therefore sees nothing better than to allow an endgame in which his advantage, if any, is minimal.

| 11. . . . | **QxQ** |
| **12. QRxQ** | |

The QR inhibits the meaningful development of the KR, and White must soon lose a move to make its useful deployment possible. Therefore, 12. KRxQ! is better, and White's greater central influence could amount to an infinitesimal plus.

12. . . .   B–N5!?

To shorten the White KB's diagonal.

13. P–B3   B–K3
14. P–N3   KR–B1

Black's thematic counterplay is against White's QBP, so this is the right method. The QR should be used on either the QR- or QN-file.

15. P–B4   QR–N1

Here 15. . . . P–QR3? is faulty in view of 16. N–R4! since Black can't guard his QN3 with 16. . . . N–Q2 because 17. P–KB5 traps the QB.

16. R–B1

Clearly indicating that White's 12th move lost a tempo. Still there is nothing better since White must prepare to contest the QB-file.

16. . . .   P–QR3
17. KR–K1   P–QN4!

Black has successfully realized this thematic advance against White's QBP. Chances are dynamically balanced. With reasonable play the result should be a draw since the absence of Queens minimizes each side's winning chances. However, careless or unstrategic play by either side could well be punished.

18. P–K5??

According to Jansa, White thought for about five minutes before pushing the KP confidently forward. The move is reckless, pointless, horrible, stupid, or a combination of all of these, and there is no satisfactory explanation for a grandmaster's making it. It accomplishes absolutely nothing and ensures the death of his KP.

Given Black's threat to exchange on White's QB4, saddling White with a weak isolated QBP, the only move worth considering is 18. PxP. After 18. . . . PxP White has 19. N–Q5!?. Jansa suggests 19. . . . NxN!? 20. PxN N–Q5 as a reply and rates the positions after 21. PxB NxN 22. PxPch KxP 23. B–Q5ch K–B1 and 21. N–N4 RxR 22. BxR B–N5 as even.

18. . . .   QPxP
19. PxKP   N–KN5

White's KP is now attacked

three times and defended only once. To protect it White has to part with his KB, thereby weakening his King position and giving Black the two Bishops in an open position. The future course of the game will show both factors to be decisive.

20. BxN   RxB
21. N–N4   R/3–B1
22. N/3–Q5?!

White will now have no chances for active play. Theoretically no better is 22. NxRP R–R1 23. PxP NxKP, but White's passed Queenside pawns afford at least some practical chances if Black misplays the position. As played White must simply await the executioner.

22. . . .   R–N2!
23. B–B4

A piece is lost after 23. PxP RxR 24. RxR P–QR4.

23. . . .   PxP

White will now have a weak isolated QBP and KP and a weakened Kingside, whereas Black has two powerful Bishops and active Rooks. Against a capable master like Black, such a situation is hopeless for White.

24. PxP

Equivalent is 24. RxP RxR 25. PxR P–N4! 26. BxP NxKP with play similar to the game.

24. . . .   P–N4!!

A strategically correct decision, which hastens White's demise. By winning White's KP for the currently unimportant KNP, Black can pump all his pieces into White's camp.

25. BxP   NxKP
26. NxPch   RxN
27. BxR   N–B6ch
28. K–B2   NxR
29. KxN?!

Allows Black's Rook to enter White's position via the King file with decisive effect. A shade better is 29. RxN, though Black's attack must soon be decisive after 29. . . . RxP!.

29. . . .   P–QR4!
30. N–Q3

If 30. N–Q5? BxN.

30. . . .   R–K1!
31. B–N5   B–N5ch!
32. K–B2   B–Q5ch
33. K–N2   R–K7ch

The R + 2B combination waylays White's King.

34. K–B1   RxQRP

With the primary threat of 35. . . . B–K7ch, and 35. R–K1 allows 35. . . . B–R6 mate.

35. N–B4   P–R3!

With the help of tactics, Black chases the Bishop away from its defense of the King. 36. BxP is met by 36. . . . RxP

with the double threats of 37.
. . . RxB and 37. . . . R–R8ch.

36. B–Q8   RxP
37. K–K1   B–K6!
White resigns

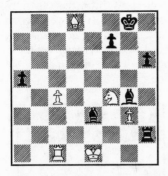

Forget the Rook—there is no
defense to the mate threat of
38. . . . R–R8.

GAME 16

White: G. Estevez
      (Cuba)

Black: R. Holmov
      (U.S.S.R.)

Played at Luhacovice (Czechoslovakia) International Tournament, May 1973.

English Opening

Using a sophisticated strategic opening, Black obtains
solid equality. White's play is
sufficiently careful and sound to
keep the chances approximately
balanced. However, Black is not
satisfied to draw against the
tournament tailender. He opens
the position on the Kingside,
mainly to the benefit of White's
Bishop. After some unsatisfactory Queen and Knight
maneuvers, Black is clearly in
trouble, and White has the realistic attacking chances. When
Black neglects to prevent a
simple Knight shot, it is suddenly mate in two!

1. N–KB3   N–KB3
2. P–B4   P–K3
3. N–B3   B–N5

A sophisticated strategic idea,
whereby Black tries to apply
pressure against White's K4-
square. This is similar to the
Nimzo-Indian Defense (see
Game 25); but with White's QP
still back home, the strategy is
not quite so firmly based on
proven positional principles.
The two most common moves
for Black are 3. . . . P–Q4 and
3. . . . P–B4.

4. Q–B2!

The best response. White prevents the doubling of his pawns
and gives the Queen a useful
central location.

4. . . .   O–O

If Black wants to keep the
Bishop he must play 4. . . . P–B4
so that the Bishop can retreat in
safety to QR4.

5. P–QR3

Forcing the Bishop off makes the point of White's 4th clear.

5. . . .   BxN
6. QxB   P–QN3!?

Black usually aims for direct central influence with 6. . . . P–Q3. Even so, White's two Bishops and flexible central pawn formation give him the typical first-move advantage. One recent example is Portisch–Larsen, Las Palmas 1976: 7. P–QN4 P–K4 8. B–N2 N–B3 9. P–K3 N–K5 10. Q–B2 P–B4 11. B–K2 P–QR4 12. P–Q3. White's a shade better and went on to win in 37.

7. P–QN4

Black's QB now gets too much scope on the center diagonal. More logical is 7. P–KN3! B–N2 8. B–N2 P–Q4 9. P–Q4 PxP 10. QxP B–K5 11. O–O with some advantage for White in Vaganian–Korchnoi, Moscow 1975.

7. . . .   B–N2
8. B–N2   P–Q3
9. P–K3   P–K4!

Holmov tried 6. . . . P–QN3 in Shamkovich–Kholmov, 1972 U.S.S.R. Championship, and in this position continued 9. . . . QN–Q2 10. B–K2 P–B4 11. P–Q4 Q–K2 12. O–O N–K5. The text is an improvement which makes it harder for White to challenge Black's center.

10. B–K2   QN–Q2
11. O–O   R–K1
12. P–Q3   P–B4

The opening phase has ended with both sides having a good position. White has the two Bishops and no weaknesses; Black's QB has a good diagonal and Black has greater center influence. The position is in balance.

13. N–Q2

With the idea of exchanging the light-square Bishops. This is a defensive idea rather than a way of playing to win. But Black's central influence makes it difficult for White to develop an active plan.

13. . . .   R–K3
14. B–B3   BxB
15. NxB   P–KR3
16. P–N5

With the long-range idea of a Queenside pawn roller by means of 17. P–QR4, 18. P–R5, etc., but Black can put an effective stop to that. More promising is the central advance 16. P–Q4!?.

16. . . .   P–QR4!
17. PxP e.p.

The opening of the Queenside in this situation is more to Black's advantage than to White's. It is difficult to recommend something attractive, however, since White's 16th move gave up the contest for Black's QB4-square, thus making a potential P–Q4 much less attractive.

17. . . .   RxP
18. Q–N3   Q–R1
19. KR–Q1   P–Q4!

This advance leads to the liquidation of White's QBP and thus leaves Black in slight, though undisputed, control of the center.

20. PxP   QxP
21. Q–B2

The exchange of Queens gives Black a comfortable endgame, especially in view of White's isolated QRP. Keeping the Queens on is unquestionably the correct practical approach.

21. . . .   Q–B3

Intending 22. . . . R–R5 or 22. . . . Q–R5, but White can prevent that. The immediate 21. . . . P–QN4! is in order. Black then threatens the positional 22. . . . R–R5 and because of his central superiority has a small but comfortable plus.

22. P–QR4!   P–K5

This impatient advance leads to nothing but the opening of the White Bishop's diagonal. A more useful way to play for the win is 22. . . . R–R1!, followed by using the Rook in the center. Objectively the position is essentially in balance, but the balance is dynamic, and so the better player—obviously Black here—has chances for the full point.

23. PxP   QxKP
24. Q–B3!

With White's first threat—thanks to the just opened diagonal—25. RxN!.

24. . . .   Q–B3

O.K. but 24. . . . R–R2 seems more efficient. The Queen is well placed in the center.

25. Q–B4   Q–R1

Here too 25. . . . R–R2 seems more efficient.

26. Q–B3!?

In effect, an interesting way to offer a draw. White is satisfied with such a result against his famous adversary.

26. . . .   N–B1?!

But Holmov is not interested in drawing against the tournament tailender. 26. . . . Q–B3 instead repeats the position. The Knight move is a step in the wrong direction, however. 26.

. . . R–R2 is again more efficient.

27. Q–N3   N–N3?!

And this is clearly wrong since it allows White's Rook to penetrate to Q7. Holmov seriously underrates his opponent. The Cuban IM can be a creative tactician; at Leningrad Interzonal 1973 he defeated both Hübner and Tal (see Game 53) in fine games. In any case, to win requires good moves, and Holmov's misplacement of his pieces invites disaster.

28. BxN!

A fresh and open mind is behind this capture. To get his Rook to Q7, White is willing to exchange off his "beautiful" Bishop.

28. . . .   RxB
29. R–Q7   Q–B3?

Giving White the eighth rank is unforgivable. It is high time to reverse gears and play 29. . . . N–B1!.

30. R–Q8ch   K–R2
31. Q–Q1!

A simple, though pretty threat, which Black overlooks. Black's position is, nevertheless, already very unpleasant. A Knight move loses the QR to 32. Q–Q3ch. The only defense is 31. . . . R–B4! since then 32. Q–Q3? attacking both Rooks can be met by 32. . . . RxP!! 33.

RxR QxR because 34. QxR?? allows 34. . . . Q–R8ch followed by mate. After 31. . . . R–B4! White's sharpest is 32. P–R4! which threatens both 33. Q–Q3 and 33. N–N5ch. White's advantage is indisputable, anyway. But what happens now is "a bit" worse!

31. . . .   R–K3??
32. N–N5ch!   Black resigns

The forced 32. . . . PxN allows 33. Q–R5 mate!

GAME 17

White: R. Holmov
     (U.S.S.R.)

Black: N. Spiridonov
     (Bulgaria)

Played at Sochi (U.S.S.R.) International Tournament, September 1973, Round 13.

English Opening

Black employs an interesting strategic concept as early as move 4 and forces White to do some independent thinking that soon in the game. White's response is too eccentric, thus showing Black's opening strategy to be quite successful. Soon Black achieves a slight positional plus by controlling the dark squares on the Kingside. White decides to castle Queenside but subsequently does not maneuver successfully. In due course Black is able to open lines and generate strong pressure against White's King. Finally Black's Queen infiltrates White's camp, and some pretty tactics spell the end of the road for White's King.

Overall a meaningful demonstration of how to beat the Russians: a strategically noteworthy opening innovation, positionally logical maneuvering, thorough preparation for the potential attack, and energy and tactical sharpness in executing it.

1. P–QB4   P–KN3
2. N–KB3   B–N2
3. P–K4   P–Q3
4. P–Q4

If Black plays 4. . . . N–KB3, one of the standard variations of the King's Indian Defense will arise. Black's move order does, however, give some flexibility in what to do next.

4. . . .   B–N5!?

An interesting, strategically creative way to apply pressure against White's QP. Objectively no better than the standard 4. . . . N–KB3, it does force White to solve new problems. This is always a good practical approach against a theoretically well-prepared opponent.

5. B–K2   N–QB3

With the obvious threat of 6. . . . BxN followed by 7. . . . NxP. If 6. B–K3 Black continues the pressure on the QP with 6. . . . P–K4. How should White proceed?

6. N–N1?!

With the idea 6. . . . BxB?! 7. NxB when White's QP is comfortably protected and White has a nice central superiority. Such abject retreats are, however, rarely sound. Spiridonov recommends indirect protection with 6. QN–Q2! as White's best and gives the following variation: 6. . . . P–K4 (6. . . . NxP?? 7. NxN and White wins a piece) 7. P–Q5 BxN 8. NxB N–Q5 9. NxN PxN 10. Q–N3 Q–B1 11. P–B5! with a slight edge to White.

6. . . .   B–Q2!

Making White's KN look rather silly back home.

7. B–K3   P–K4!
8. P–Q5   N–Q5
9. N–KB3   NxNch

Black decides to play on the dark squares on the Kingside.

An equally good approach is to undermine White's center with 9. . . . NxB 10. QxN P–KB4!.

10. BxN   B–R3!

The point of Black's moves 7 through 9. With the center diagonal now closed, Black gladly exchanges his bad Bishop for White's good one. The net result will leave Black comfortable on the dark squares, his remaining Bishop having more scope than White's.

11. N–B3?!

Leads to new and serious weaknesses. The safe move is 11. Q–Q2. Double-edged but playable is 11. O–O!? since after 11. . . . BxB 12. PxB White may have some counterplay along the KB-file.

11. . . .   BxB
12. PxB   Q–R5ch!
13. P–KN3   Q–N4

Black's Queen is actively placed, and White's advanced KNP will be attackable in just a moment. Overall Black is already clearly superior. He has the better Bishop and active Queen; White has only weaknesses.

14. Q–K2   P–KR4!
15. O–O–O

Obviously the Queenside is the only place where the King will feel at least half safe.

15. . . .   P–R5
16. P–KN4

Opening lines will only help Black get at White's weaknesses.

16. . . .   N–B3
17. KR–N1?!

Why use a Rook to protect a pawn when 17. P–KR3 will do the job?

17. . . .   K–K2

Black wants to connect Rooks and start working on White's Queenside, so he doesn't want to castle there himself. However, for the moment he also isn't sure whether he wants to castle on the Kingside. The text seeks a middle ground. Hindsight tells us, however, that 17. . . . O–O! is quite safe and would save Black a move or two over the game.

18.	K–N1	KR–Q1
19.	Q–Q2	B–K1
20.	R–QB1	P–R4!

Black's 19th move freed Q2 for the Knight so that it can get to a more useful location on QB4, where it will also be able to watch White's King. The text move ensures that the Knight won't be bothered by White's P–QN4.

21.	P–KR3	N–Q2
22.	P–N3	N–B4
23.	K–N2?	

The King is less safe here than on QN1. A better defensive formation is 23. R–B2!.

| 23. | . . . | P–QB3! |

The beginning of the undermining of White's King position.

| 24. | R–B2 | K–B1! |

A good precautionary move. Black ensures that White's Knight will never get to Q5 with *check*.

| 25. | B–K2 | R–R3! |
| 26. | K–N1 | |

White admits his error on move 23 but at the cost of two tempos. This has given Black enough time to get his attack going.

26.	. . .	R–N3
27.	R–QN2	P–R5!
28.	B–Q1?!	

Too defensive. Even worse is 28. P–N4? because of 28. . . . P–R6. White has to try 28. NxP!?. Black is much better after 28. . . . NxKP! 29. Q–Q3 (29. Q–B2? QxP!) N–B4 30. NxN PxN 31. P–K4 PxP! 32. KPxP R–KB3!, but White at least has a protected passed QP and some chances. As played, he has none.

| 28. | . . . | BPxP! |
| 29. | KPxP | |

After 29. NxQP Black moves the Rook away and then threatens . . . NxKP. In addition, after 29. NxQP White is stuck with isolated, double KPs. With the text White improves his pawn formation, but . . .

| 29. | . . . | R–R1! |

. . . Black starts on the final phase of his attack. White can't prevent the opening of the QR-file and the doubling of Black's Rooks thereon.

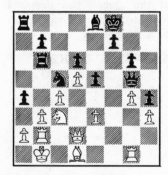

30.	R–B1	PxP
31.	PxP	R/3–R3
32.	R–R2	

The Rooks must be opposed, but the resulting lack of control of White's QN5 allows Black to further denude White's King.

32. ...	RxR
33. NxR	P-N4!
34. P-N4	

From now on there is no chance for successful defense.

34. ...	N-K5
35. Q-Q3	N-N6
36. R-K1	Q-B3!
37. B-N3	Q-B7
38. R-QB1	PxP
39. BxP	B-N4!

With the help of tactics, Black finishes the job nicely. The threat is 40. . . . RxN!, and 40. BxB allows 40. . . . QxN mate. So . . .

40. R-B2	BxB
41. QxB	Q-K8ch
42. K-N2	QxP

Not only is Black a pawn up, but the Queen has decisively penetrated White's position. The end is near.

43. N-B3	Q-R2!

Threatening 44. . . . Q-R8ch 45. K-N3 R-R6 mate. If now 44. N-N1 Spiridonov gives 44. . . . R-N1 45. P-N5 N-K5! 46. QxN RxPch 47. K-B1 Q-N8ch as winning for Black. White decides to shorten the agony with . . .

44. K-B1?!	Q-N8ch
45. K-Q2	

Obviously 45. N-Q1 allows 45. . . . R-R8ch, and 45. K-N2 leads to 45. . . . Q-R8ch 46. K-N3 R-R6 mate.

45. ...	N-B8ch
White resigns	

The forced end is 46. K-K2 Q-K6ch! 47. KxN R-R8ch 48. K-N2 Q-N6 mate.

Chapter 8

Keres, Paul

Who hasn't heard of Paul Keres: grandmaster par excellence, noted author, and extraordinary good-will ambassador for chess? It is safe to say that the only thing that he didn't achieve in the world of chess was to become world champion. In the match tournament for the world championship in 1948 he tied for 3rd–4th with Reshevsky behind Botvinnik and Smyslov. Thereafter he participated in every Candidates event through 1965 but was never able to become the challenger. Always a best man, never the groom.

Born in Narva, Estonia, on January 7, 1916, Keres quickly reached international stardom, and his tie for 1st–2nd with Fine at AVRO Tournament in 1938 established him as one of the world's leading players. Defeating Euwe by 7½–6½ in a 1939/40 match further confirmed this. Keres was a three-time winner of the U.S.S.R. Championship, in 1947, 1950, 1951. His numerous international successes include first places at Madrid 1943, Amsterdam 1954, Mar del Plata 1957, Hastings 1965/66, Budapest 1970, and Tallinn 1975, to name just a few. His first prizes in major tournaments total over forty! Keres became familiar to Americans as a result of his participation in the 1963 Piatigorsky Cup tournament at Los Angeles (tied for first) and in Church's Fried Chicken tournament at San Antonio 1972 (5th).

Keres has always been a very popular and active writer. His books include a series on openings, selections of his best games, and *Practical Chess Endings*. He died from a heart attack at Helsinki, Finland, on June 5, 1975. His last published FIDE rating was 2580.

GAME 18

White: P. Keres
(U.S.S.R.)

Black: L. Popov
(Bulgaria)

Played at Dortmund (West Germany) International Tournament, May 1973, Round 6.

Sicilian Defense
(Taimanov Variation)

Popov uses a dynamic variation, and when White does not play energetically enough, Black gains dynamic equality. Early in the middlegame Keres could draw by repeating moves, but as White against a less famous opponent, he feels that he must try to win. Such hopes are forlorn, however, and Popov plays a perfect game. He gains some advantage by virtue of his central influence and his chances for a Kingside attack. When Keres's defense is not the best, a beautiful combination decides the day.

1. P–K4	P–QB4
2. N–KB3	P–K3
3. N–B3	

Played often. Even so the normal 3. P–Q4 seems more flexible and better to me.

3. . . .	P–QR3
4. P–Q4	PxP
5. NxP	Q–B2

The new Taimanov Variation. The Bulgarian IM has made it his specialty and feels quite comfortable in it. For maximum success—especially when playing someone who is better—it is important to select a variation which "feels comfortable."

6. P–KN3

White's next step is usually to develop the KB and then castle. The fianchetto is quite popular but without the development of Black's QN not quite as efficient as otherwise. For 6. B–K2, see Tal–Hübner, Leningrad 1973, Game 54.

6. . . .　　　N–KB3

O.K., but more effective is 6. . . . B–N5!, pretty much forcing 7. KN–K2 and then 7. . . . N–KB3. White's formation is then a bit passive.

7. B–N2	P–Q3
8. O–O	B–Q2

Black goes about trying to develop his Queenside first. 8. . . . N–B3?! is not accurate since after 9. R–K1 B–K2 White opens the KB diagonal and gains the advantage with 10. NxN PxN 11. P–K5! PxP 12. RxP!. 9. . . . B–Q2?! is even worse since White has 10. N–Q5!.

9. R–K1　　　B–K2

Black's move order takes away any chances White may

have for tactics. Again 9. . . .
N–B3?! allows 10. N–Q5! PxN
11. PxPch N–K4 12. P–KB4
with clear advantage to White.

| 10. P–QR4 | N–B3 |
| 11. NxN | BxN |

Unquestionably the solid way
to recapture and therefore to be
played against a Keres. How-
ever, 11. . . . PxN!? may also be
playable. Subsequently, in
Round 13 against the West
German master Süss, that is how
Popov played, and after 12. Q–
K2 P–K4 13. P–N3 O–O 14.
B–N2 KR–K1 15. QR–Q1 B–
N5 16. B–B3 B–R6 17. B–N2
B–N5 the players agreed to split
the point.

12. P–N3

This and the following are
too passive to give Black any
trouble. Only with 12. P–R5!
P–QN4 (otherwise 13. B–K3)
13. PxP e.p. QxP 14. R–R3!, as
in Korsunski–Sideif-Zade, Baku
1975, can White hope for some
advantage.

12. . . .	O–O
13. B–N2	P–QN3
14. Q–Q4	KR–Q1
15. QR–Q1	Q–N2

The opening phase has ended
satisfactorily for Black. He has
some pressure against White's
KP and will get in . . . P–QN4,
thereby gaining some play on
the Queenside. Even though
Black has nothing beyond the

third rank, everything is harmoniously placed, and there are
no weak spots in Black's camp.
Black has full dynamic equality.

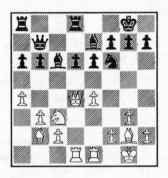

16. R–Q2

Not a meaningful location for
the Rook, but it is difficult for
White to come up with concrete
plans.

16. . . .	P–QN4!
17. PxP	PxP
18. P–QN4	

Not a pretty move since it
weakens White's QB4 and the
pawn itself is weak here. Nevertheless, Black's 18. . . . P–N5
had to be prevented.

18. . . .	QR–B1
19. R–R1	R–R1
20. R/2–Q1?!	

As the better player *and*
White, Keres feels honor-bound
to play for the win. But the position is, if anything, considerably
more comfortable for Black
than for White. White's best
practical approach is to play 20.
R–K1!? and hope that Black

will be satisfied to repeat the position after 20. . . . QR–B1 21. R–R1 R–R1, etc. Chances are good that he would do so.

20. . . .	N–K1!
21. Q–K3	B–B3
22. P–R4	P–R3
23. R–K1	

White is still suffering from an inability to do anything.

23. . . .   N–B2!

Not so for Black, who is ready for 24. . . . N–R3 winning the QNP. White must exchange Rooks.

24. RxR   NxR!

Now the Knight is ready for . . . N–N3 and . . . N–B5. Thus White, again, must rush to simplify.

25. N–Q1	BxB
26. NxB	N–N3
27. R–R1	P–Q4!

Black has gotten in this thematic central advance and stands at least equal. White must search for ways to hold the balance.

28. Q–Q4!

White gains by closing the center, and now he threatens 29. P–K5! with advantage since Black's Bishop would be very passive. Inferior are both 28. PxP?! BxP 29. BxB NxB 30. Q–Q4 Q–B3 with White having weaknesses both on the Queen-

side and Kingside and 28. P–K5?! P–Q5! 29. BxB QxB 30. Q–K2 N–Q4 31. N–Q3 Q–B5 with serious weaknesses in White's Queenside.

28. . . .   P–K4!

A fine way to keep the position open. This reactivates Black's Bishop and underscores White's weaknesses on the Kingside.

| 29. QxKP | PxP |
| 30. R–Q1! | R–K1! |

But not 30. . . . RxRch? 31. NxR and in the endgame Black's weaknesses are more exploitable than White's, and White's Queen has a commanding central location.

31. Q–QB5?!

Up to here White has defended quite well, but from now on, apparently tired and frustrated by Black's perfect play, he quickly goes under. White does threaten 32. R–Q6 but actually allows Black's Knight to head where it wants to with a gain of tempo. 31. Q–Q6 is better.

31. . . .	N–Q2
32. Q–K3	N–K4
33. R–Q6?!	

Starting to leave his King without protection. 33. R–R1 is safer.

| 33. . . . | Q–R1! |
| 34. Q–N6? | |

Allows the following combination which leads to a forced loss. Defensive resources are still offered by moves such as 34. R–Q1, 34. Q–QB3, and 34. Q–B5.

34. . . .   **Q–R8ch**
35. N–Q1   **P–K6!!**

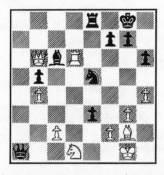

Suddenly White has no defense. Thus if 36. QxKP N–B6ch or if 36. BxB P–K7. And after 36. B–B1 Popov gives as simplest 36. . . . N–B6ch 37. K–N2 N–Q5ch 38. RxB QxN!. The text is equally hopeless.

36. PxP   **BxB**
37. KxB

The tactical 37. R–Q8 is foiled by 37. . . . B–B3 38. RxRch BxR 39. Q–Q8 K–R2!.

37. . . .   **Q–R1ch!**
38. K–N1   **N–B5**
     White resigns

White's Q, R, and N stand so awkwardly that he loses a whole Rook: 39. Q–Q4 NxR 40. QxN R–Q1, etc.

GAME 19

White: L. Portisch
     (Hungary)

Black: P. Keres
     (U.S.S.R.)

Played at Petropolis (Brazil) Interzonal Tournament, July 24, 1973, Round 1.

Queen's Gambit Declined (Semi-Tarrasch Variation)

For a repeat performance against the same opponent Portisch prepares a strategic novelty in the early opening. Keres is not able to solve the requirements of the position, and when he ventures on a dubious Queen sortie his position nearly becomes critical. Portisch sacrifices a pawn for strong initiative, regains it soon, and forces a vastly superior endgame. It is doubtful whether the endgame can be held even with perfect defense, but Keres is too demoralized to put up any reasonable effort, whereas Portisch is sharp all the way through. Portisch demonstrates very well how to beat the Russians: a strategically meaningful opening idea, clear and incisive middlegame, transposition into a superior endgame, and energetic play there.

1. P–QB4   **N–KB3**
2. N–QB3   **P–K3**
3. N–B3   **P–B4**

With this move Keres shows his interest in Tarrasch or Semi-Tarrasch formations. Instead, 3. . . . P–Q4 brings about the orthodox Queen's Gambit Declined, and 3. . . . B–N5 gives us Game 16.

4. P–KN3   P–Q4

Continuing with his plan. In the middle 1970s 4. . . . P–QN3 followed by 5. . . . B–N2 became popular.

5. PxP   NxP

Leading to the Semi-Tarrasch. The capture by the Knight prevents, at least for the moment, the imposition of an isolated QP. However, Black has less central influence than after the "pure" Tarrasch, which would result after 5. . . . PxP 6. P–Q4.

6. B–N2   B–K2
7. O–O   O–O
8. P–Q4   N–QB3
9. NxN

Thus far both sides have developed simply and normally. Here, however, White had to make his first decision. The text leads to an exchange of Knights and a strengthening of Black's center and gives Black an isolated QP. This strategically simple approach is part of Portisch's prepared plan and is fully playable. However, theoretically better chances for an advantage are offered by the more active and potentially sharper 9. P–K4!?, whether Black captures White's Knight or retreats his to QN3.

9. . . .   PxN

The only reasonable recapture. After 9. . . . QxN? 10. B–K3! White has a sizable lead in development and great potential for his KB to rake Black's Queenside.

10. B–K3!?

The novelty Portisch prepared especially for this game. White applies additional pressure against Black's QBP, thus in effect forcing it to declare its intentions. White also overprotects his Q4-square. Less than a year earlier at San Antonio 1972 against the same opponent, Portisch played 10. PxP BxP 11. B–N5 P–B3 12. R–B1 B–N3 13. B–Q2, gained a minute advantage, and won when Keres didn't defend the middlegame accurately. The text move is quite successful in its maiden appearance. Current theory, however, contends that 10. PxP! is White's best chance for a slight advantage.

10. . . .   B–B3?!

Finding himself in an unfamiliar situation, Keres goes for counterplay. The future proves him wrong to do so. Equally unsatisfactory is 10. . . . Q–N3?! 11. PxP BxP 12. BxB

QxB 13. P–QR3 and Black's isolated QP was a permanent weakness in Petrosian–K. Grigorian, 1973 U.S.S.R. Championship, even though Black did squeeze out a draw on move 49. The blockading 10. . . . P–B5! is correct. Then after the intended 11. N–K5?! (11. P–N3 with equality is better), 11. . . . B–B4!, Black's coming play on the Queenside already gives him a slight edge, as in Tal–Alburt, 1975 U.S.S.R. Championship (draw in 31).

11. PxP!   BxP
12. R–N1

As a consequence of the last two moves White's Rook now exerts significant pressure against Black's Queenside and will in due course penetrate there.

12. . . .   B–B3
13. N–K1

In effect forces the QP forward and thus increases the scope of White's KB. However, Black does gain some time and space. Therefore, 13. N–Q4!? seems stronger as in Ornstein–Schneider, 1975 Swedish Championship. After 13. . . . Q–R4? (13. . . . R–K1 is better) 14. BxP R–Q1 White can gain a decisive advantage with 15. BxN!.

13. . . .   P–Q5
14. B–B4   Q–R4?

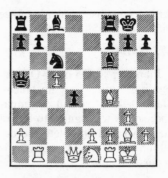

A Queen sortie difficult to understand and explain. Keres is too fine a player not to realize that such a move—development is incomplete—is not positionally justified. Perhaps he felt adventurous in Round 1 or felt too dissatisfied with his position to consider playing normal moves. In any case, it is imperative to complete development. In order, therefore, is 14. . . . R–K1 15. N–Q3 and now either 15. . . . B–N5 or 15. . . . N–R4 followed by 16. . . . B–Q2 and 17. . . . B–B3. In either case, Black's disadvantage is small.

15. N–Q3!

Be my guest! White gets a very strong initiative for the pawn. Moreover, it is hard to see how Black can develop his Queenside without giving a pawn back.

15. . . .   QxRP
16. B–Q6   R–K1

Keres criticizes this and suggests instead 16. . . . R–Q1 17. N–B4 B–K4. White clearly achieves a substantial advantage with 18. B–Q5!, however.

17. N–B4

Planning N–Q5 or B–Q5, depending on circumstances. Black lacks a fruitful continuation, so his willingness to return the pawn and complete the development of the Queenside is understandable.

17. . . .	B–B4
18. RxP	B–K5
19. BxB	RxB
20. Q–N1	

Excellent practical play and also no doubt the theoretically strongest move. The middle-game looks fairly unclear, but in the endgame White's control of the seventh rank and the passed QBP give him a significant advantage. Black must exchange Queens since 20. . . . Q–R3? is worse: 21. QxR QxR 22. N–Q5!.

20. . . .	QxQ
21. R/1xQ	R/5–K1

Keres does not like this either and recommends 21. . . . R–QB1. But then 22. R–Q7! followed by doubling Rooks on the seventh also leaves Black in quite a precarious situation. If White plays perfectly—as Portisch does—there just seems to be no satisfactory defense.

22. R–B7	R/K–QB1
23. R/1–N7	RxR
24. RxR	

Black's Knight must now give way, and White's QBP can then move forward. Black originally planned to play 24. . . . N–N5 but then decided that 25. N–Q3! was too strong: 25. . . . NxN 26. PxN followed by pushing the QBP, or after 25. . . . N–Q4 26. R–N7! and again the QBP advances. The retreat 24. . . . N–Q1 is met by 25. N–Q5 P–KR4 26. R–Q7 planning both 27. NxBch PxN 28. B–K7 and 27. N–B7 followed by 28. N–R6. Keres's actual move loses at least as quickly and surely.

24. . . .	N–R4
25. N–Q5	B–Q1
26. N–K7ch!	

Getting rid of Black's Bishop is the simplest way to win. If now 26. . . . K–B1 27. N–B6ch K–K1 28. NxB KxN 29. RxBP, or if 26. . . . K–R1 27. R–Q7 P–KR3 28. N–Q5 K–N1 29. N–N4 followed by 30. P–B6.

26. . . .	BxN
27. BxB	P–KR3
28. P–B6!	

Passed pawns must be pushed.

28. . . .	R–N1
29. B–Q6	K–R2

Black has no way to prevent the loss of material. Two other choices are 29. . . . R–N8ch 30. K–N2 R–QB8 31. R–B8ch K–R2 32. P–B7 and the pawn soon queens, and 29. . . . R–N3 30. R–B8ch K–R2 31. P–B7 RxB

32. R–R8ch KxR 33. P–B8=
Qch K–R2 34. Q–B5ch, win-
ning the Knight.

30. RxBP!

The mark of master tech-
nique: giving up one advantage
(the passed QBP) for an even
greater one (decisive material
and positional superiority).

30. . . .   **R–N8ch**
31. K–N2   NxP
32. R–B7!   N–Q1

The winner after 32. . . . R–
N3 is 33. B–B8 and after 32.
. . . R–QB8, 33. B–K5!.

33. RxP

The position Portisch had in
mind. White is a pawn up and
has eliminated Black's passed
pawn. Black's QP is very weak
and White's R and B combination has good chances to get at
Black's KNP. Black is ultimately lost, though Keres manages to do it with extra speed.

33. . . .   R–N4?!

Somewhat better is 33. . . .
K–N3 34. B–K5 N–K3, though
35. P–N4! followed by 36. P–
B4 is decisive.

34. P–B4   N–N2
35. B–K5   R–N5
36. BxQP!   P–N4
37. K–B3   K–N3
38. R–R6ch   K–B2
39. P–K3   Black resigns

Black is two pawns down already and about to lose a third.

Chapter 9

Korchnoi, Viktor

Probably the greatest political sensation ever in the chess world was Viktor Korchnoi's announcement on July 27, 1976, that he had decided not to return to the Soviet Union. At that time he had just finished playing in (and winning) the IBM Tournament at Amsterdam, Holland. Though he had carefully managed to bring out all his chess literature, his wife and son remained (and still remain) in Leningrad. At the time of the decision he was among the top three players in the world—which just amplified the shock effects of the decision.

Korchnoi was born in Leningrad on July 23, 1931, and studied history at the university there, but he has been a professional chess player all his life. He became an international grandmaster in 1956 and has participated in all the Candidates events since 1962. He was closest to ultimate success in 1974 when he lost in the finals to Karpov by the minimum result of 12½–11½. Not surprisingly his string of successes are many: four-fold Champion of the U.S.S.R. (1960, 1962, 1964, 1970), on five winning Olympiad teams, on five winning European championship teams. Korchnoi's international first places include Bucharest 1954, Havana 1963, Wijk aan Zee 1968, Palma de Majorca 1969, 1973 Leningrad Interzonal (tie with Karpov). In matches he has defeated Reshevsky, Tal, Geller, Petrosian (twice), Hübner, Mecking, Polugaevsky, and Spassky.

His first literary work is an autobiography published in 1977 in Holland. His 1977 FIDE rating is an exceptional 2645.

GAME 20

White: J. Rukavina
(Yugoslavia)

Black: V. Korchnoi
(U.S.S.R.)

Played at Leningrad (U.S.-S.R.) Interzonal Tournament, June 18, 1973, Round 12.

Queen's Gambit Declined (Meran Variation)

The most dramatic attacking game of the Leningrad Interzonal. After an unbalanced and fighting opening, Black achieves approximate equality. However, he indulges in time-wasting maneuvers, and White builds up a strong attacking formation. As the decisive action approaches, both contestants have exhausted almost all their time and have only seconds left for the coming complications. Here Rukavina shows that he has nerves of steel. He sacrifices a Rook, follows it up accurately, and wins convincingly when Korchnoi misses the right defense. Later analysis showed the sacrifice not to be fully sound, but in a practical game, with seconds left on the clock, genius-level defenses are not to be found. For this game Rukavina received, deservedly, the prize for the most creative achievement.

1. N–KB3	P–Q4
2. P–Q4	N–KB3
3. P–B4	P–K3
4. N–B3	P–B3
5. P–K3	

Black's move order discourages the routine 5. B–N5 and thus White satisfies himself with allowing the Meran Variation. It is not that 5. B–N5 is not playable, but that with 5. . . . PxP!? 6. P–K4 P–QN4 7. P–K5 P–KR3 8. B–R4 P–N4 Black can force hair-raising complications. Modern players do not have anything per se against complications—witness the popularity of so many obscure variations in the Sicilian Najdorf—so the lack of popularity of this so-called "Botvinnik Variation" is simply a question of fashion. In the years to come it may reappear in modern tournament practice.

5. . . .	QN–Q2
6. B–Q3	PxP

Black's 6th and 7th moves form the idea behind the Meran. Black allows White to establish a strong central presence with an early P–K4, while he gets ready to challenge White's center from the flank with a . . . P–QB4.

7. BxBP	P–QN4
8. B–Q3	B–N2

The early lines went 8. . . . P–QR3, followed by 9. . . . P–QB4. Modern tournament practice has preferred the developmental text.

9. P–K4

White logically and consistently establishes a strong central presence. Nevertheless the quiet 9. O–O is at least equally good. For this see Game 34, Portisch–Polugaevsky, Portoroz 1973.

9. . . . P–N5
10. N–QR4 P–B4

Doubly attacking White's center: Q4 from the flank and K4 by Bishop and Knight. Thus White's next is forced.

11. P–K5 N–Q4
12. PxP

White has two fundamental choices here: either to capture Black's QBP with the Knight or pawn or to ignore it with, for example, 12. O–O. After the latter Black usually continues 12. . . . PxP and White 13. R–K1. This is a good flexible way to handle the position for White and perhaps he retains a slight edge. The capture with 12. NxP gives Black excellent chances for equality after 12. . . . NxN! 13. PxN BxP since 14. B–N5ch leads to nothing after 14. . . . K–K2 when Black has excellent control of the central squares to compensate for his King location. The text move is White's third possibility. It is probably the most innocuous one because

White's QN has nothing to do on the edge of the board.

12. . . . Q–R4!
13. O–O BxP
14. R–K1

Because of the active location of Black's pieces, White has little opportunity for an initiative. 14. NxB NxN just further develops Black, and 14. P–QR3 B–K2! 15. B–Q2 O–O 16. R–K1 KR–Q1 17. Q–N3 QR–N1 18. B–K4 B–QB3 19. PxP BxP gives Black sound equality, as in Uhlmann–Larsen, Monte Carlo 1968.

14. . . . N/4–N3
15. NxN QxN

The chances here are approximately in balance. Black has excellent development and central presence. His one slight drawback is that he is short of potential defenders on the Kingside and so to castle there immediately is fraught with clear dangers; e.g., after White's N–KN5.

16. Q–K2   R–QB1
17. P–QR3!?

Immediately challenging
Black to a sharp fight. The developmental 17. B–Q2 is safer.

17. . . .   BxN!?

Black in turn responds with a
fighting move. There are two
advantages to the text: White's
potentially useful attacking
Knight is exchanged and White's
pawn structure is weakened.
But the demerit is also clear: by
exchanging his marvelous QB
Black allows White's Q and KB
strong pressure against Black's
Kingside. All in all it's a move
to play in going for a risky win.
The balancing, safe move is 17.
. . . P–QR4.

18. PxB!

Forced since 18. QxB? allows
18. . . . B–Q5 19. Q–N3 PxP!
with advantage to Black: 20.
RxP BxKP!, etc.

18. . . .   P–N6?!

Sealing off the Queenside is
fine with White since it allows
him to concentrate on his attacking chances against Black's
Kingside. Here 18. . . . B–Q5
is harmless since White can protect his KP easily with 19. P–
B4. Black has no particular way
to strengthen his pressure, so
here is a good time for 18. . . .
O–O!. The unbalanced position
then offers dynamically even
chances.

19. R–Q1   R–B2

Protecting the Knight so that
castling doesn't allow White
BxRPch followed by RxN.

20. B–KB4   O–O
21. R–Q2   N–N1?

The consequence of 18. . . .
P–N6?! is that Black has difficulties finding active play. But
the Knight retreat is pointless,
time wasting, and wrong. 19.
. . . KR–B1! is correct followed
by 20. . . . N–B1!. Then Black's
King gets needed protection and
the doubled Rooks can get some
play along the QB-file.

22. QR–Q1   N–B3
23. Q–K4   P–N3
24. B–KN5!

White is efficiently fashioning
strong play against Black's
King, particularly on the dark
squares.

24. . . .   R–Q2?!

Rukavina questions this move
since Black chases the Queen
pretty much where it wants to
go. The immediate 24. . . .
B–K2 saves tempo.

25. Q–KB4!   B–K2

25. . . . R–Q5?! is a further
waste of time because of 26.
B–K4!.

26. B–B6   BxB
27. PxB

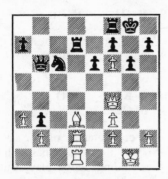

White's triple isolated KBPs are a horrible strategic weakness, *but* the KBP on the sixth is potentially a mortal enemy of the Black King. Rukavina has quite consistently aimed at reaching this type of position correctly believing that his attacking power will prevent Black from getting at his pawn weaknesses. At this point White has a significant advantage, and Black must find the only moves to prevent being mated.

27. . . .   K–R1!

27. . . . Q–Q1? is refuted by 28. BxP!.

28. B–K4!

Excellent central play. White positions his Bishop actively and invites an exchange of Rooks, which would increase White's dominance because Black's remaining Rook would be tied to protecting his King.

28. . . .   N–Q5
29. K–N2

The King will not be particularly well placed here.

Therefore, 29. K–R1!? is possibly better.

29. . . .   R–KN1
30. P–KR4

Played to prevent a potential . . . P–KN4 but has the disadvantage of loosening White's King position. The centralizing 30. Q–K5! is strongest. If then 30. . . . N–B3 31. BxN RxR 32. RxR QxB 33. R–Q6 Q–B1 34. Q–Q4 and White has complete control of the board. Therefore, 30. . . . R/1–Q1 is necessary, but after 31. P–KR4! White is a couple of tempos ahead of the game. Starting here both sides were about out of time, and so their failure to play perfect chess is understandable.

30. . . .   Q–B4
31. Q–N5   P–K4!?

To allow the endgame bind after 31. . . . QxQ?! 32. PxQ R/1–Q1 33. P–B4 is plain suicide.

32. P–B4!   N–K3
33. QxKP!

White may have been able to sacrifice the Queen with 33. RxR NxQ 34. BPxN, but the situation is not clear after 34. . . . Q–B5!. And why should White give up his Queen when he has a won position by retaining it?

33. . . .   RxR
34. RxR   Q–B8
35. B–Q5!?

With seconds remaining on his clock White is brave enough to sacrifice a whole Rook, and Caissa rewards such bravery. Objectively, though, the active, logical 35. R–Q7! is correct. Black then lacks a satisfactory continuation: if 35. . . . NxPch 36. K–R2 N–K7 37. RxBP! Q–N8ch 38. K–R3 Q–B8ch (38. . . . P–KR4 allows 39. QxPch!! PxQ 40. R–R7 mate) 39. K–N4 P–R4ch (if 39. . . . QxP 40. RxPch! KxR 41. Q–KR5 mate!) 40. K–N5!.

35. . . .   QxR

There is no objective basis for criticizing this natural move, especially since it keeps the draw in hand. Subsequently, however, it was discovered that with 35. . . . P–N4!! Black could win; e.g., 36. RPxP NxNP! 37. PxN QxR and Black's attack would come first. But how is it possible to notice something as exotic as 35. . . . P–N4!! when there is no time to think?

36. BxN   Q–Q1??

This blunder, however, is inexcusable. Obviously 36. . . . PxB?? allows 37. P–B7ch R–N2 38. P–B8=Q mate, and not so obviously 36. . . . R–K1? loses to 37. Q–B7!! Q–K7 38. QxBP! Q–K5ch 38. K–N3 and Black will be mated on KN7. 36. . . . Q–Q8! is fairly logical and obvious though, and after 37.

BxBP Q–N5ch 38. K–B1 Q–Q8ch Black has a clear perpetual check.

37. BxBP   R–B1
38. Q–K7!

Winning by force and obviously overlooked by Black. There is no defense to the coming 39. BxKNP!.

38. . . .   P–KR4
39. BxKNP   Q–Q4ch
Black resigns

There is little question that after 40. K–R2 Q–N1 Black is lost: 41. P–B7 Q–N2 42. Q–N5, etc. Even so the circumstances surrounding the resignation are interesting and illustrative of the tremendous nervous energy a master expends in tough games in tough tournaments. After Korchnoi played 39. . . . Q–Q4ch (by far the only reasonable move) he decided that he didn't like it after all, moved the Queen back to Q1, and from there to QN3 (a horrible move which allows three mate-in-ones!). This both perplexed and shocked Rukavina, who was in terrible time pressure also. What Rukavina did was to repunch Korchnoi's clock and gesture to indicate that the completed move (39. . . . Q–Q4ch) must stand. At this point the controlling arbiter was about to interfere, but Korchnoi simplified matters by quickly resigning. Eyewitnesses report that this episode so unnerved Korchnoi, that he spent the next several hours walking it off on the streets of Leningrad. This must have been excellent medicine, for Korchnoi quickly recovered his form and nerves, won a number of games, and finished in a tie for first place with Karpov.

GAME 21

**White: V. Korchnoi
(U.S.S.R.)**

**Black: T. Ghitescu
(Rumania)**

Played in European Team Championship at Bath (England), July 7, 1973, Round 2.

King's Indian Defense (Normal Variation)

Ghitescu adopts a variation which is a specialty of Rumanian masters, and after very exact and careful play he gains clear equality. White seems to

have little else but to acquiesce to wholesale exchanges and a dead-drawn endgame. However, Korchnoi cannot get himself to do so. Instead, in order to play for the win he starts retreating his pieces. Suddenly, Black is better. A further error allows a devastating pin which leads to the loss of a pawn. But Korchnoi "prefers" to lose a piece and must resign on move 33. From complete equality to a painful loss in just nine moves —White's harsh penalty for refusing to look for truth on the chess board.

1.	P–Q4	N–KB3
2.	P–QB4	P–KN3
3.	N–QB3	B–N2
4.	P–K4	P–Q3
5.	N–B3	O–O
6.	B–K2	

White's development carries the plain name "Normal Variation." The name is apt for two reasons: *(1)* White's development is simple, unassuming, and center-oriented. He will bring out his minor pieces first and then look at the subsequent plan for action. *(2)* When the King's Indian had its resurgence after World War II, this variation was the most common.

6. . . .   P–K4

Having castled, Black initiates thematic pressure against White's center. The initial target is invariably White's Q4.

7. O–O

By far the most flexible response. White can, however, obtain a slight endgame advantage with 7. PxP PxP 8. QxQ. Closing the center immediately with 7. P–Q5 is called the Petrosian Variation and was quite fashionable in the late 1950s.

7. . . .   PxP!?

The thematic move to apply pressure to the center is 7. . . . N–B3, which is also the usual move here. Fairly common also is 7. . . . QN–Q2. The text is a specialty of Rumanian masters. Generally it is not advantageous to give up the fight for a central square—such as White's Q4 here—without gaining something in return. Here Black hopes to get quick pressure against White's K4.

8. NxP   R–K1
9. P–B3

There is no other satisfactory way to protect the KP. Obviously awkward is 9. B–B3, and 9. Q–B2 is also without problems for Black. Denker–Gheorghiu, 1971 U.S. Open continued 9. . . . QN–Q2 10. B–K3 P–B3 11. KR–K1 N–B4 12. P–B3 P–QR4 with a fine game for Black.

9. . . .   P–B3!

Planning to annihilate White's center starting with 10. . . .

P–Q4. White has two logical responses.

10. K–R1

This is one of them. By removing the King from the KN1–QR7 diagonal White eliminates many of the tactical possibilities which would result after Black's . . . Q–N3. The alternative is 10. N–B2, which directly aims at preventing Black's 10. . . . P–Q4. Nevertheless, Black still must proceed thus; otherwise White's central superiority will quickly become overpowering. After 10. . . . P–Q4! 11. BPxP PxP 12. PxP B–B4 Black had good play for the pawn in Botez–Gheorghiu, 1966 Rumanian Championship: 13. B–QB4 Q–N3ch 14. K–R1 N–R3 15. P–KN4?! QR–QB1.

10. . . .   P–Q4

10. . . . QN–Q2 is possible, but the text is unquestionably the most consistent approach.

11. BPxP   PxP
12. B–QN5

By forcing Black to interpose on his Q2, White wins Black's QP. This turns out to be only temporary, however. Instead of the text move, Yugoslav GM Bukic recommends 12. B–KN5. It seems to me that Black retains equality after 12. . . . PxP.

12. . . .   QN–Q2!?

Black must interpose something since 12. . . . R–B1?! al-

lows 13. P–K5, and after 12.
. . . R–K2?! too strong is 13.
B–N5!. But what should Black
interpose? Theory considers
only 12. . . . B–Q2, but then 13.
PxP! leads to a slight plus because Black has difficulties in
recovering his pawn. The text
is an interesting attempt at
strengthening Black's play. He
refrains from any overt action
to immediately recover material and develops his Queenside with gain of time by pushing back White's KB. Black
expects that in due course
White's advanced QP will be
unsupportable.

13. PxP	P–QR3
14. B–R4	P–QN4
15. N–B6	Q–N3
16. B–N3	B–N2

This is basically the critical
position for judging Black's
opening idea. He has completed
his development, his pieces
stand harmoniously, and with
an imminent . . . BxN he can
recover the sacrificed pawn.
Clearly White must give back

the material, but can he trans-
form the material advantage
into a positional one?

17. P–QR4

Leads to nothing but a general exchange of Queenside material. The only worthwhile idea
is 17. B–N5!, as GM Gheorghiu
suggested, with the idea 17. . . .
BxN?! 18. PxB QxP 19. N–Q5!
with some advantage to White
because of his active piece
placement. (The immediate
threat is 20. R–B1 followed by
21. N–B7.) Instead of 17. . . .
BxN?! Black should continue
with 17. . . . N–B4 or 17. . . .
P–QR4!?. His chances for
equality then are excellent.

17. . . .	N–B4!
18. B–N5	NxB
19. QxN	BxN
20. PxB	QxP
21. PxP	PxP
22. RxR	

The position is rather equal
and symmetrical and a draw
here would be a consistent result. Neither side has any realistic winning chances. If instead
22. QxNP Black's simplest response is 22. . . . RxR! 23. RxR
QxQ 24. NxQ R–N1, and Black
will soon recover the QNP for
dead equality: 25. N–B3 P–
R3!, etc.

| 22. . . . | RxR |
| 23. R–B1 | |

With this move White shows
his determination to play for a

win. Again complete equality
results after 23. QxNP QxQ 24.
NxQ R–N1, etc.

23. . . .   P–R3!
24. B–K3

A blunder is 24. NxP?? PxB!
and Black's Queen is safe because of the back-rank mate
after 25. RxQ?! R–R8ch, etc.
The first rank weakness will
plague White throughout the
game.

24. . . .   Q–B5!
25. Q–Q1?

Black has played excellently
all the way through, and White
has to concede the honorable
draw after 25. QxP QxQ 26.
NxQ R–N1. But Korchnoi cannot face such a prospect. However, playing for a win by retreating one's pieces invariably
leads to the opposite.

25. . . .   P–N5!

Of course. Black now gains
space on the Queenside and
across the board. Black is already better.

26. N–R4

Equivalent is 26. N–K4.

26. . . .   Q–K3!
27. N–N6   R–K1
28. N–B4?

Walks into a deadly pin. The
safe 28. B–N1! is required. Obviously Black has some advantage, but White should be able
to protect his weak spots.

28. . . .   R–QB1!
29. Q–Q3

29. P–QN3 allows 29. . . .
RxN! 30. RxR QxB.

29. . . .   N–Q4!
30. B–Q2

About equivalent to 30. R–
K1 NxB 31. NxN BxP.

30. . . .   BxP!

A pretty move based on
back-rank mate motifs: 31.
NxB? RxRch 32. BxR Q–K8ch
33. Q–B1 QxQ mate.

31. R–K1?

After 31. R–QN1 or 31. R–
KB1 White has a miserable
position a pawn down. But what
happens now is worse.

31. . . .   N–B5!

Another back-rank combination leads to a decisive win of
material. 32. RxQ NxQ leads to
a hopeless endgame, and 32.
BxN? obviously leads to mate.
Only marginally better than the
text is 32. Q–Q6 QxN! 33. BxN

B–N2 and the passed QNP leads to a sure win.

32. Q–B2?!   QxN
33. R–K8ch

If 33. QxB, 33. . . . N–Q6 is decisive.

33. . . .   K–R2
White resigns

After 34. RxR Black mates with 34. . . . Q–B8.

GAME 22

White: R. Hübner
(West Germany)

Black: V. Korchnoi
(U.S.S.R.)

Played in Public Training Match at Solingen (West Germany), December 1973, Match Game 3.

Ruy Lopez
(Open Variation)

Korchnoi plays into a variation that Hübner has had success with in the past. The result here too is that Black does not gain full equality out of the opening. White has control of the dark squares, the superior Bishop, pressure against Black's QP, and attacking chances on the Kingside. With careful maneuvering Black's position should be defensible, but Korchnoi does not feel comfortable

in the position and puts up very weak resistance. Hübner first wins a pawn, then gains two pieces for a Rook, and also obtains a killing attack against Black's Kingside. Soon Black's situation is so hopeless that he resigns even as he makes a desperate Rook sacrifice. Overall the game is an easy task for Hübner, and his clever opening selection deserves much credit.

1.	P–K4	P–K4
2.	N–KB3	N–QB3
3.	B–N5	P–QR3
4.	B–R4	N–B3
5.	O–O	NxP

This Open Variation was briefly discussed in Game 13. It has never been as popular as the Closed Variation. Formerly its leading practitioner was ex-World Champion Dr. Max Euwe. Of the present leading grandmasters, only Korchnoi uses it—and secondarily at that. As a matter of fact Korchnoi is the author of the section on the Open Variation in the *Encyclopedia of Chess Openings* published in 1974.

6. P–Q4!

To hope for any advantage White must hurriedly open lines against Black's King. 6. R–K1 N–B4 leads to nothing.

6. . . .   P–QN4

The normal way of handling the Open. There is no brutal

refutation of the Riga Variation: 6. . . . PxP 7. R–K1 P–Q4 8. NxP B–Q3!?; nonetheless White is demonstrably better after the following complications: 9. NxN BxPch 10. K–R1 Q–R5 11. RxNch PxR 12. Q–Q8ch QxQ 13. NxQch KxN 14. KxB.

**7. B–N3   P–Q4
8. PxP   B–K3**

We have now the normal position in this variation. Black's disadvantage stems from an inherent looseness in his position: Queenside, QP, Knight on K5, possibly an insufficiently protected Kingside. As partial compensation Black does have fairly smooth development, but White's position is without noticeable weaknesses, so there is little that Black can hope to accomplish against it.

White has the choice of two main approaches. The older, solid move is 9. P–B3, which strengthens White's Q4 and allows the KB to retreat to QB2. The alternative is the game continuation.

9. Q–K2

This variation became fashionable after its successful use in the 1948 Match Tournament for the World Championship. It prepares a dynamic undermining of Black's QP by means of 10. R–Q1 and 11. P–B4.

**9. . . .   B–K2
10. R–Q1   O–O?!**

After the debacle here, Korchnoi never ventured this subvariation again. In Match Game 5 here and in Match Game 4 against Mecking in the 1974 Candidates Matches, he switched to 10. . . . N–B4, eventually equalizing. Both games were drawn.

**11. P–B4   NPxP
12. BxP**

The first important position in our subvariation. The pressure against Black's QP is quite real, and there are no smooth ways to minimize it. Therefore, considerable theoretical work has been done on the Queen sacrifice 12. . . . PxB 13. RxQ KRxQ, but after 14. N–B3! White's chances are indisputably superior. Black's most common defensive method is 12. . . . Q–Q2 13. N–B3 NxN 14. PxN P–B3 15. PxP BxP. In *E.C.O.* Korchnoi's analysis concludes that this variation gives Black eventual equality. But since he himself doesn't follow his recommendations, his confidence in them must not be total.

12. . . .   B–QB4

Another reasonable continuation that Korchnoi had previously played with success. The exchange of the dark-square Bishops gives Black some defensive time but weakens considerably the dark squares in his position. The idea is playable but does not lead to full equality.

13. B–K3   BxB
14. QxB   Q–N1

The double attack on the KB and QNP forces White's reply.

15. B–N3   Q–N3

In Matanovic–Korchnoi, Yugoslavia–U.S.S.R. 1966, Korchnoi played 15. . . . N–R4, and after 16. QN–Q2 Q–R2! 17. QxQ RxQ 18. QR–QB1 P–QB4 19. NxN NxB Black had equality. Subsequently in Hübner–Demarre, World Student Championship, Dresden 1969, White improved with 16. N–K1! (threat 17. P–B3) NxB 17. PxN Q–N3 18. QxQ PxQ 19. P–QN4! P–B3 20. P–B3 N–N4 21. PxP PxP 22. N–B3 and gained a clear endgame advantage. Thus Hübner was looking forward to a repeat performance. However, Korchnoi used the text move in the 1973 U.S.S.R. Championship, which concluded shortly before this match, and thus is the first one to vary. Hübner does demonstrate that in his hands it is White for choice, anyway.

16. Q–K2!

Tukmakov–Korchnoi, 1973 U.S.S.R. Championship, went 16. QxQ PxQ 17. N–R3 (17. BxP?? QR–Q1 18. B–N3 BxB and Black wins) 17. . . . KR–Q1 18. N–B2 N–R4 19. N–N4 (19. N/2–Q4!? with a small plus is better) 19. . . . N–B5! 20. BxN PxB 21. NxP RxRch 22. RxR P–R3! 23. N–N4 R–R5 and Black had equality (24. P–QR3 P–B6!). However, having lost the first two match games, Hübner wants more than a minute endgame advantage.

16. . . .   QR–Q1

An alternate approach, suggested by Petrosian, is 16. . . . N–K2 with . . . P–QB4 as a followup.

17. N–B3!   NxN
18. PxN   Q–B4

Korchnoi's attempted improvement on the 18. . . . N–K2 of Tal–Geller, Budva 1967, in which White was clearly better after 19. QR–N1 Q–R4 20. P–B4 KR–K1?! 21. N–N5!. With the text Black further protects the QP and thus threatens 19. . . . B–N5 with counterplay, while he prevents White's P–QB4. Even so Black's position is without many prospects, and the QRP will soon need protection.

19. P–KR3!   B–B1

Thereby planning some play against White's KP after a . . . KR–K1. 19. . . . P–QR4, is equivalent.

20. Q–Q3!

Aiming at Black's KR2 after a B–QB2 or N–KN5. Black's Kingside is now clearly short of defenders.

20. . . .   KR–K1
21. R–K1

With White's KP protected, the potential N–KN5 becomes a stronger threat.

21. . . .   P–N3

There is no way to avoid this weakening.

22. QR–Q1!

White has a lovely harmonious position with all his pieces actively placed. White has potential against Black's Kingside,

Queenside, QP, and dark squares. All that Black can do is to laboriously try to protect his weak spots.

22. . . .   P–QR4?

And this just creates a new one on his QN4. The defensive 22. . . . N–K2 is in order.

23. B–R4!

With the simple but devastating threat of 24. Q–N5!, which would win at least a pawn.

23. . . .   B–Q2??

Even so there is no reason to panic. Unpinning the Knight is in order; i.e., either 23. . . . R–K2 or the safer 23. . . . R–B1. Black's position is quite unpleasant, but at least he has a position.

24. QxP

Wins a pawn and the game. Black's house of cards collapses completely.

24. . . .   Q–N3
25. N–N5!

Making hay while the sun shines is the surest way to riches. The weaknesses of Black's Kingside are irreparable.

25. . . .   R–KB1
26. Q–B4!

Threatening 27. RxB and 27. Q–R4, among others.

26. . . .   N–N1

Black has *sacrificed* a pawn to get this position?

27.	R–N1	Q–R3
28.	Q–R4	P–R4
29.	RxN!	

Adding a decisive material superiority to his positional one. Only *Black's* extreme time pressure makes him play on: he has no time to recognize the hopelessness of his situation!

29.	. . .	RxR
30.	BxB	Q–Q6
31.	N–K4!	R–N3
32.	P–K6!	PxP
33.	Q–K7	Q–Q4
34.	N–N5	RxP

Black resigns

White has a multitude of wins, among them 35. BxPch RxB 36. Q–R7ch K–B1 37. NxRch K–K1 38. NxPch.

Chapter 10

Kuzmin, Gennady

Born on January 19, 1946, in Mariinsk, Gennady Kuzmin had outstanding chess years in 1973 (when he became a grandmaster) and in 1974. He tied for second (with Petrosian, Polugaevsky, Karpov, and Korchnoi) in the 1973 U.S.S.R. Championship, finished a strong seventh in the 1973 Leningrad International, tied for 1st–4th at Hastings 1973/74, and was an undefeated Board 6 on the Soviet team at Nice Olympiad 1974.

Poor health (heart problems) has led to results considerably below those of 1973/74, even though his FIDE rating, at 2550, remains high.

GAME 23

White: E. Cobo
 (Cuba)

Black: G. Kuzmin
 (U.S.S.R.)

Played at Capablanca Memorial Tournament, Cienfuegos (Cuba), February–March, 1973.

King's Indian Defense (Normal Variation)

Black decides to surprise his opponent with an opening novelty. But the "novelty" is so antipositional that Black is significantly worse almost immediately. A further error makes it impossible for him to develop his Queenside smoothly. On the other hand, White systematically obtains the advantage along the Q-file and on the Queenside. Black's premature attempt at counterplay is quashed efficiently, and then all of Black's weaknesses come home to roost. Kuzmin had a successful tournament at Cienfuegos; Cobo did not. In this game, however, White shows that poor chess moves will be punished quite severely. Starting with move 7 Black is never in the game.

1. P–QB4   N–KB3
2. N–QB3   P–KN3
3. P–K4   P–Q3
4. P–Q4   B–N2
5. N–B3   O–O
6. B–K2

With some transposition of moves the normal variation of the King's Indian has been reached. We already saw this variation in Game 21, in which Black continued with the usual 6. . . . P–K4.

6. . . .   P–B3

Less common but playable. Black still plans . . . P–K4 but first establishes control of his Q4.

7. O–O   Q–N3?

Officially this is an opening innovation, but it is so bad that it must be called an opening error. The Queen has no chance of leading the attack on White's QP and will be driven back with loss of time. As mentioned above, 7. . . . P–K4 is correct. If Black is in the mood to experiment, then 7. . . . P–QR3 intending . . . P–QN4 is a reasonable try.

8. Q–B2!

Protects the KP and QNP and frees Q1 for the KR. White gains the advantage with simple, good moves.

8. . . .   R–K1
9. P–KR3!

To play B–K3 without being bothered by . . . N–KN5.

9. . . .   P–K4
10. PxP!   PxP
11. B–K3   Q–B2
12. KR–Q1

The resolution of the center tension is theoretically on Black's terms. But here White gains a clear advantage in development and control of the Q-file. His advantage is considerable.

12. . . .   QN–Q2?

Black will now have extreme difficulty developing his Queenside. 12. . . . B–K3 is imperative.

13. P–QN4!

To establish a grip on Q6.

13. . . .   N–B1
14. B–B5   N/3–Q2

Clumsy, but otherwise the KP can't be protected.

15. B–Q6   Q–Q1
16. P–B5

A dream position for White out of a closed opening. He has a bind on the Queenside and control of the Q-file, whereas Black's forces are completely passive.

16. . . .   **Q–B3**
17. B–B4!

Excellent nonroutine play. White prepares to exchange, as soon as it appears, Black's only potentially active piece.

17. . . .   **N–K3**
18. BxN   **QxB**
19. N–QR4

On the way to QB4 where it will control Q6 and attack the KP. Other good ideas are 19. P–QR4 and 20. P–N5 and even the immediate 19. P–N5!?.

19. . . .   **N–B1**
20. N–N2   **P–B3**
21. N–B4   **Q–B2**
22. P–QR4   **B–K3**
23. N/3–Q2   **QR–B1**

Black has laboriously managed to bring out his Queenside pieces, but overall he is very cramped, his prospects bleak.

24. P–R5

Clearly planning P–QR6. The immediate 24. P–B4! is also very strong.

24. . . .   **BxN**

Hoping to develop his Knight to the vacated K3-square. After 24. . . . P–QR3 White can play 25. P–B4!.

25. NxB   **N–K3**

To allow White's next is quite undesirable, but so is 25. . . . P–QR3 26. P–B4!.

26. P–R6!   **N–Q5?!**

Black's first and last attacking move in this game. It makes matters worse by giving up control of White's KB4, but human nature wants at least to threaten something.

27. Q–Q3   **R/K–Q1**
28. P–B4!

With Black's Queenside in ruins, White turns to the center where he establishes a new Black weakness—the KP. White's play is a model of logic and simplicity.

28. . . .   **N–K3**
29. PxP   **PxP**
30. Q–B1!

This quiet retreat wins material by force, since the KP can't be protected.

30. . . .	QxQch
31. KxQ	R–Q2
32. BxP	

The well-deserved first fruit.

32. . . .	BxB
33. NxB	RxRch
34. RxR	PxP
35. R–Q6!	

Forcing the Knight back.

| 35. . . . | N–Q1 |
| 36. R–Q7 | |

With the penetration of the Rook the game is over. Black's best now is 36. . . . P–QR4 37. PxP N–K3. But after 38. N–Q3! White is a clear pawn ahead and has the vastly superior position.

| 36. . . . | R–N1?! |
| 37. RxQRP | **Black resigns** |

37. . . . RxP loses to 38. R–R8, and Black has no reasonable move to counter White's threatened 38. RxQRP.

GAME 24

White: G. Kuzmin
(U.S.S.R.)

Black: B. Larsen
(Denmark)

Played at Leningrad (U.S.-S.R.) Interzonal Tournament, June 17, 1973, Round 11.

Sicilian Defense

Larsen reacts to an unusual variation with an even less common subvariation and quickly succeeds in throwing White off a steady course. As a result White remains a pawn down and has nothing to show for it. A momentary lapse by Black does allow White to gain good drawing chances. But after White muffs his chance, Black scores a convincing endgame win. An effective fighting win very much in Larsen's style with psychological overtones throughout.

1. P–K4	P–QB4
2. N–KB3	N–QB3
3. B–N5	

A continuation significantly less common than 3. P–Q4. It has two major points: to weaken Black's pawn formation with a timely BxN and to quickly complete Kingside development by castling.

| 3. . . . | N–B3!? |

The most popular defenses are 3. . . . P–K3 and 3. . . . P–KN3. We'll see an example with the latter in Game 44, Hecht–Spassky, Dortmund 1973. But the text is very much in the Larsen tradition: he selects a move which, though playable, is not currently popular and thus forces the opponent to start solving practical problems at a very early stage.

4. P–K5

Something must, of course, be done about the attacked KP, and this is one response. The protecting 4. N–B3 allows 4. . . . N–Q5! with equality since after 5. NxN PxN Black gains time because of the attack on the QN. White's most flexible and perhaps best plan is Bronstein's 4. Q–K2!?.

4. . . .   N–Q4!

At first glance 4. . . . N–KN5!? to attack the KP seems attractive. However after 5. BxN! QPxB 6. P–KR3! N–R3 7. O–O P–KN3 8. P–Q3 B–N2 9. N–B3 Black's KN remains out of action and this yields White the better chances, as in Seret–Puhm, 1975 French Championship.

5. O–O

This quiet move leads to nothing, but even after the more active 5. N–B3 Black keeps a steady equality with 5. . . . N–B2!: 6. P–QR4 P–KN3 7. O–O B–N2 8. R–K1 O–O 9. P–Q3 N–Q5 10. B–QB4 P–Q4 11. PxP e.p. QxP, as in Haag–Padevsky 1958.

5. . . .   Q–B2

Here too there is nothing wrong with 5. . . . N–B2!, but Larsen characteristically selects a more unbalancing plan.

6. R–K1   P–K3
7. P–QN3?!

Rather too slow. Larsen's fighting approach is starting to bear fruit. White should himself play actively with 7. N–B3! but has allowed Black to pre-empt the fight plan.

7. . . .   P–QN3

To get the QB onto a useful central diagonal.

8. B–B1?!

Again very passive. Both 8. B–B4 with the plan 9. BxN and 10. N–B3 and 8. B–Q3 with the idea 9. B–K4 are better.

8. . . .   B–N2
9. B–N2   P–QR3
10. N–R3   B–K2
11. N–B4   O–O

A psychologically interesting moment. Black has completed his development healthily and now plans to liquidate White's center outpost with 12. . . . P–B3. Black can then expect to have a slight plus. Such an outcome is logical because White has consistently refrained from meeting the challenge to his move-one initiative.

12. N–Q6?

After running from a fight for his first eleven moves White finds that he doesn't like his position. So he makes a complete about face and sacrifices a pawn—a valuable central pawn at that—to open the position. However, since he has fulfilled none of the prerequisites for such an opening to be effective, his chances for success are minute, and the text move must be rated as the losing moment.

12. . . .	BxN
13. PxB	QxP
14. P–Q4	PxP

15. NxP	N–B5!
16. NxN	QxN

So Black has a sound extra pawn and his QB has a marvelous diagonal. None of White's tactics have a chance of success: 17. BxNP? is refuted by 17. . . . N–R6ch, and 17. Q–Q4 leads to nothing after 17. . . . N–R6ch 18. K–R1 P–B3 19. Q–KR4 N–N4.

17. Q–N4	N–N3
18. P–QB4	P–Q3
19. QR–Q1	P–K4
20. R–K3	P–B4!

With his extra central pawn it is actually Black who should have the superior attacking chances.

21. Q–N5	R–B3
22. R–N3	P–B5
23. R/3–Q3	

White's situation is critical. 23. R–N4? loses to 23. . . . B–B1 and 23. R–R3 is rather pointless. So White hopes for some miracle along the Q-file.

23. . . .   N–K2?

By moving too quickly Black throws away almost all of his advantage. As Larsen tells it, he saw the following sacrifice but overlooked something. After the accurate 23. . . . N–R1!, planning the attacking . . . R–N3 and the defensive . . . N–B2, White's game would be in the last moments. But after the text move, the fight is renewed.

24.	RxP!	RxR
25.	RxR	QxR
26.	BxP	

The mate threat on KN7 allows White to win Black's Knight, thus leaving White with only the small material disadvantage of B and P for R. Also very important is that White's Q and QB are very active and several of Black's pawns are weak. White's chances for a draw are excellent here.

26.	. . .	Q–N3
27.	QxN	B–K5

After 27. . . . R–K1 28. QxB RxB 29. QxRP White has two pawns for the Exchange and Black has no decisive continuation. A serious alternative is 27. . . . BxP 28. BxB P–B6 29. QxPch QxQ 30. BxQ, but, as both Larsen and Tseitlin note, White can hold after either 30. . . . PxB 31. B–Q4! P–N4 32. PxP PxP 33. P–QR4!, and after the disappearance of the Queenside pawns Black has no winning chances, or after 30. . . . KxB 31. BxP R–Q1 32. B–Q5

and White has two pawns for the Exchange and can keep out Black's Rook.

28. P–B5!

Superior to 28. BxBP?! R–K1 29. Q–N5 QxQ 30. BxQ B–N8 when Black has excellent winning chances since he either wins the QRP or gets his Rook to the eighth rank.

28.	. . .	PxP

A way to *lose* is 28. . . . R–K1?? 29. B–B4ch K–R1 30. BxNPch.

29. BxBP?

Spoiling the fruits of his previous ingenious play. Correct is the obvious 29. B–B4ch K–R1 and then 30. BxNPch QxB 31. QxB. Larsen feels that White's drawing chances are excellent because all Black's pawns are so weak.

29.	. . .	R–K1
30.	Q–Q6	

30. QxP? loses to 30. . . . BxP!.

30.	. . .	QxQ
31.	BxQ	R–Q1
32.	B–B4ch	

32. BxBP? loses a piece after 32. . . . R–Q8 and 33. . . . B–Q6.

32.	. . .	B–Q4!!

Gets rid of a pair of Bishops and leads to a winnable R vs. B endgame in which White has only one pawn for the Exchange. Instead after 32. . . . K–R1 33. P–B3 White has some drawing chances since Black's King is far from the KP after 33. . . . RxB 34. PxB.

33. BxBch   K–R1
34. P–N3

Unfortunately for White 34. BxP? RxB wins a piece since White must part with his Bishop to save his King.

34. . . .   RxB
35. B–B4   P–N4!

In general, with pawns on both sides of the board, one pawn for the Exchange is insufficient to hold the game. Invariably the stronger side is able to penetrate somewhere. So too here. There is no way to set up a satisfactory defensive formation. White's 37th and 38th moves do lose some time, but in the larger picture that is inconsequential. White is theoretically quite lost, and his *practical* chances also are scant.

36. K–N2   K–N2
37. P–QR4   P–QR4
38. K–B3   R–KR3
39. K–N2   K–B3
40. P–R3   K–K4!

Black's King cannot be stopped from reaching a useful location. The position is simple enough that Larsen did not even bother to adjourn the game.

41. B–N8   K–Q5
42. B–B4   R–KB3
43. B–N8   K–B6
44. B–B4   K–Q7

On the way to K8. White can prevent this only for a short while.

45. K–B1   P–R4
46. B–K2   P–R5
47. PxP   PxP
48. B–B4   R–B6!
49. K–N2   R–B6
50. P–B4?!

Speeds up the loss, but there is no long-term defense, anyway.

50. . . .   K–K8
51. P–B5   R–N6ch
52. K–R2   R–KB6
White resigns

White's in zugzwang after 53. B–K6 K–B7 and must decide whether to lose the QNP or the KBP (giving up the KRP means giving up the King!). Either way, the resulting position is completely hopeless.

GAME 25

White: S. Gligoric
    (Yugoslavia)

Black: G. Kuzmin
    (U.S.S.R.)

Played at Leningrad (U.S.-S.R.) Interzonal Tournament, June 22, 1973, Round 14.

Nimzo-Indian Defense (Normal Variation)

This is a strategic effort all the way through. After the opening White has an isolated QP, but the active placement of his pieces gives him a slight edge overall. At an appropriate moment White dissolves his isolated pawn and should still retain the advantage of the somewhat freer position. But a moment's carelessness by Black allows White to transpose into a Q + P endgame in which White wins a pawn by force. Theoretically the position is an ultimate win for White, but the road is long. Apparently dejected however, Kuzmin resigns after adjournment and thus deprives us of seeing Gligoric's technique and himself of any chances for a half point.

1.	P–Q4	N–KB3
2.	P–QB4	P–K3
3.	N–QB3	B–N5

The Nimzo-Indian Defense, first brought into tournament practice by Latvian-born Danish grandmaster Aron Nimzovich. Introduced over fifty years ago, it has stood the test of time and is today an even more popular opening than in its early years. The basic point of the Bishop move is to exert indirect pressure on White's key K4 central square. Black is quite prepared to exchange his KB for White's QN in order to retain this pressure. If this saddles White with doubled QBPs, then Black can try to attack them. White, on the other hand, has the Bishop pair and greater central influence. All in all, an interesting, dynamic fight is assured—thus its continual popularity.

4. P–K3

Rubinstein's continuation, by far the most popular modern approach. In effect, White says, "I'm not going for any drastic refutation of 3. . . . B–N5 but will first complete my development and then decide what to do next."

4. . . .   P–B4

This immediate challenge to White's center is currently the most popular move. Somewhat more in the original Nimzovichian manner is 4. . . . P–QN3 and 5. . . . B–N2. The flexible 4. . . . O–O is also playable.

5.	B–Q3	O–O
6.	N–B3	P–Q4
7.	O–O	

White has now completed his basic development, and it is now Black's turn to make decisions. The two reasonable approaches are to develop the QN and to start to clear center tension. Thus 7. . . . N–B3, 7. . . . QN–Q2, 7. . . . BPxP, and 7. . . . QPxP seem logical. And in fact at various times all of these have been popular. In this game Black chooses a line which became common in the middle 1970s.

| 7. . . . | QPxP |
| 8. BxP | P–QR3 |

With the logical plan of 9. . . . P–QN4 and 10. . . . B–N2. However, this cannot really be executed, and the move can easily turn out to slightly weaken the Queenside and lose time. More effective is the straightforward 8. . . . PxP 9. PxP P–QN3.

9. B–Q3

Good also is the preventive 9. P–QR4!. In Spassky–Petrosian, 1975 U.S.S.R. Spartakiad, White obtained a clear advantage after 9. . . . PxP 10. PxP Q–R4?! 11. B–KN5 N–Q4 12. N–K4! N–Q2 13. Q–K2 R–K1 14. KR–B1 N–B1 15. N–B5! and won in 41 moves.

9. . . .   QN–Q2

Black's problem is that the immediate 9. . . . P–QN4?! is met by 10. N–K4!, when there is no good way to complete

Queenside development without losing the QBP.

| **10. P–QR4** | **PxP** |

10. . . . P–QN3?! misplaces the KB after 11. N–R2! B–R4 12. P–K4!.

| **11. PxP** | **P–QN3** |

To fianchetto the QB seems logical, but this leads to a very passive location for the QN. Perhaps better, therefore, is 11. . . . N–N3 12. Q–K2 N/N3–Q4 13. B–KN5 B–K2 14. KR–K1 R–K1, as in Portisch–Panno, 1968 Lugano Olympiad, where White's attacking chances were fewer than in this game.

12. Q–K2	**B–N2**
13. R–Q1	**R–K1**
14. B–KB4	**N–B1**
15. N–K5	

This type of position, with White having an isolated QP but with some space advantage, is well known in chess literature. Here two special factors tilt the position clearly in White's favor: the weakness of

Black's QRP prevents active play by the QR, and Black's QN (now at KB1) has no active prospects. If now 15. . . . N–N3 16. NxN RPxN 17. B–K5! and Black has just weakened his Kingside.

15. . . .   N–Q4
16. B–Q2!   P–B3

If Black exchanges White's QN, then after 17. PxN White's center is strengthened. The text does lead to a slight weakening of the Kingside and KP, but White's Knight cannot be tolerated too long on the active K5-square.

17. N–B4   B–K2
18. NxN!

Black was planning 18. . . . N–N5, which would bother White's KB and QP quite unpleasantly. Therefore it is in White's interest to exchange the Knight. Compared to the position after Black's 15th, Black's Kingside has been weakened.

18. . . .   QxN
19. Q–N4   P–B4

With this and the following moves, Black is able to gain some space for his KB and N, but again at the cost of further weakening his Kingside and the important K4-square. None of these factors by itself is large, but Black is forced to accumulate more and more weaknesses. White is clearly, though not decisively, better.

20. Q–N3   B–R5
21. Q–R3   QR–Q1
22. B–B3   N–N3
23. N–K3!

Black, of course, threatened 23. . . . N–B5, and 23. NxP?? is a blunder because of 23. . . . Q–B3 followed by 24. . . . N–B5. Therefore White liquidates his isolated QP, thereby opening the position so that several of Black's weaknesses can be exposed to direct action. This is a well-known technique to handle isolated-QP positions.

23. . . .   Q–Q3
24. P–Q5!   Q–K2

Renewing the threat of . . . N–KB5.

25. B–B4!   N–B5
26. Q–B3   NxQP
27. BxN   BxB
28. NxB

Obviously Black will recapture, but how? The answer will be critical to the result of the game.

28. . . .   RxN?

The losing moment. Generally speaking, the defending side should exchange pieces in order to lessen the pressure; thus Black's move seems strategically in order. However, the tactical possibilities in moves 30 to 33 are of overriding importance here. Correct is 28. . . . PxN! since then 29. P-KN3 leads to nothing after 29. . . . B-B3, and 29. QxBP? is downright bad because of 29. . . . R-KB1. Therefore, the best that White has is 29. RxP RxR 30. QxRch Q-KB2 31. Q-Q4, and after 31. . . . B-Q1! Gligoric rates White's position as only slightly better. The usual strategic factors lead to the plus: Black's Queenside has been weakened, there is looseness on the Kingside too, and White's Q and B are actively placed. Black's potentially saving factor is that little attacking material is left with which for White to realize on his advantages.

29. RxR   PxR

Now after 30. QxPch we would be back into the previous note. But White has something better: he can now chase Black's pieces back.

30. P-KN3!   B-B3
31. R-K1!   Q-Q2
32. RxRch   QxR
33. QxPch   K-R1

Worse is 33. . . . Q-B2 34. Q-R8ch and White will obtain a passed pawn on the Queenside.

34. BxB   PxB
35. QxP

And so one of Black's weaknesses—the KBP—has fallen, and White is a sound pawn up. Theoretically this should be a win, but because the extra pawn is on the same side as the King, the technical problems involved are considerable. The "defending" Queen is such a strong attacking piece that the stronger side has always to worry about allowing perpetual check. In the moves to come before the time control at move 40, White is essentially satisfied to keep the status quo.

35. . . .   Q-B3
36. P-N3   K-N2
37. P-R4   P-QR4
38. K-R2   Q-Q3
39. Q-K4   Q-B4
40. K-N2   Q-Q3
41. Q-N4ch   K-R3
42. Q-B5   Black resigns

White sealed his 42nd move and Black decided to resign without resuming play. There were two main factors involved in this decision: respect for Gligoric's technique and disgust at himself for the error on move 28. Gligoric indicates that his winning method would have consisted of placing his KNP on N4, his KRP on R5, and his KBP on B3 and then playing his King to KR3 and his Queen to K3 via K4. Presumably then he would be ready to advance his KBP and possibly the KNP. All of this is good, but even so a slight misstep is often all that is required for perpetual check to rear its ugly head. Black would certainly have not been criticized if he had decided to play on.

GAME 26

White: G. Kuzmin (U.S.S.R.)

Black: G. Forintos (Hungary)

Played in European Team Championship at Bath (England), July 13, 1973, Round 7.

Queen's Gambit Declined (Orthodox/ Tartakower Variation)

In the opening White tries to employ a modern strategic approach, but a premature central break allows Black to equalize. When White becomes careless in an approximately even middlegame position, Black uses relatively simple tactics to win two pieces for a Rook. Black consolidates his material advantage well, first in the middlegame and subsequently in the endgame. White resigns when he must lose a valuable Queenside pawn. A rather easy win against a Soviet grandmaster. Black played normally and well; White did not.

1.	P–Q4	N–KB3
2.	P–QB4	P–K3
3.	N–KB3	P–Q4

Turning down the opportunity for the Queen's Indian with 3. . . . P–QN3 in preference to the Orthodox Defense to the QGD.

4.	N–B3	B–K2
5.	B–N5	O–O
6.	P–K3	P–KR3

This move with the 7th move followup has been a modern-day mainstay for a long time. There is, however, some resurgence of the "ancient" 6. . . . QN–Q2. For one example see Game 33, Polugaevsky–Portisch, Portoroz Play-off 1973.

7. B–R4   P–QN3

In the position after White's 7th move Black stands satisfactorily from the standpoint of King safety and center influence. In fact Black's only serious developmental problem is what to do with his QB. Over fifty years ago Tartakower hit on the idea of the QB fianchetto, and this has been Black's most popular approach ever since.

8. B–K2!

Apparently innocuous, but in combination with the next move a creative strategic idea of Korchnoi's. The move order employed here is the most accurate one, since after 8. BxN BxB 9. PxP PxP 10. B–K2 Black can place his QB more actively with 10. . . . B–K3.

For a long time the main line was 8. PxP NxP 9. BxB QxB 10. NxN PxN 11. R–B1 B–K3 12. Q–R4 P–QB4 13. Q–R3 R–B1, and with 14. B–N5!? White scored a dramatic and convincing win in Fischer–Spassky, Match Game 6, 1972. However, improvements were subsequently discovered for Black, and it has become easier for Black to equalize after 8. PxP NxP than after Korchnoi's plan.

8. . . .	B–N2
9. BxN!	BxB
10. PxP	PxP

Instead 10. . . . QBxP?! gives White too much influence in the center. What is the strategic basis of White's play? The clearing of the central tension has fixed White's pawn formation so that Black's Bishop pair is pretty much biting on granite.

On the other hand, White's Knights are very flexible, and the KN can, for instance, be brought to KB4 to pressure Black's QP. As a result of 7. . . . P–QN3 Black has a slight structural weakness on the Queenside, and if Black plays . . . P–QB3, then the Queenside weakness will be accentuated. White can then choose a Queenside pawn advance or a central break with P–K4, after due preparation, of course. Overall, in the hands of a fine strategic maneuverer, White's position offers many more chances for meaningful progress than Black's.

11. Q–N3

O.K., but more flexible is 11. O–O first to see what setup Black will choose.

11. . . .   P–B3

Permanently protecting the QP at the cost of weakening the Queenside and deadening the QB. An alternate approach is 11. . . . R–K1 followed by 12. . . . Q–Q3.

12. O–O   N–Q2

In an earlier round, Pytel (Poland)–Szabo (Hungary) went 12. . . . R–K1 13. QR–B1 N–Q2 14. KR–K1 N–B1 draw! The conclusion makes some practical sense: White's position is somewhat better, but Black is the better player!

13. P–K4?!

Without the development of
the Rooks, this central break
lacks punch and Black can
easily equalize. 13. QR–Q1 or
13. QR–B1 is indicated.

| 13. . . . | PxP |
| 14. NxP | P–B4! |

Opening the QB's diagonal
gives Black even chances.
White's most fighting response
is 15. P–Q5 with the advanced
passed QP being partly weak
and partly strong. The text
move is rather toothless.

15. N–Q6	Q–N1!
16. NxB	QxN
17. B–B4	

White is in no shape for a
sharp sortie such as 17. N–K5?!.
Forintos gives the following refutation: 17. . . . BxN! 18. B–
B3 Q–B2 19. BxR BxPch 20.
K–R1 RxB 21. P–N3 BxP 22.
PxB Q–B3ch, and Black has
two pawns for the Exchange
and the better position.

| 17. . . . | QR–Q1 |
| 18. B–Q5 | Q–R3! |

There is no reason for Black
to acquiesce to the passive 18.
. . . Q–N1.

19. QR–Q1?

This automatic developing
move suffers from tactical deficiencies. 19. B–B4! is cor-
rest and required. Black then
has the choice of "playing the
game" after 19. . . . Q–R4 20.
P–Q5 or satisfying himself with
a draw after 19. . . . Q–N2 20.
B–Q5, etc.

| 19. . . . | PxP! |
| 20. NxP?! | |

Not completely satisfactory
but somewhat better is 20. B–
B4 Q–R4 21. NxP N–B4 22.
Q–K3, though, Black's advantage is clear after 22. . . . KR–
K1. White, however, is still
ignorant of Black's coming
combination.

20. . . .	N–B4
21. Q–KB3	RxB!
22. QxR	R–Q1

Strange as it may seem, White's Queen has no square to retreat to from which it can protect the Knight. Thus Black gains the clear material advantage of two minor pieces for a Rook. Black has no fundamental weaknesses, so with normal, careful play his material advantage must tell.

23. Q–B6   BxN

Usually it is better for the stronger side to keep a Rook to go with the minor pieces, since this way the potential activity of the weaker side's "extra" Rook is minimized. Here 23. . . . RxN? is clearly inferior since after 24. RxR BxR 25. Q–K8ch K–R2 26. P–QN4 N–K3 27. QxP White is already better: 27. . . . Q–B5? 28. R–K1!, etc.

24. P–QN4   N–K3
25. R–Q2   Q–R6!
26. R–N1   B–B3!

Here it's difficult for Black to make any progress without liquidating the pin along the Q-file. Black has seen that his position is quite safe after the Rook exchange.

27. RxRch   NxR!
28. Q–B4

28. Q–K8ch K–R2 also leads to nothing for White. Every one of Black's pawns and minor pieces is protected; thus White

will have no chances for successful counterplay. With his next move Black makes his Queen more mobile.

28. . . .   Q–R5!
29. P–R4   N–K3

Black could prevent White's next with 29. . . . P–KR4. But getting in P–KR5 is without real significance for White, since he has no good way to bother Black's King.

30. P–R5   N–Q5!
31. R–K1   Q–Q2!
32. Q–Q3   Q–B3
33. Q–K4?!

Entering an endgame here ensures that White will have no practical chances for survival. Keeping the Queens on is an absolute must. Theoretically White is lost, of course, but the presence of Queens always affords some practical chances.

33. . . .   QxQ
34. RxQ   K–B1
35. P–R4   P–R3!

Preventing White from fixing Black's Queenside pawns after 36. P–N5.

36. P–N5   P–R4!

And not 36. . . . PxP?! 37. PxP NxP?! because of 38. R–QN4, and after the liquidation of the Queenside, White's chances for a draw are excellent. After the text, Black's Queenside pawns are safe from ex-

changes, and he can start working on White's potentially attackable QRP.

37. K–B1	N–K3!
38. K–K2	N–B4
39. R–KN4	K–K2
40. K–K3	K–K3
41. K–K2	

White can do nothing and
must await the executioner.

41. . . .	K–Q4
42. R–KB4	N–K3
White resigns	

White's QRP cannot be
saved: 43. R–KN4 B–Q5! followed by 44. . . . N–B4.

Chapter 11

Lutikov, Anatoly

Though born in Leningrad on February 5, 1933, Lutikov has been living in the Moldavian S.S.R. throughout his active chess career. In 1973 at the age of 40, fairly late for a Soviet, he became an international grandmaster.

Lutikov has always been a strong master, and paradoxically he has generally done better in international tournaments than in national events. Altogether he has participated in seven U.S.S.R. Championships. His best international results are 2nd at Wijk aan Zee 1967, 2nd–3rd at Amsterdam 1968, 1st at Dubna 1973, 1st–2nd at Leipzig 1973, and 1st at Albena 1976. Lutikov's 1977 FIDE rating is 2540.

GAME 27

White: W. Uhlmann
(East Germany)

Black: A. Lutikov
(U.S.S.R.)

Played at Leipzig (East Germany) International Tournament, October 1973.

English Opening

Right out of a strategic opening, White delivers a masterful demonstration of the value of the initiative. The initiative is transformed into an extra pawn and the extra pawn, by means of an instructive R + P endgame, into the win. Of course, Black's opening play is questionable; nevertheless, White's refutation is outstanding in every way.

1. P–QB4   P–Q3

Quite an unusual response but perfectly playable. The game will generally enter, by transposition, one of the more standard openings.

2. N–QB3   P–K4

The English opening has been reached. By transposition we have reached Game 6, Smejkal–Balashov, Sochi 1973. 2. . . . P–KN3 instead leads to King's Indian formations.

3. N–B3

Undoubtedly more active than the 3. P–KN3 of Game 6. The usual approaches for Black now are 3. . . . P–KN3, 3. . . . P–KB4, and a Knight move to B3. But Lutikov often has original tastes in the opening.

3. . . .   B–N5

Most likely not the best move but considerably more logical here than in Game 6. Here, at least, the Bishop is attacking something.

4. P–Q4!

Starting active central play as quickly as possible. Logical for Black now is 4. . . . N–Q2, which develops as it defends. White can then choose between 5. P–K3 and 5. P–KN3.

4. . . .   BxN?!

Black is intent on making capital gains from his 3rd move, but the exchange is not strategically well motivated. Black achieves an unbalanced position all right, but it is unbalanced in White's favor!

5. KPxB!?

With this recapture White gives his first priority to rapidly completing his development. There is also nothing wrong with 5. NPxB, the capture toward the center.

5. . . .   PxP?

Black thinks only of strategy and forgets about everything else. With this move Black ensures himself a sound 4-pawn vs. 3-pawn Queenside majority, and his three Kingside pawns will readily hold White's four. Unfortunately for Black, White now gains a devastating advantage in development; this will be of infinitely greater importance than the respective pawn formations. Correct for Black is one of the normal Knight developing moves.

6. QxP   N–QB3
7. Q–K4ch   KN–K2

It doesn't matter what Black interposes, White always has the same response; e.g., 7. . . . Q–K2 8. N–Q5! or 7. . . . B–K2 8. N–Q5!.

8. N–Q5!   Q–Q2

Since Black is not able to complete the development of his Kingside (8. . . . P–KN3?? 9. N–B6 mate), he must rush to get his King to safety on the Queenside.

9. B–Q2   O–O–O
10. O–O–O   K–N1?!

No benefit derives from placing the King here. Therefore Black should save the tempo with something like 10. . . . R–K1 or 10. . . . Q–K3.

11. B–B3   NxN
12. QxN!

White wants to keep as many lines open as possible so that the Bishops can develop maximum scope. Therefore 12. PxN is less accurate.

12. . . .   R–N1?!

With the logical plan 13. . . . P–KN3 and 14. . . . B–N2, but White convincingly demonstrates that there is no time for it. The best there is, is to accept a lifeless but materially equal endgame after 12. . . . Q–K3 13. R–K1! QxQ 14. PxQ.

13. P–B5!

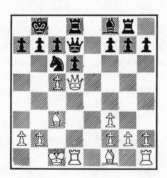

Opening lines for the primary threat of 14. B–B4. Black has no satisfactory response.

13. . . .   B–K2
14. B–B4   B–B3

Rather than defend further with 14. . . . QR–KB1, Black tries to buy some breathing room at the cost of a pawn. Neither alternative is attractive.

15. QxBP   QxQ
16. BxQ   R/N–B1
17. BxB   PxB
18. B–Q5!

Making it very unattractive for Black to recover the sacrificed material with 18. . . . PxP?! 19. BxN PxB, since Black's Queenside majority has been devalued by the triple isolated QBPs, and White's 4-to-2 Kingside pawn majority offers good potential for creating passed pawn(s).

18. . . .   N–N5
19. P–QR3!   NxB
20. RxN   PxP
21. KR–Q1!

Of all the pieces, the Rooks especially need open spaces and active prospects to demonstrate their inherent value. White prefers to keep his Rook(s) as active as possible, even though he may not be ahead any material. 21. RxP is unquestionably playable since after 21. . . . R/B–K1 White has the parry 22. R–Q1!, but White is confident that the active text offers more.

21. . . .   RxR
22. RxR   K–B1?

Playing an inferior ending a pawn down is hopeless. Black has to hold on to his material with 22. . . . P–N3. Uhlmann then gives this variation: 23. R–Q7! P–KR4 24. R–R7 R–N1 25. P–KN3 R–N4 26. P–B4 R–B4 27. K–B2 with White considerably better. This is quite true, but Black's 4-to-2 Queenside pawn majority definitely confers some practical chances for successful resistance.

23. RxP

So White has transformed his initiative into an extra pawn. Even though White has a doubled pawn on the Kingside, the fact that he has a 4-to-2 majority there gives him an excellent chance of creating two passed pawns. On the other hand, Black is too passive to hope for a viable passed pawn on the Queenside. Even so the win is not routine, but Uhlmann clearly and impressively demonstrates the use of an active Rook.

| 23. . . . | K–Q2 |
| 24. K–Q2 | R–B2?! |

Black could establish a more easily protectable Queenside pawn formation if he played 24. . . . P–N3! here.

| **25. R–QR5!** | **P–QR3** |
| **26. P–KN4!** | |

White's Rook is actively placed, and White's King has a flexible location in the center where it can head in the direction that offers the most realistic chance for results. Therefore White should start using his strength: the Kingside pawn majority.

26. . . .	K–K1
27. P–B4!	R–Q2ch
28. K–K3	K–B2
29. P–KR4!	R–Q8
30. P–R5!	P–R3
31. R–QB5	P–B3
32. R–B3!	

With the dual plans 33. R–N3 and 33. R–Q3.

| 32. . . . | R–KN8 |

Black tries to keep his Rook active. This is perfectly logical and sound. The passive 32. . . . R–Q2 might allow him to hold out longer, but no bonus points are given for length of a game; of importance to the practical player is the creation of chances for his opponent to go wrong. For instance, if now 33. K–B3?, Black has 33. . . . P–KB4! when White's Kingside pawn formation is ruined and Black should draw without too much difficulty: 34. PxP R–KR8! 35. K–

N4 K–B3 36. R–QN3 R–N8ch, etc.

33. R–N3!

White also correctly gives preference to his Rook's activity.

33. . . .   P–N4

This weakening is practically forced since the attempt to bring the Rook back with 33. . . . R–K8ch 34. K–Q4 R–K2 leads to a position in which White's King easily penetrates the Queenside starting with 35. K–B5!.

34. R–B3   R–K8ch?

Allowing White's pawns to remain whole robs Black of all hope for anything. Absolutely necessary is 34. . . . RxP 35. RxP R–R5!. After 36. R–B5 Black still is in great difficulties; e.g., 36. . . . R–R6ch 37. K–K4! R–QN6?! 38. K–B5! followed by 39. R–B7ch. Even so he's much better off than in the game.

35. K–B3   R–QN8

After 35. . . . R–K3 Uhlmann

gives this convincing variation: 36. P–B5 R–Q3 37. K–K3! K–K2 38. P–N4!! (to immobilize Black's Queenside pawn majority) followed by 39. R–Q3 and a won K + P endgame.

36. P–N4   R–QR8
37. K–K4   Black resigns

White threatens 38. K–B5 followed by 39. RxP. After the only reasonable defense, 37. . . . R–K8ch 38. K–B5 R–K3, White has a choice of wins. One is 39. P–N5 getting two passed pawns; another 39. R–Q3 (with the threat 40. R–Q7ch R–K2 41. R–Q6) 39. . . . K–K2 40. K–N6 winning the KRP or 40. R–K3 getting a won K + P endgame.

Chapter 12

Petrosian, Tigran

Tigran Petrosian was born on June 17, 1929, in Tiflis, Georgia, of Armenian parents. In the late 1940s as his chess prowess developed, he moved to Moscow and has been living there ever since. Nevertheless, he considers himself very much a "true Armenian." Since becoming an international grandmaster in 1952 Petrosian has been among the very top in the chess world. The very top—the World Championship—was reached in 1963 by defeating Botvinnik (12½–9½) and retained in 1966 by turning back Spassky's challenge (12½–11½). Petrosian's six-year reign ended in 1969 when he lost to Spassky by 12½–10½.

Other accomplishments of his great chess career include four-time U.S.S.R. Champion (1959, 1961, 1969, 1975), on nine winning Soviet Olympiad Teams, participant in all applicable Candidate competitions from 1953 through 1977, winner of international tournaments from Buenos Aires to Wijk aan Zee. He has played in the United States five times: U.S.A.–U.S.S.R. Team Match 1954, Los Angeles International, Piatigorsky, Cup 1963 (tied for first with Keres), Santa Monica International 2nd Piatigorsky Cup 1966 (tied for 6th–7th), San Antonio International, Church's Fried Chicken, 1972 (tied for first with Karpov and Portisch), and Lone Pine 1976 (first prize worth $8,000).

In 1968 Petrosian obtained the academic degree Master of Philosophical Science with his thesis on *Chess Logic: Some Problems of the Logic of Chess Thought*. That same year he became Editor-in-Chief of *64*, a weekly newspaper for chess and checkers. He remained in that largely honorary capacity until July 1977. Petrosian collaborated with Vik Vasiliev on *Tigran Petrosian: His Life and Games*, published in the Soviet Union in 1969 and in an expanded English translation in 1974.

His 1977 FIDE rating is 2645.

GAME 28

White: D. Marovic
(Yugoslavia)

Black: T. Petrosian
(U.S.S.R.)

Played at Amsterdam (Netherlands) IBM International Tournament, July 1973, Round 8.

King's Indian Defense (Kavalek-Soltis Variation)

A tough, rough, gutsy win over a Russian. The course of this game does not demonstrate the most effective way to score against a typical Soviet grandmaster. On the other hand, former World Champion Petrosian can hardly be called "typical," and to try to defeat him more than "usual" chess is required. Be that as it may, Marovic doesn't mind having his King position opened up or allowing Black two powerful center pawns. He has seen that Black's shaky King position gives White good practical winning chances. This is what happens. In mutual time pressure, Black allows White to sacrifice a Knight for Black's center pawns, and this opens Black's position for the remaining White pieces. When Black defends inaccurately, he is quickly swept overboard by White's sharp, resolute play.

1. P–QB4	P–KN3
2. N–KB3	B–N2
3. P–Q4	P–Q3

By placing his QP here immediately, Black indicates his interest in a King's Indian–like pawn formation. The flexible 3. . . . N–KB3 leaves the way open for a . . . P–Q4 and a Grünfeld formation.

| 4. N–B3 | N–KB3 |
| 5. P–KN3 | |

Instead with 5. P–K4 White can transpose into the Normal Variation, seen in Games 21 and 23. The text move, preparing the KB fianchetto, is another good, positional approach.

| 5. . . . | O–O |
| 6. B–N2 | P–B3 |

As is often true in the King's Indian, Black has a choice of going for either . . . P–QB4 or . . . P–K4. For instance, the immediate 6. . . . P–B4 leading to the Yugoslav Variation is quite playable. We'll see this later in Game 51, Taimanov–Smejkal, Leningrad 1973 and Game 52, Tal–Torre, Leningrad 1973. The most straightforward way to go for . . . P–K4 is 6. . . . QN–Q2 followed by 7. . . . P–K4. 6. . . . N–B3 is also quite possible and popular. After 7. O–O P–QR3 we have the Panno Variation, to be seen in Game 60, Quinteros–Tukmakov, Leningrad 1973. The text move is a rarer guest in modern tournament practice. Black can still be planning . . . QN–Q2 and . . . P–K4 but probably has something else in mind.

7. O–O   Q–R4

A move which was first brought into modern tournament practice by GM Lubomir Kavalek in the 1960s and which has been steadily and successfully employed by American IM Andrew Soltis in the 1970s. In recognition of both of their contributions, the name Kavalek–Soltis Variation is appropriate. The idea behind the move is to swing the Queen over to the Kingside (to KR4) and to support the advance . . . P–K4. Depending on White's response, Black will choose one of the two.

8. P–KR3

White's best move, according to the most modern theory. It contains the nasty tactical point that after 8. . . . Q–R4? 9. N–KN5! Black is helpless against the coming 10. B–B3!. In other variations, too, the move serves the useful purpose of taking White's KN4-square away from Black's minor pieces.

8. . . .   B–B4?!

Unusual, not to say extravagant. Black plans the exchanging 9. . . . N–K5, and if now 9. B–Q2 Q–R3 10. P–N3 N–K5

and Black stands well. However, to play . . . B–KB4 there is no reason to move the Queen to QR4 first. In this context, 7. . . . B–B4!? is more logical. In the game position, the centrally indicated move is 8. . . . P–K4. That's what Kavalek and Soltis play.

9. N–Q2!   P–K4
10. P–Q5

An early blockade of the center is often perfectly satisfactory for Black. Here, however, because of the awkward location of his Queen and QB, Black will be forced to lose a couple of tempos. Therefore White will be able to retain his first-move advantage.

10. . . .   P–B4
11. P–R3   N–R3
12. P–K4   B–Q2
13. N–N3   Q–Q1
14. B–N5

The opening phase is over. White has clear space advantage in the center and on the Queenside. White is potentially able to start play in the center and Kingside with P–KB4 or on the Queenside with P–QN4. Black's only hope lies on the Kingside, but he must be careful that any lines that he opens do not rebound to White's advantage. Overall, White has the theoretically and practically superior chances, but Black is still fully in the game.

| 14. . . . | Q–K1 |
| 15. K–R2 | P–R4 |

An attempt at Kingside play. The KR2-square is freed for the Knight's retreat, and the KRP can be pushed forward to KR5.

16. R–K1	N–R2
17. B–K3	Q–Q1
18. N–Q2!	

The Knight is needed on the Kingside. At first glance 18. N–B1 with the idea 19. N–Q3 looks attractive since from Q3 the Knight can be used both for the Queenside (P–QN4) and Kingside (P–KB4). However, Black has 18. . . . P–R5! 19. P–KN4 B–KB3! followed by 20. . . . B–KN4 and Black has a meaningful control of the dark squares on the Kingside. After the text move, 18. . . . P–R5 can be met by 19. P–KN4! B–KB3 20. N–B3! and Black will be stymied on the Kingside, whereas White will start his Queenside action with an early P–QN4.

| 18. . . . | P–N3 |
| 19. P–B4! | |

Having a choice, White prefers the more active plan of going for Petrosian's King. Against Petrosian that seems to be the best approach. Only a Fischer can hope to defeat him in positional maneuvering. The move, however, is double edged, since after Black's response, the position gets opened a lot.

| 19. . . . | P–R5! |
| 20. NPxP! | |

20. P–KN4?! PxP! again gives Black control of the dark squares.

20. . . .	QxP
21. N–B3	Q–K2
22. Q–Q2!	

Puts the Queen on a useful square and allows the QR to join the fray. To exchange the center pawns is not in Black's interest since after 22. . . . PxP?! 23. BxKBP White threatens very strongly 24. P–K5, and the preventive 23. . . . P–B3 weakens Black's Kingside and locks in the KB. Therefore with his next move Black prepares for and anticipates White's PxP.

22. . . .	QR–Q1
23. PxP	PxP
24. R–K2	B–B1

Planning to maneuver the QN to QB2, K1, and then to the excellent blockading post Q3. With his next White prevents that plan since 25. . . . N–B2? will lose to 26. P–Q6.

| 25. N–QN5! | P–B4!? |

A very double-edged break. Black sees that White has a protected passed QP and the initiative on the Queenside, and thus he wants to create counter-chances on the Kingside. It is not really clear who will benefit from the coming line opening. A quieter alternative is 25. . . . N–N1. With hindsight we know that the QN never enters the game, and this is an obvious handicap to Black. With 25. . . . N–N1 the Knight can be brought closer to the action.

26. PxP   PxP
27. P–Q6!?

With only about ten minutes left, Marovic decides on this risky advance. The QP is less safe here than on Q5, and Black also gets control of his K3-square. 27. B–B2! P–K5 28. R–KN1! seems positionally more justified, with White having the more realistic attacking chances.

27. . . .   Q–B3
28. B–B2   P–K5
29. B–R4   Q–N3?!

The Queen will not be well placed here since White's QR will go to KN1. After the game, Petrosian recommended 29. . . . Q–R3! as better. The extremely complicated position then seems to yield dynamically even chances. In practice, the player in better command of his nerves is usually successful. In this game, it will be White.

30. N–N5   N–B3
31. R–KN1

White now has the superior attacking chances; however, with both sides in time pressure, the result is most uncertain.

31. . . .   K–R1
32. Q–K1   N–R4?

As Petrosian tells it, he was so transfixed by the thought of getting his KB to check on K4, that he paid no attention to White's possibilities. Reasonable defensive moves are 32. . . . R/Q–K1 and 32. . . . Q–K1.

33. NxKP!!

Although nearly out of time, White keeps his cool. Annihilation of the center pawns allows White a decisive opening of lines. In time pressure Black puts up weak resistance, and White is quickly rewarded for his bravery.

33. . . .   PxN
34. BxP   Q–K3
35. R–K3!

The mate threat on KR3 must be dealt with first.

35. . . .   R/Q–K1

If 35. . . . B–Q5 White wins after 36. BxR BxR 37. QxB RxB 38. R–N6! Q–K4ch 39. K–N1.

36. B–K7!   R–B4?!

The threat was 37. B–N6, but a better defensive try is 36. . . . Q–K4ch! 37. K–R1 RxB! 38. PxR QxKP since now 39. B–N6 can be met by 39. . . . Q–N2ch.

37. BxR   QxKB
38. R–N5   Q–B2
39. Q–R4   K–N1?

Giving up a piece for nothing. Better is 39. . . .Q–B5ch 40. QxQ NxQ 41. R–K4 N–K3 42. R–N6 N–B1! though the endgame after 43. BxN! RxB 44. R–K7 will be lost in due course.

40. RxN

And White is up an Exchange and two pawns and has a winning attack. Even so Black's next can be only understood as a nervous reaction to the recent happenings.

40. . . .   BxRP?

Without even the slightest hope for a trap since White can take the Bishop with complete safety in any one of three ways.

41. KxB   Black resigns

Chapter 13

Polugaevsky, Lev

Since 1962 when he became an international grandmaster, Lev Polugaevsky has been in the front line of Soviet chess players. Born in Mogilev on November 20, 1934, and by education an engineer, Polugaevsky has lived his adult life in Moscow as a professional master. Among his significant chess accomplishments are U.S.S.R. Champion in 1967 and 1968 (he has participated seventeen times), three-time member of U.S.S.R. Olympiad teams, participant in the Candidate Matches of 1974 and 1977 (defeating Mecking in 1977 by 6½–5½), and winner of twenty international tournaments.

His autobiography *In the Grandmaster's Laboratory* was published in the Soviet Union in 1976. Polugaevsky's 1977 FIDE rating is 2620.

GAME 29

White: G. Sax
(Hungary)

Black: L. Polugaevsky
(U.S.S.R.)

Played at Hilversum (Netherlands) International Tournament, June 12, 1973, Round 1.

Sicilian Defense (Najdorf Variation)

Polugaevsky plays the opening creatively and quickly reaches an excellent position. By move 20 he is ahead a pawn and has what must be called a clearly won game. However, at that moment the worm turns. Sax repeatedly finds the best practical chances, and the position begins to drift away from an exceedingly easy win. As Sax continues to do his best and Polugaevsky keeps blundering, a position in which Black must play correctly to keep the balance arises. Finally White is better and after adjournment, White brings home the point with effective Queen and Knight maneuvers. A good practical fighting effort by Sax. For Polugaevsky, a clear indication of poor sporting form—something the further course of the tournament repeatedly confirmed.

1.	P–K4	P–QB4
2.	N–KB3	P–Q3
3.	P–Q4	PxP
4.	NxP	N–KB3
5.	N–QB3	P–QR3

Polugaevsky is one of the world's leading experts on the Black side of the Najdorf. The Najdorf is unquestionably his primary weapon against the KP.

6. P–B4

The move to choose if White wants active play, but it has a clear positional basis. The positional 6. B–K2 is quieter. The most popular, complicated move is 6. B–KN5; it arises in the next game. The clear strategic point of 6. P–B4 is to get in P–K5, which chases away Black's KN and possibly allows further advance to K6. Black has two general approaches to this strategic threat.

6. . . .	Q–B2

One approach is obvious enough: Black plays . . . P–K4 himself either here or later. However, that move's disadvantages are clear: Black's Q4-square is permanently weakened

and the scope of the KB decreased. More popular now is to prevent White's K5 by applying pressure against that square, as in this game.

7.	B–Q3	P–KN3
8.	O–O	B–N2
9.	N–B3	QN–Q2
10.	Q–K1!	

Again aiming for P–K5, and in case of . . . P–K4, the Queen will have good Kingside prospects on KR4. What should Black's response be?

10. . . .	N–B4!?

An original and creative idea, first employed in this game. Rather than prevent White's P–K5, Black, by effectively regrouping his Knights, tries to take the sting out of that advance. Safer, however, is 10. . . . O–O.

11. K–R1?!

It is desirable to move the King out of a possible check, but the time loss here is not justifiable. In a later game, Sax–Minic, Zagreb 1975, Sax improved with the immediate 11. P–K5! PxP 12. PxP KN–Q2! 13. B–KB4 N–K3 14. B–N3 and obtained a clear advantage after 14. . . . N–N3? (the double-edged 14. . . . Q–N3ch is better) 15. P–QR4!.

11. . . .	P–QN4!
12. P–K5	PxP
13. PxP	KN–Q2
14. B–KB4	B–N2!

Black has achieved active and harmonious development and can look to the future with confidence. Experts have suggested two reasonable moves here for White. GM Szabo recommends 15. Q–K3. IM Minic prefers 15. Q–N3, with the probable continuation being 15. . . . N–K3 16. QR–K1 O–O 17. B–K4 BxB 18. RxB Q–B3. In both cases the complicated position offers equal chances.

15. N–N5?

Sax selects this premature attacking sortie instead, and the punishment is swift.

15. . . .   Q–B3!
16. R–B3?!

The mate threat prevents defenses like 16. Q–N3?: 16. . . . NxP! 17. BxN BxB. The minor evil is still the retreat 16. N–B3!.

16. . . .   P–R3!
17. KN–K4   NxB
18. PxN   NxP
19. BxN   BxB
20. R–QB1

The net result of White's ambitious 15th and 16th moves is that he has lost his valuable KP for nothing. Moreover, Black has the Bishop pair and a generally lovely position. White's position is theoretically so bad that it could easily be called hopeless.

When I discussed the course of this game with Sax in the summer of 1976, he said that at this moment he had only one minute left to complete his next twenty moves, whereas Polugaevsky had loads of time. When I questioned him further by asking, "Didn't you actually have two minutes or so?" he thought a while and replied, "No, I think only one minute, because all that I wanted to do was to make the time limit [as a matter of chessmaster's honor] and then resign." Thus the game here starts an interesting psychological turning point. Sax feels 100 percent certain of an imminent loss and with nothing to lose starts playing freely. Polugaevsky, sure of a win, tries not to take the slightest chance. Objectively, White is quite lost for many moves to come, but he has the important factor of momentum. On the other hand, Black becomes less and less certain of the position, and his nerves finally go completely to pieces.

20. . . .   Q–N3
21. P–QR4   R–QB1

O.K., but why not 21. . . . P–N5! to shunt the QN to some inactive square?

22. PxP   PxP
23. R–Q1   P–N5

O.K., but Black can win additional significant material—with no meaningful danger—by 23. . . . P–B4!.

24. N–R4   Q–Q5
25. R–K3   O–O

The unprotected KB gives White a shade of active play. More accurate is 25. . . . B–B5! first and after 26. R–K2 O–O since then 27. Q–R4 is harmless because of 27. . . . B–N4!.

26. KN–B5   B–B5
27. RxP   B–Q4

White has his pawn back, but Black's active Bishops control the board. Even so, the position is sufficiently open that White has some practical hope. And he's become tactically sharp so that he doesn't miss a chance.

28. N–K4!

The Black QB's diagonal must be closed. After 28. N–Q7 decisive is 28. . . . R–B7!.

28. . . .   B–QN6

Looks like the last straw for White since 29. R–R1? loses to 29. . . . BxN 30. RxB R–B8. But with no time on his clock, White "sees" a momentary respite with . . .

29. R–Q7!   Q–K4?!

Obviously not 29. . . . QxR?? because of 30. N–B6ch, but the Queen now gets kicked around and winds up in poor location. The active 29. . . . Q–K6! is correct, when White is at the end of his tricks. Then material loss is unavoidable and White retains a miserable position.

30. P–Q4   Q–N2?!

That's a hell of a place to put a Queen. Black has clearly lost his bearings around here. There seems to be nothing wrong with 30. . . . Q–KB4, and if 31. P–N4 Q–QN4.

31. N/R–B5   BxR
32. QxB

Not 32. N–K6? PxN 33. RxQch KxR and Black has a significant material advantage, since 34. QxB? loses to 34. . . . R–B8. After the text move White must still be lost because it is not clear what he has for the Exchange. Even so, with Black's Queen misplaced on KN2, White has some hope. And hope is what is needed in theoretically lost positions.

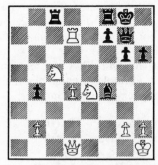

32. . . .   QR–Q1??

Walking into a triple fork is awful. It clearly indicates the condition of Black's nerves and is the best possible explanation for the things that happen. 32. . . . KR–K1! is correct to prevent the potential N–K6 and threaten an immediate win with 33. . . . RxN/K! 34. NxR R–B8.

33. P–KN3!

A useful zwischenzug which prevents back-rank mates later on.

33. . . .   B–K6
34. N–K6   PxN?

The weakening of Black's K3-square gives White's remaining Knight forking chances there. Safe, sound, and correct is the obvious 34. . . . RxR 35. NxQ KxN. After 36. P–Q5 P–B4! Black's two Rooks are somewhat superior to White's Queen, though White should draw.

35. RxQch   KxR
36. N–B5!   R/Q–K1
37. Q–N3   R–B8ch?

Black is too materialistic here and pays no attention to the strategic consequences. Correct is 37. . . . BxP! 38. NxPch RxN 39. QxR BxP 40. Q–K7ch R–B2 41. QxP B–B3. White has a slight material advantage, but there is so little material and the pawn formations are so similar that White has no real chances to win.

38. K–N2   R–K8
39. NxPch   K–R2
40. P–Q5

A position won for White. The passed QP is a terror, the Q and N combination paralyzes Black's Rooks, and Black's QNP is unprotectable. White wins smoothly and safely.

40. . . .   B–N4
41. QxP   R–K7ch
42. K–R3   R–K4
43. Q–Q6   B–B3
44. P–QN4!

Passed pawns must be pushed! Black has no hope of coping with both passed pawns and can just as well resign.

44. . . .   K–N1
45. P–N5   P–R4
46. N–B5   R–B4
47. N–Q7   K–B2
48. Q–B7   B–Q1

48. . . . RxP? loses to 49. Q–QB4 among others.

49. Q–QB4   P–N4
50. Q–Q3   P–N5ch
51. K–N2   K–N3

51. . . . R–B6 allows 52. Q–R7 mate!

| 52. P–N6 | K–N4 |
| 53. P–Q6 | |

If Black won't resign, White will make two Queens! The move also prevents Black's . . . B–QB2.

53. . . .	R–B6
54. Q–Q2ch	K–N3
55. P–N7	Black resigns

GAME 30

White: J. Timman
   (Netherlands)

Black: L. Polugaevsky
   (U.S.S.R.)

Played at Hilversum (Netherlands) International Tournament, June 1973, Round 5.

Sicilian Defense (Najdorf Variation)

In a complicated, active, modern variation, a sharp fight is to be expected. Timman tries a new idea on move 12, but there is no upcoming fight. Three moves later Black has lost his Queen! A rare but perfect example of chess blindness, by a very fine grandmaster.

1. P–K4	P–QB4
2. N–KB3	P–Q3
3. P–Q4	PxP
4. NxP	N–KB3
5. N–QB3	P–QR3
6. B–N5	

Throughout the 1960s and 1970s this has been by far the most popular weapon against the Najdorf. It is sharp and active. White clears the back rank on the Queenside for quick castling there. This will get the King to reasonable safety and allow the QR to participate in a potential attack against Black's center, an area where Black's King will most likely be. In addition the QB gets ready to pin the Knight; after the logical followup 6. . . . P–K3 7. P–B4, the threat of P–K5 is in the air.

| 6. . . . | P–K3 |
| 7. P–B4 | QN–Q2 |

Black has a wide choice here. Also good and playable are 7. . . . B–K2, the supersharp 7. . . . Q–N3 (Fischer's QNP Variation), and the sharp 7. . . . P–N4 (Polugaevsky Variation, something he plays only part of the time).

8. Q–B3

The most common and probably best move. White is ready to castle, and the Queen prevents an immediate 8. ... P–N4? because of 9. P–K5. However, periodically White chooses 8. Q–K2. We'll see two examples of this: Game 37, Savon–Mecking, Petropolis 1973, and Game 64, Tukmakov–Browne, Madrid 1973.

8. ...   Q–B2
9. O-O-O   P–N4
10. B–Q3

Year in, year out the normal move was 10. P–KN4 until in Game 15 of his 1972 match against Fischer, Spassky tried the text move and obtained an excellent position, even though the game was eventually drawn. Ever since then, 10. B–Q3 has become the new main line. That doesn't necessarily mean that it is better than the "old" 10. P–KN4, but it is new and different. In chess, as in clothing, some change in fashion is required to prevent boredom. Currently also getting play is the supersharp 10. BxP!? with hairraising complications and unclear positions.

10. ...   B–N2
11. KR–K1

All White's pieces are harmoniously developed centrally or toward the Black King. If now 11. ... P–N5?! White gets

an overpowering attack after 12. N–Q5!; therefore Black must choose a more modest plan.

11. ...   P–R3

Spassky–Fischer went 11. ... B–K2 12. Q–N3 O-O-O 13. BxN! NxB 14. QxP, and it is unclear whether Black has sufficient compensation for the pawn. The text is Polugaevsky's novelty, which already had given him a full point in Geller–Polugaevsky, Kislovodsk 1972.

12. Q–R3!

And this is Timman's novelty, prepared in conjunction with fellow Dutch grandmaster Donner just the night before! This was an excellent guess as to what Polugaevsky would play. The reward for such excellent foresight is quite often a good score. Geller had played the obvious 12. B–R4, but after 12. ... B–K2 13. N–Q5?! NxN 14. PxN BxB White's attack was insufficient and Black, with an excellent defense, repulsed it.

12. ...   O-O-O

The King must speed to safety, since White was threatening 13. P–K5! PxP 14. NxKP!.

13. BxN

All part of the previous night's plan. A subsequent game

(our No. 45), Spassky–Donner, Amsterdam (IBM) 1973, went 13. P–B5?! P–K4 14. N–K6??.

13. . . .   NxB
14. N–Q5!

Still the previous night's work. Of course, the KP is pinned: 14. . . . BxN? 15. PxB NxP allows 16. NxKP! and 14. . . . NxN 15. PxN BxP 16. P–QR4! gives White excellent compensation for the pawn in a sharp position. Even so this last line is the way to go. But Polugaevsky, flustered by the unexpected turn of opening events, tries something else.

14. . . .   Q–R4??
15. N–N3!   Black resigns

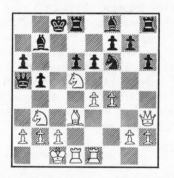

Black's Queen is trapped and lost! He can choose 15. . . . Q–R5 16. N–N6ch or 15. . . . QxP 16. N–B3, but either way he gets only one minor piece for it. Getting a Rook for the Queen with 15. . . . QxR is also obviously inadequate.

GAME 31

White: L. Polugaevsky
(U.S.S.R.)

Black: L. Szabo
(Hungary)

Played at Hilversum (Netherlands) International Tournament, June 1973, Round 10.

King's Indian Defense (Sämisch Variation)

Black tries a dubious opening idea, and as early as move 10 White establishes a significant advantage. But his strategy over the next ten moves is so uncertain that White loses a pawn, fails to get any compensation for it, and then leaves an Exchange en prise. Szabo takes full advantage of the offered chances and wins convincingly. But Polugaevsky is not to be recognized—his nightmarish tournament continues.

1.	P–QB4	P–KN3
2.	P–K4	B–N2
3.	P–Q4	P–Q3
4.	N–QB3	N–KB3
5.	P–B3	

As so often happens in modern master practice, a "normal" position is reached via an unusual order of moves. The Sämisch has been Polugaevsky's primary weapon against the King's Indian, so Szabo should be well prepared. Now Black almost invariably plays 5. . . .

O–O and after 6. B–K3 has to decide what to do next. But Polugaevsky knows all the normal variations quite well, and so Szabo plans a little surprise. He reasons that White is so out of form in this tournament that he may not find the right responses.

5. . . .   P–N3!?

With the strategic plan . . . P–QB4. After the preliminary 5. . . . O–O 6. B–K3, the plan with 6. . . . P–N3 is a well-known, popular way to defend against the Sämisch. Is it even better a move earlier?

6. B–Q3!

An accurate response. Now 6. . . . P–B4? is refuted by 7. P–K5! when White's KB will get to K4 with decisive effect. Since White himself now threatens P–K5, Black's choices consist of 6. . . . P–K4?! (a change of plans), 6. . . . B–N2, and the text.

6. . . .   P–QR3

Giving the Rook a flight square on QR2.

7. KN–K2   P–B4?!

With 7. . . . O–O 8. B–K3 P–B4 Black can transpose into known channels, but he is determined to be original and to challenge White's ingenuity.

8. P–K5!   QPxP

The effect of not interpolating 5. . . . O–O 6. B–K3 is now very apparent. In the usual lines, Black Knight can retreat in comfort to K1, but here that square is not vacant!

9. PxKP   N–N1

A sad necessity since after 9. . . . KN–Q2?! 10. B–K4 R–R2 11. P–B4! Black's Queenside is tied up in knots. After the text, 10. B–K4 is harmless because Black has the freeing Queen exchange.

10. B–B4?!

Starting here White loses the thread of the game and goes downhill move by move. Protecting the KP thusly is both awkward and antipositional. The obvious 10. P–B4! is strong. White then has a significant advantage: he is well ahead in development and has clear central superiority.

10. . . .   B–N2
11. O–O

Now the KP will be unprotectable. 11. Q–Q2!? N–Q2 12. Q–K3 is worth consideration. This threatens 13. P–K6, and after 12. . . . P–K3 13. B–K4! BxB 14. QxB White will have time for 15. B–N3 and 16. P–B4.

11. . . .   N–Q2

Obviously White's KP cannot be protected; therefore, it is logical to devalue Black's Kingside pawn formation with 12. P–K6! PxP and then continue with 13. N–K4!?. After 13. . . . BxP 14. R–QN1 the situation is unclear, but White has undeniable compensation for his missing pawns. Instead White tries to protect the KP indirectly but overlooks some elementary tactics.

12. Q–R4?!   P–QN4!
13. Q–B2

A sad necessity. After 13. PxP?! PxP 14. QxP? Black wins a Bishop with 14. . . . B–QR3.

13. . . .   P–N5
14. B–K4!   BxB
15. NxB   BxP
16. QR–Q1

At the moment Black has won the valuable KP, and White must strain hard to get some compensation in his superior development. 16. BxB NxB is fruitless since 17. NxP?

allows 17. . . . Q–N3 winning the pinned Knight.

16. . . .   BxB
17. NxB   K–B1!

An excellent dual-purpose defensive move. Black ensures that a White Q–QR4 doesn't pin Black's Knight and allows an eventual castling by hand. White now has two reasonable plans. With 18. NxBP Q–N3 19. RxN QxNch 20. K–R1 N–B3 he can accept an approximately even middlegame, or he can play 18. R–Q2 with the idea of 19. KR–Q1, getting fair compensation for the pawn.

18. Q–R4?!

The Queen is only superficially well placed here; in fact, it's quite uncomfortable.

18. . . .   R–R2
19. R–Q5?!

A truly clumsy move. The Rook takes this useful square away from the Knight and sets itself up for a fork. 19. R–Q2 is correct, and after 19. . . . Q–B2! 20. N–Q5!. Then White still has some practical compensation for the pawn.

19. . . .   Q–B2

Attacking the Knight and threatening 20. . . . N–N3. White is clearly in trouble.

20. N–Q3?

Leaving the Exchange en prise is plain stupid. The only correct move is 20. KR–Q1!. Then 20. . . . N–N3? is refuted by 21. R–Q8ch K–N2 22. Q–K8. Black's only correct move is 20. . . . KN–B3!. After 21. NxN NxN 22. R–Q8ch K–N2 White has no compensation for the missing pawn. But it is better to be down a pawn than a pawn *and* Exchange.

20. . . .	N–N3
21. Q–B2	NxR
22. PxN	K–N2!

Up enough material Black correctly consolidates his King position and brings the extra Rook into the game.

| 23. N/3xBP | N–B3 |
| 24. Q–B4 | Q–K4! |

Black is even willing to give up a pawn to get his Rooks active play. Once Szabo got his chance he started to exploit his superiority with fine accuracy and energy.

25. NxN	QxN
26. QxNP	R–QB1
27. R–Q1	R/2–B2
28. N–K4	Q–K4

| 29. N–B3 | Q–K6ch |
| 30. K–B1 | |

The King isn't safe here, but neither is it safe on KR1; e.g., 30. K–R1 R–B5 31. Q–N7 R–Q5! 32. R–KN1 R/1–B5! 33. QxRP R–KR5!.

| 30. . . . | R–B5 |
| 31. Q–N7 | Q–K4! |

Threatening the KRP and 32. . . . R–QN1 followed by 33. . . . RxP. Something has to give.

32. R–K1	QxRP!
33. QxKP	R–QN1
34. R–K2	Q–N6!

Materially White is only a shade worse, but positionally he is in a severe bind. He can hardly move a thing; e.g., 35. K–N1? RxN! 36. PxR R–N8ch, or 35. R–Q2? RxN! 36. PxR R–N8ch 37. K–K2 R–K8ch. Black is meanwhile threatening to push his KRP and rip open White's King position. White's best chance for prolonging his hopes is 35. Q–K3!.

35. P–Q6?

Passed pawns must be pushed; *except* when they will be lost, as here.

| 35. . . . | R–Q5! |
| 36. P–Q7 | Q–B2 |

The end of the QP and the game. Everything White does from now on can be dispensed with.

37.	R–K6	RxQP
38.	Q–B6ch	K–N1
39.	R–B6	

Equally hopeless is 39. RxP R–Q7!.

39.	. . .	Q–Q1
40.	N–K4	R–Q8ch
41.	K–K2	Q–Q6ch
42.	K–B2	Q–Q5ch!

A mark of sensible practical play. Why try to mate White when the endgame is "kid's stuff"?

43.	QxQ	RxQ
44.	P–QN3	P–B4
45.	N–N5	

After 45. N–B6ch K–N2 46. RxP R–KB1 White's Knight is trapped.

45.	. . .	R–Q7ch
46.	K–N3	RxRP
47.	R–B7	RxP
48.	NxP	

White is down an Exchange and a passed pawn. His chances for a successful attack are less than one in a million.

48.	. . .	R–N3
49.	R–R7	P–R4
50.	N–N5	P–R5!
51.	N–R3	P–R6
52.	N–B4	P–N4
53.	N–Q5	R/N–N7
54.	N–B6ch	K–B1
55.	N–R7ch	K–K1
56.	NxP	RxPch
57.	K–B4	R–R8
58.	KxP	P–R7
59.	N–K6	R–K8
60.	R–R8ch	K–Q2

White resigns

GAME 32

White: O. Panno
  (Argentina)

Black: L. Polugaevsky
  (U.S.S.R.)

Played at Petropolis (Brazil) Interzonal Tournament, August 12, 1973, Round 14.

Reti Opening

At the start of this game Polugaevsky was one of the tournament leaders and to draw with Black would satisfy him completely. It is rather surprising, therefore, that he chooses a double-edged variation. But once in it, he must soon acquiesce to an inferior, unpleasant endgame. Panno takes full advantage of the risk-free, superior position and brings home the win with a technically flawless performance. All the way through White has a lovely position.

1. N–KB3   P–Q4
2. P–B4   P–Q5

This double-edged response clearly defines the Reti. Black's move is playable according to theory; even so, under the circumstances, 2. . . . P–QB3 or 2. . . . P–K3 is safer and more practical.

3. P–K3

White immediately challenges the intruder. A sound alternative is 3. P–KN3 P–QB4 4. B–N2 in order to complete the development of the Kingside first. Instead of 4. B–N2, White played 4. P–K3!? N–QB3 5. PxP NxP 6. NxN QxN 7. P–Q3 B–N5 8. P–B3!? in the decisive Round 17 game, Polugaevsky–Portisch. This position is quite unclear, but White won in good style in 39 moves.

3. . . .   N–QB3
4. PxP   NxP
5. NxN   QxN
6. P–Q3

Preparing to chase the Queen away with 7. N–B3 and 8. B–K3. 6. N–B3 is usually equivalent. In Game 68, L. Espig–Vasiukov, Dubna 1973, Black continued with 6. . . . B–N5?! and White with 7. Q–R4ch.

6. . . .   P–K4
7. N–B3   N–B3?

This sound-looking, normal Knight-developing move is a serious opening error. The key question here is whether White can gain control over his important Q4-square. Since the text does nothing to prevent this, the answer is "yes" with a significant advantage to White. The correct way was demonstrated later in Andersson–Portisch, Madrid 1973: 7. . . . P–QB3 8. B–K3 Q–Q3 9. B–K2 N–K2! (on the way to KB4!) 10. N–K4 Q–B2 11. O–O N–B4 12. B–Q2 B–K2 with full equality.

8. B–K2   P–B3
9. B–K3   Q–Q1
10. P–Q4!   PxP
11. QxP!

White now is master of the board. His Queen is powerfully placed, and if the Queen is exchanged, his QB will be equally powerfully located. The greater central influence (pawn on QB4), edge in development, and more active pieces will lead to a marvelous situation for White. Black's Knight, though apparently on a good central square, has nothing to do there. If the Knight could get to KB4, Black would have equality, but his faulty 7th move robbed Black of this chance.

11. . . .   QxQ?!

The resulting endgame will be depressingly lifeless for Black. A considerably better practical alternative is 11. . . . Q–R4!.

12. BxQ   B–K2
13. O–O–O   O–O
14. P–KR3!

Not only preventing a . . . B–KN5 or . . . N–KN5 by Black but also planning a Kingside pawn advance consisting of P–KN4, P–KB4, P–KB5. This would tend to completely suppress the activity of Black's pieces.

14. . . .   B–K3
15. KR–K1   P–QR3
16. P–B4!

All of White's pieces are usefully developed, and the pawn advance starts.

16. . . .   B–QN5?!

This does not work out well, but it is difficult to suggest something good. 16. . . . P–QN4?! is also inadequate because of 17. B–B3 with the dual threats of 18. P–KB5 and 18. BxP. The minor evil is 16. . . . KR–K1, protecting the KB.

17. P–N4!   P–QN4
18. P–KB5!   BxQBP
19. BxB   PxB
20. BxN!   PxB
21. R–K4!   BxN
22. PxB

White has played the previous exchanges like a real trooper and has a significant advantage because of the better pawn formation, more active Rook(s), and potentially the more active King. Any one of these factors is insufficient to win, but the combination is deadly. In realizing his superiority, Panno demonstrates the finest technique possible. Black doesn't have a chance.

22. . . .   KR–Q1
23. RxP   RxRch
24. KxR   R–QB1

Black must start defending his weaknesses. Grossly insufficient is the "active" 24. . . . R–Q1ch 25. K–B2 R–K1 because of 26. RxP R–K6 27. RxBP RxRP 28. RxRP, etc.

25. R–R4   R–R1
26. R–Q4

Attempting to get to Q6. 26. R–N4 or 26. K–B2 is equally good.

26. . . .	R–N1
27. K–B2	R–N4
28. R–QB4!	

But here 28. R–Q6?! is inaccurate since Black gets ample counterplay by attacking the QRP as follows: 28. . . . R–R4! 29. K–N3 R–N4ch 30. K–B4 R–R4! 31. K–N3 R–N4ch 32. K–B2 R–R4 33. K–N1 R–N4ch, and if 34. K–R1, then 34. . . . R–B4! is adequate.

| 28. . . . | R–R4 |

After 28. . . . P–B4? 29. P–QR4 R–R4?! Black's Rook is stalemated, and White wins by penetrating with his King, starting with 30. K–Q3.

29. P–QR4   P–R4

The QBP cannot be saved; thus Black correctly looks for counterchances on the Kingside.

30. K–N3!   P–R5!?

By protecting his QRP White wins a pawn, whereas Black hopes to get an advanced passed KRP by eventually penetrating with his King or Rook and winning White's KRP.

| 31. RxP | K–N2 |
| 32. R–Q6 | |

Black is in zugzwang and so must lose another pawn. A simpler and more effective way to accomplish the same result is 32. K–N4! since this places the White King one square farther forward for the coming Queenside pawn advances.

| 32. . . . | R–K4 |
| 33. RxRP! | |

33. R–Q1 R–K6 34. R–KR1 is very passive, and 33. R–Q3 is ineffective because after 33. . . . R–K8 Black's Rook is very active and can threaten . . . R–KN8 and . . . R–KN6. Thus White correctly gets himself another passed pawn and then returns his Rook to stop Black's pawn.

33. . . .	R–K6
34. R–Q6!	RxP
35. R–Q1!	K–R3

Or 35. . . . R–K6 36. P–R5 P–R6 37. P–R6 R–K7 38. R–QR1 P–R7 39. K–N4! (Panno) when White's King will assist his pawn to queen.

36.	P–R5	R–K6
37.	P–R6	R–K1
38.	R–QR1	P–R6
39.	K–N4!	

White's King must help the pawns. Premature is 39. P–R7? R–QR1 40. K–N4 P–R7, and White can't prevent the coming 41. . . . RxP!.

39.	. . .	K–N4
40.	P–R7	P–R7
41.	K–N5!	KxP

Now after 41. . . . R–QR1 White has 42. K–N6.

| 42. | P–B4 | KxP?! |

42. . . . K–N6 43. P–B5 K–N7 is thematic, but after 44. P–B6 P–R8=Q 45. RxQ KxR 46. K–N6, etc., White will wind up a Queen ahead.

| 43. | R–R1 | **Black resigns** |

White will win the KRP (43. . . . R–KR1 44. RxP anyway) and then queen his pawns.

GAME 33

White: L. Polugaevsky
(U.S.S.R.)

Black: L. Portisch
(Hungary)

Played at Portoroz (Yugoslavia) Play-off Match Tournament for selection of qualifiers for Candidates Matches, September 7, 1973, Round 3.

Queen's Gambit Declined (Orthodox Variation)

Portisch has especially prepared an old variation with which to surprise his opponent, who is known for his fine knowledge of all modern openings. The surprise is effective, and Black achieves virtual equality out of the opening and into the early middlegame. In a dynamically even position, Polugaevsky tries an interesting sacrifice. The sacrifice is good enough for equality, but White, who is short of time, does not continue accurately, and soon it is Black who gains the superior chances. Pressed for time White defends very poorly. At adjournment Black has a won endgame. A fine fighting game by Portisch, who shows himself off to advantage in the opening, middlegame, and endgame.

| 1. | P–Q4 | N–KB3 |
| 2. | P–QB4 | P–K3 |

3. N–KB3	P–Q4
4. N–B3	B–K2
5. B–N5	O–O
6. P–K3	QN–Q2

Around the turn of the century, when the QGD first became a popular opening, this was the way Black defended. It is a solid approach whose disadvantage is that Black's QB remains locked in.

7. R–B1   P–QR3!?

This is the ancient subvariation Portisch prepared especially for this play-off. Black plans to play . . . QPxP and then . . . P–QN4, bringing the QB into action on QN2. More common is 7. . . . P–B3 with the probable followup 8. B–Q3 PxP 9. BxBP N–Q4 10. BxB QxB 11. N–K4 P–QN3 12. O–O and a slight plus for White as in Portisch–Ljubojevic, Milan 1975.

8. P–QR3

Caught by surprise, Polugaevsky reacts cautiously. The move has little point, however. One logical alternative is to enter the Exchange Variation with 8. PxP, making Black's 7th move something of a waste of time. The next time Polugaevsky had White against Portisch—in Round 9—that is what he chose and after 8. . . . PxP 9. B–Q3 P–B3 10. Q–B2 R–K1 11. O–O N–B1 12. QR–K1 had a slight edge. For more complicated

play, 8. P–B5!?, as in Hort–Portisch, Madrid 1973, is reasonable.

8. . . .	P–B3
9. B–Q3	P–R3
10. B–R4	PxP
11. BxP	P–QN4
12. B–R2	

On Q3 the Bishop gets in the way, and 12. B–K2 is passive. The text move has no disadvantage.

12. . . .	P–B4
13. O–O	B–N2
14. PxP	NxP
15. N–Q4	R–B1
16. P–B3	

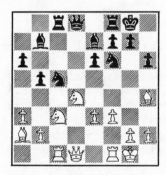

The pawn formation is rather symmetrical and both sides have sound development and no weaknesses. White may have a minute advantage since he can get a slight center superiority after P–K4. However, having no weaknesses, Black shouldn't have much trouble holding the balance.

16. . . .	Q–N3
17. P–QN4	

Preventing 17. . . . P–N5.

| 17. . . . | QN–Q2 |
| 18. B–B2 | B–Q3! |

Black locates his KB more aggressively, pointing it at White's KR2.

19. P–K4	Q–B2
20. P–N3	Q–N1
21. Q–K2	N–K4!?

The Knight impudently challenges White to do something about it. The text is enterprising and psychologically effective. Objectively somewhat stronger is the flexible 21. . . . KR–Q1! and only after 22. KR–Q1, 22. . . . N–K4.

22. KR–Q1

The sharp 22. P–B4? fails to 22. . . . N/4–N5 23. P–K5 NxB 24. RxN RxN! 25. RxR N–K5 with advantage to Black. GM Gufeld has, however, correctly pointed out that White could exploit the absence of Black's QN from the Queenside by playing 22. N–N3!, and after 22. . . . N–B5 23. N–B5! or after 22. . . . N/4–Q2 23. N–R5!, in either case with some advantage to White who then controls more space.

| 22. . . . | KR–Q1 |

Now 23. P–B4? is again faulty after 23. . . . N/4–N5!, etc., but with 23. N–N3! White can keep the game in strategic balance: 23. . . . N–B5 24. N–B5, etc. Instead, White com-

mits a tactical and psychological error. Up to the play-off, Polugaevsky had been quite successful against Portisch; therefore, despite his shortage of time, he decides on the following sacrifice. Clearly he's confident that he can sweep Black off the board. But Portisch defends and maneuvers perfectly; it is White who, affected by time pressure, goes to pieces quickly.

23. NxKP!?	PxN
24. BxPch	K–R1
25. P–B4	

If White wants to get this in he must do so immediately since after 25. BxR BxB!, 26. P–B4? is impossible because of 26. . . . B–N5.

| 25. . . . | RxN! |

This countersacrifice eliminates White's central pawn advance and keeps the position in balance.

26. RxR	NxP
27. R–K3	NxB
28. KxN	

The material balance shows that White has a Rook and pawn to balance Black's two minor pieces, and materially this is slightly insufficient. However, White's Rooks have nice open files; thus White has sufficient compensation. If Black's Knight now retreats, to 28. . . . N–B3, White plays 29. B–B7! followed by 30. R–K8ch and after exchanging Queens and one set of

Rooks, White, with a Rook remaining has good prospects against Black's Queenside. Therefore Portisch prefers a sharper plan, particularly in view of White's time shortage.

28.	...	N–B5!?
29.	BxN	PxB
30.	QxP	R–KB1

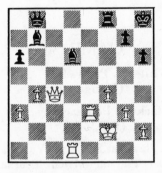

With the pawn that he just won, White now has a slight material advantage. However, all of Black's pieces are very active, and the immediate threat is 31. . . . BxBP!. The game hangs in balance. But with only 5 minutes left, White has the more difficult practical problems to solve.

31. R–Q4?

This direct defense finds an elementary refutation. Correct is 31. K–K1! with complicated, dynamically equal play. After 31. . . . B–B1!? White keeps the balance with 32. Q–B6!? (Gufeld).

31. . . .   B–K4!

Attacks the Rook, which dares not move off the fourth rank because of 32. . . . BxP!.

32.	R/4–K4	BxR
33.	RxB	Q–N3ch
34.	K–N2	B–B3

Of course, Black now has a clear material advantage. But White, paradoxically enough, has no more weaknesses, and so Black's task in winning this position is quite difficult.

| 35. | R–K6 | Q–N4 |
| 36. | QxQ?! | |

Exchanging under these terms is not attractive since Black will gain both of White's Queenside pawns in exchange for his own. A better approach is 36. Q–B6!.

36.	. . .	PxQ
37.	R–N6	R–R1
38.	RxP	RxP
39.	P–R4??	

White goes completely to pieces here. By weakening his KNP, he gives Black a ready-made attacking object. The correct pawn move is 39. P–N4! with the idea of exchanging one set of pawns with 40. P–N5. Also reasonable is 39. R–Q5 followed by 40. P–N5.

39.	. . .	B–B6
40.	R–N6	B–K8
41.	R–N6	

What a stupid location from which to protect a pawn. The

game is adjourned here and upon resumption Black wins quite easily. White only has one pawn for the piece, and the awkward location of his pieces gives him no hope for any kind of resistance.

41.	. . .	BxQNP
42.	P–R5	B–K8
43.	K–R3	K–N1
44.	K–N2	K–B2
45.	K–R3	R–K6
46.	K–N2	R–K3!
47.	R–N4	R–R3!
48.	R–R4	

Another stupid spot for the Rook, but Black was threatening to go after the KRP with 48. . . . R–R4.

48.	. . .	R–R7ch
49.	K–R3	B–B7
50.	R–N4	R–R4
51.	K–N2	B–Q5
52.	R–R4	B–B3
53.	R–R1	R–R8!
54.	R–R3	

White resigns

At long last White decides to give up the ghost, without even

bothering to await Black's reply. Black has several winning methods, one of which (given by Szabo) is 54. . . . K–K3 55. K–B3 K–B4 56. P–N4ch K–K3 57. R–R2 R–R6ch 58. K–K4 R–R5ch 59. K–B3 RxPch! 60. KxR B–K4ch and 61. . . . BxR.

GAME 34

White: L. Portisch (Hungary)

Black: L. Polugaevsky (U.S.S.R.)

Played at Portoroz (Yugoslavia) Play-off Match Tournament for selection of qualifiers for Candidates Matches, September 11, 1973, Round 6.

Queen's Gambit Declined (Meran Variation)

A perfect example of how to beat the Russians. White selects a strategically sound opening in which he has prepared a significant improvement and obtains a slight but risk-free advantage. An erroneous freeing attempt by Black is refuted by a sharp combination, with the result that White enters an endgame up a pawn. This minimal material advantage is realized in a technically faultless manner.

1. P–QB4	N–KB3
2. N–QB3	P–K3
3. N–B3	P–Q4
4. P–Q4	P–B3
5. P–K3	QN–Q2
6. B–Q3	PxP
7. BxBP	P–QN4
8. B–Q3	B–N2
9. O–O!?	

Except for transpositions, this game has followed our Game 20, Rukavina–Korchnoi, Leningrad Interzonal 1973, in which White continued with the centrally active 9. P–K4. Portisch prefers a less committal approach, especially since he has an opening novelty in mind.

9. . . .	P–N5
10. N–K4	NxN

Before this game this was thought to be a routine equalizing method. It is O.K. but only as long as Black continues accurately. A good equivalent is 10. . . . B–K2 11. NxNch NxN 12. P–K4 O–O 13. Q–B2 P–KR3 14. R–Q1 and now 14. . . . P–B4! with approximate equality.

11. BxN   B–K2?!

To first chase the Bishop back with 11. . . . N–B3! is imperative and only after 12. B–Q3 to play 12. . . . B–K2. This transposes into the equalizing line given in the previous note.

12. N–Q2!

Portisch's key novelty! The primary point is to allow the KB to remain on the KR1–QR8 diagonal since this makes it difficult for Black to achieve the freeing . . . P–QB4. Moreover, the Knight can find very good placement on either QB4 or K4. Formerly the routine 12. P–QN3 O–O 13. B–N2 was played and Black had no difficulty equalizing after 13. . . . N–B3 14. B–Q3 P–B4!; e.g., 15. PxP BxP 16. R–B1 B–K2 17. N–K5 Q–Q4, as in Panno–Olafsson, Portoroz 1958.

12. . . .	O–O
13. P–QN3	R–B1?!

The Rook placement here is more awkward than good. After the game 13. . . . N–B3 14. B–B3 N–Q4 was recommended as Black's best, and this appeared soon thereafter in Polugaevsky–Sveshnikov, 1973 U.S.S.R. Championship. Black equalized after 15. B–N2 P–QB4! 16. PxP BxP 17. N–B4 Q–K2 18. R–B1 QR–B1, etc., and drew in 36. However, the immediate 15. N–K4!, preventing Black's . . . P–QB4, does retain an edge for White.

14. N–B4	N–B3
15. B–B3	N–Q4
16. P–QR3!	

Out of this apparently quiet strategic opening, White has gained the following advantages: a clear superiority of central space, superior pawn formation, and pressure along the QR-file. Since these have been obtained for "free," White is significantly better.

16. . . .   P–QR4

The QRP will be weak here, but 16. . . . PxP is equally unattractive. The sharp 16. . . . P–QB4?! is met by the simple 17. PxBP!

17. B–Q2   P–QB4?

Black is too weak to afford this active advance. White now wins material by force with an effective combination. Black's best is the defensive 17. . . . R–R1.

18. QPxP!   BxP
19. NxP!!   B–R3

Worse is 19. . . . QxN 20. PxP followed by 21. PxB, and White has a strong Bishop pair to go with his extra pawn.

20. PxP!   BxNP

There is little pleasure in 20. . . . BxR since after 21. PxB White has two terrific passed pawns for the Exchange.

21. BxB   NxB
22. QxQ   KRxQ
23. KR–Q1   RxRch
24. RxR

The combination has brought the clear advantage of a passed QNP. Interestingly, the forces at work are the same as in Game 13, Geller–Portisch, Portoroz 1973. But whereas, Geller couldn't do anything with his extra QNP, Portisch realizes his advantage with fine technique.

24. . . .   K–B1
25. P–R3   R–B4
26. R–Q8ch   K–K2
27. R–QN8

Should Black now exchange Rooks, Knights, or nothing? The answer is not easy, but inasmuch as the exchange of pieces generally favors the stronger side, Black's offer to exchange Rooks cannot be right. 27. . . . N–Q6!? seems like the most practical continuation.

27. . . .   R–QN4?!
28. RxR   BxR
29. P–N3!   K–Q3
30. N–N7ch   K–B2
31. N–B5

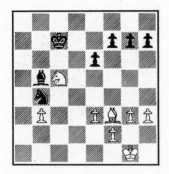

At the moment Black may appear to have a defensible position, but that is only a mirage. White's QNP is quite safe, and so Black has no counterplay, whereas by offering exchanges White will force Black's defenders to give way.

31. . . .   P–R3

Necessary to prevent White's Knight from getting to White's KN5.

32. B–N2!   N–R7
33. B–B1   K–B3
34. BxBch   KxN

Equally dismal is 34. . . . KxB 35. N–Q3 N–N5 36. N–K5 P–B3 37. N–B3!, and if 37. . . . P–K4 then 38. N–R4! and the Knight will go after Black's Kingside pawns. The value of the text move is that White's Bishop will not be able to directly menace Black's pawns. But even so, the passed QNP will be decisive, since the

Bishop will be able to protect it, and then White's King will be available for various active forays.

35. B–K8   P–B3
36. B–Q7!   P–K4
37. P–R4   P–K5

This does prevent a White K–KB3 but at the cost of a weak pawn on K5. The pluses and minuses are about in balance. A move to keep the status quo is 37. . . . N–B6.

38. K–N2   N–B8
39. B–K6   N–Q6?

39. . . . K–N5 is more logical since the various K + P endgames after 40. P–R5 NxP 41. BxN KxB seem drawn; e.g., 42. P–B3! P–B4! 43. P–N4! K–B5!! 44. PxBP K–Q4!, etc. An immediate 40. K–R3 is foiled by 40. . . . N–Q6. Thus White must be satisfied with 40. B–Q5 NxP 41. BxP. Black is very weak on the light squares, and so White's King has good chances of penetrating Black's Kingside. Even so, Black keeps reasonable practical defensive chances. As played, Black allows White to set up a bind on the Kingside, and then Black is totally defenseless.

40. P–R5!   N–K8ch
41. K–R3   K–Q3

White's King has to head toward the center anyway; thus 41. . . . N–Q6 42. K–N2 N–K8ch 43. K–B1, etc., simply forces White to execute the correct maneuver.

42. B–B5   K–K4
43. P–KN4!

Keeping the bind. 43. B–R7?! P–B4! is inferior.

43. . . .   N–B7

The "active" 43. . . . N–Q6 can be met by both 44. K–N2 and 44. P–B4ch.

44. K–N2	**K–Q4**
45. B–R7	**N–N5**
46. K–B1!	**N–B3**
47. K–K2	**N–N5**
48. K–Q2	**N–R7**
49. B–B5	**Black resigns**

Here the lights went out in the tournament room, so the game was adjourned; however, Black resigned without continuing. With Black's pieces forced to watch his weak KP, White's King can assist in the advance of the QNP; for instance, 49. . . . N–N5 50. K–B3 N–R7ch (50. . . . N–Q6 51. P–B3!) 51. K–N2 N–N5 52. K–R3, etc.

Chapter 14

Savon, Vladimir

There are times in a person's life when he brings off a superhuman effort. For Vladimir Savon this was the 1971 U.S.S.R. Championship. Unnoticed and unheralded, he played fantastic chess and was a deserved and decisive winner, finishing 1½ points ahead of the field—a field that included Tal, Smyslov, Karpov, Stein, Bronstein, Polugaevsky, Geller, Tukmakov, and Vaganian. Savon's results since have not come close to matching this one, but he has established himself as a good quality grandmaster.

Born on September 26, 1940, in Chernikov, Ukraine, he still lives in the Ukraine (Kharkov). Savon became an international grandmaster in 1973 and played in the 1972 Chess Olympiad. His international experience is not vast, his best results being 2nd–4th at Mar del Plata 1971, 2nd at Sukhumi 1972, 2nd–3rd at Erevan 1976, and 2nd–3rd at Ljubljana-Portoroz 1977. Savon's 1977 FIDE rating is 2540.

GAME 35

White: W. Uhlmann
   (East Germany)

Black: V. Savon
   (U.S.S.R.)

Played at Capablanca Memorial Tournament, Cienfuegos (Cuba), February–March 1973.

English Opening

Savon tries an esoteric approach against the English Opening but comes out with a clear central inferiority and nothing to show for it. Uhlmann applies additional pressure with some fine maneuvering, and Savon makes his situation worse by an unmotivated exchange of Bishop for Knight. Black's attempts at Queenside counterplay are parried with deft action in the center. Twice Uhlmann eschews winning endgames to keep the action in the middlegame and thus, he hopes, to take advantage of Black's time pressure. Objectively such an approach carries some dangers, but in this particular situation White is rewarded. Black volunteers a serious weakening of his Kingside and then oversteps the time limit in a rather helpless position.

1. P–QB4	N–KB3
2. N–QB3	P–KN3
3. P–K4	P–K4

A somewhat esoteric plan, though playable. The conventional 3. . . . P–Q3 4. P–Q4 leads to the King's Indian Defense.

| 4. N–B3 | N–B3?! |

But this is carrying originality too far. Correct is 4. . . . P–Q3 5. P–Q4 QN–Q2 with transposition into a King's Indian type of variation.

| 5. P–Q4! | PxP |

Giving up the center so early is nothing but an admission of the bankruptcy of Black's strategic idea associated with 4. . . . N–B3?!. But unfortunately 5. . . . P–Q3 is met by 6. PxP!, and now 6. . . . QNxP leads to

the same type of position, and 6. . . . PxP allows 7. QxQch! KxQ 8. B–N5 and a most unpleasant pin (8. . . . B–N2?? 9. N–Q5 wins).

6. NxP	B–N2
7. B–K3	O–O
8. B–K2	R–K1
9. P–B3	

White already has a significant central advantage as the result of Black's 4th and 5th moves. Most importantly, Black cannot hope to attack White's center, and Black's QN even gets in the way of his trying to generate Queenside counterplay.

| 9. . . . | P–Q3 |
| 10. O–O | N–K4?! |

Giving up pressure on White's Q4 just allows White a freer hand to position his pieces for maximum effectiveness. 10. . . . B–Q2 is more logical.

| 11. Q–Q2! | P–QR3 |
| 12. QR–Q1 | B–Q2 |

The opening phase has ended significantly in White's favor:

he has a clearly superior and secure center and every one of his pieces is usefully deployed, whereas Black is cramped and lifeless. The next step is to apply additional pressure by redeploying the pieces. With his next White sets up an annoying Bishop pin.

13. B–N5!   N–B3

Stamping his 10th as a waste of time. Black tries to reduce the pressure by attempting a Knight exchange.

14. N–N3

White correctly wants to keep up the pressure and thus retains the Knight. A more useful retreat though is 14. N–B2!, an idea that White gets a couple of moves later.

14. . . .   P–QR4
15. N–Q5!

More pressure.

15. . . .   P–R5
16. N–R1!   B–K3
17. N–B2

So White's Knight has found the correct spot after all. On QB2 the Knight guards the important Q4-square and can go to K3 where it overprotects the Q5 outpost. Black is still without counterplay.

17. . . .   BxN?!

Black is anxious to remove the annoying Knight before White can play 18. N/B–K3

and recapture on Q5 with the Knight. But after the text, White has even more central influence and the two Bishops in a position which will be soon rather open. Black's position is unpleasant in any case, but 17. . . . N–K4 followed by 18. . . . N/4–Q2 seems like a better defensive plan.

18. BPxB   N–K4
19. K–R1!

Good practical precaution. Black's counterplay must come by means of . . . P–B3, and White ensures that Black can't play . . . Q–QN3 with check.

19. . . .   Q–N1
20. N–K3   P–B3

With White's Queen no longer controlling the KR6-square, Black may seem to have a chance here for 20. . . . P–R3, but that is not so. Uhlmann gives this refutation: 21. BxN! BxB 22. P–B4 N–Q2 23. B–N5 Q–Q1 24. N–N4 B–N2 25. P–K5! P–R4 26. P–K6!!, since 26. . . . BPxP 27. PxP RxP?! loses to 28. B–B4, and little better is 26. . . . PxN 27. BxN R–K2 28. P–B5! and Black's weakened Kingside will soon crumble.

21. PxP   PxP
22. BxN!

A little combination based on the strategic factor that Black's remaining Knight will be unprotected on Q2. Instead, White gains nothing from 22.

QxP QxP 23. R–Q2 Q–N3 24. BxN QxN!.

22. . . .   BxB
23. P–B4   N–Q2
24. P–K5!   B–K2

After 24. . . . B–N2 White has many good continuations, among them 25. QxP QxP 26. B–B3. But the clumsy text can't be any better.

25. PxP   QxQP

The game is immediately over after 25. . . . BxP? 26. N–N4! P–R4 (or 26. . . . B–B1 27. B–B3) 27. N–R6ch K–N2 28. NxP! KxN 29. B–B4ch, etc.

26. Q–B3

Counting on Black's time pressure, White wants more than the won endgame after 26. QxQ! BxQ 27. RxB RxN 28. B–B3 N–B1 29. RxBP when White's a pawn ahead with the better position. The course of the game proves Uhlmann right, but objectively it isn't the smartest thing to do.

26. . . .   Q–B3!?

The only defense. After 26. . . . Q–B4 Uhlmann gives this pretty line: 27. B–B4! N–N3 (27. . . . B–B3?! 28. BxPch!) 28. N–N4! P–R4 (28. . . . Q–KR4 29. N–K5 is a positional crush) 29. BxPch! KxB 30. N–R6ch with mate to follow.

27. Q–B2

Here, too, a larger advantage is to be gained by entering the endgame by means of 27. B–B3!.

27. . . .   B–B1!

The counter on White's Knight allows Black to save all material and reasonably consolidate his position. Now 28. N–N4 is parried by 28. . . . Q–B4! with an attack on White's Queen. White seems to have overlooked this in playing his 26th move.

28. N–B4   R–R2
29. B–B3   R–N1
30. P–KN3

Black stands well enough and after 30. . . . R–N5, for example, his disadvantage is relatively minor. But he commits a characteristic time-pressure error.

30. . . .   P–R4?

Unmotivated pawn pushes are a hallmark of serious time pressure. With no time to think, it is easy to push a pawn. But the damage often is great. Here Black's Kingside is decisively weakened, and White immediately exploits this circumstance.

31. P–B5!   N–B4
32. PxP   QxKNP
33. Q–B2!

But here, with Black's Kingside in shreds, White correctly wants more than 33. QxQ PxQ 34. BxBP.

33.	. . .	R–N5
34.	N–K5	Q–N2
35.	R/Q–K1	

Black overstepped the time limit and lost.

As Black was playing 35. . . . R/2–N2, his flag fell and he was forfeited. Not that it mattered much, since after 36. BxRP RxP, for example, White can win an Exchange with 37. BxPch or go for more with 37. Q–B5.

GAME 36

White: V. Savon
(U.S.S.R.)

Black: G. Garcia
(Cuba)

Played at Capablanca Memorial Tournament, Cienfuegos (Cuba), February–March 1973.

Pirc/Modern Defense

Faced with an oblique counter against his strong center, White reacts correctly in the beginning, but soon completely forgets what the game of chess is about. He ignores the center, King location, King safety, and piece coordination. Black takes advantage of White's "purposeful" carelessness and walks all over his opponent. In fewer than forty moves it's all over.

1.	P–K4	P–KN3
2.	P–Q4	B–N2
3.	N–QB3	P–Q3
4.	P–B4	

Postponing Black's . . . N–KB3 gives both Black and White some options to the normal Pirc (1. P–K4 P–Q3 2. P–Q4 N–KB3 3. N–QB3 P–KN3). Here Black could enter the Pirc itself with 4. . . . N–KB3 or head toward less explored waters with 4. . . . N–QB3 or 4. . . . P–QB3 or . . .

| 4. . . . | P–QR3?! |

With the plan of . . . P–QN4 and . . . B–QN2, leaving the QBP in reserve for other things. The text is played intermittently, but I'm somewhat skeptical about its theoretical value. It seems too passive given White's strong center.

5.	N–B3	P–QN4
6.	B–Q3	B–N2
7.	Q–K2	P–QB4

7. . . . N–Q2 is more frequently played, after which White keeps the advantage with 8. P–K5.

8. PxP   PxP
9. P–K5!

A position favoring White: he has a strong secure center and harmonious development, whereas Black's expanded Queenside can very easily become a weakness instead of a strength. In Tal–Szabo, Sochi 1973, played after this game, Black continued 9. . . . N–QB3?! 10. B–K3! N–Q5 11. NxN PxN and now 12. R–Q1! leads to clear superiority, according to Tal. Garcia's move is better.

9. . . .   N–R3!?
10. P–QR4!

10. B–K4 is good, but the text, by getting Black to weaken his Queenside, is even better.

10. . . .   P–N5
11. N–K4   Q–B1
12. P–B3

Starting here White begins to lose the thread of the position. The text itself is playable, but the followup is not. 12. B–K3?? is a gross error because of 12. . . . P–B5. Correct are such obvious moves as 12. O–O or 12. P–QN3 and 13. B–N2. In either case White has more space and stands better.

12. . . .   O–O
13. PxP?!

Weakens White's Q4-square and removes Black's pawn weakness on his QB4. Castling is infinitely better.

13. . . .   PxP
14. B–Q2?!

A modest location for the Bishop. 14. B–K3 or 14. O–O is better.

14. . . .   N–B3
15. R–QB1

Why not 15. O–O?

15. . . .   N–B4!

Black has been developing his pieces toward important central squares and stands excellently. If now 16. BxNP, Black plays 16. . . . Q–Q1! 17. B–B3 N/3–Q5! 18. NxN NxN 19. BxN QxB and with the two Bishops and active Queen has more than sufficient compensation for the pawn. White's soundest continuation is still 16. O–O. With the unmotivated text he continues on a suicidal course.

16. P–N4??   N–R3
17. P–R3   P–B4!

Obvious and strong. White already lacks a satisfactory continuation.

| 18. | N–B5 | PxP |
| 19. | PxP | NxKP! |

The punishment, taking full advantage of the weakness-prone White position.

20.	NxN	BxR
21.	B–B4ch	K–R1
22.	N–K6	Q–N2!
23.	NxR	RxN
24.	P–N5??	

Allowing Black's Knight on the edge a triumphal return to the center is part of White's strategy of self-destruction. The only reasonable move is 24. BxRP, thereby reestablishing material equality. White's position is shaky, but he has some chances to weather the storm. After the text he has none.

24.	. . .	N–B4
25.	N–B7ch	RxN
26.	BxR	N–Q5
27.	Q–K3	P–N6

White has won the Exchange and is immediately on the brink of defeat. There is no defense to the threat of 28. . . . N–B7ch.

28.	BxQNP	NxB
29.	R–B4	NxB
30.	QxN	P–KR4!

Black now has a decisive positional *and* material advantage. His last move is an efficient way to take care of any potential difficulties on his first rank. White's resulting KRP is a toothless tiger.

31.	PxP e.p.	B–KB3!
32.	R–N4	Q–R2
33.	K–Q1	Q–B4!
34.	R–N8ch	K–R2
35.	Q–Q3	B–K5!

Black's Queen and Bishops control the board, and with elementary though pretty tactics Black enlarges his material advantage. If now 36. QxB Q–Q3ch wins the Rook. White can only postpone this plan for a move.

| 36. | Q–QN3 | B–B7ch! |

| 37. | QxB | Q–Q3ch |

White resigns

GAME 37

White: V. Savon
    (U.S.S.R.)

Black: H. Mecking
    (Brazil)

Player at Petropolis (Brazil) Interzonal Tournament, August 2, 1973, Round 7.

Sicilian Defense (Najdorf Variation)

White makes all kinds of errors in losing this game: psychological, strategic, and tactical. He chooses a sharp variation with which he is unfamiliar, then when speed is essential he plays slowly, and finally he overlooks some of his opponent's tactical threats. The result is a hopeless endgame and assured loss. On the other hand Black's play is faultless throughout: active and consistent in executing the ideas behind the opening, sharp in carrying out combinations, and decisive in endgame technique.

1.	P–K4	P–QB4
2.	N–KB3	P–Q3
3.	P–Q4	PxP
4.	NxP	N–KB3
5.	N–QB3	P–QR3
6.	B–N5	

White's first error. Objectively the move is fine—it is White's most popular continuation—but it is not part of Savon's normal repertoire (he prefers 6. B–K2 or 6. P–B4), and it quickly becomes apparent that he is not comfortable with it.

6. . . .		P–K3
7.	P–B4	QN–Q2
8.	Q–K2	

The usual move is 8. Q–B3, as we discussed under Game 30.

Spassky has recently recommended 8. B–B4!? as a promising alternative, with the dual points that after 8. . . . P–N4 White can bring a promising piece sacrifice with 9. BxKP! PxB 10. NxKP and that 8. . . . Q–N3 is met by 9. Q–Q2! QxP 10. O–O giving White excellent play for the pawn.

Savon spent 15 minutes on 8. Q–K2, indicating that he hadn't expected Black's 7th move and already felt unprepared. The primary point of the text is to aim for an early P–K5. In addition the Queen is somewhat less exposed here than on KB3. But there are also clear drawbacks: Black gets in . . . P–QN4 quickly, White's KB is blocked off, and if it is developed via KN2, then White's QB4-square will be weakened. This latter point will become apparent in the game.

8. . . .		Q–B2
9.	P–KN4	

Playable, but 9. O–O–O is more flexible and useful. White must eventually castle on the Queenside and doing it immediately gives him more options later. We'll see 9. O–O–O in Game 64, Tukmakov–Browne, Madrid 1973.

9. . . .		P–N4
10.	P–QR3	

Prevents a . . . P–QN5 but at the significant cost of a tempo. 10. O–O–O!? is worth consider-

ing, and after 10. . . . P–N5 11.
N–Q5!?. White gets a significant
edge in development—and
therefore a strong attack—for
the sacrified piece.

10. . . .	B–K2
11. B–N2	B–N2
12. O–O–O	R–QB1!

To establish immediate pressure along the QB-file and
threaten counterplay with 13.
. . . Q–B5 is imperative. Less
exact is 12. . . . N–N3, which
led to an advantage for White
after 13. B–R4 P–R3 14. B–N3
O–O–O 15. B–B3 P–N4 16.
PxP PxP 17. P–K5! in Kuzmin–
Stean, Hastings 1973/74.

13. B–R4?!

Planning 14. P–N5 and/or
14. B–N3, but there is insufficient time. White spent more
than half an hour on it, without
apparently appreciating the
strength of Black's response. Instead, 13. BxN! is correct. (13.
KR–K1 also seems playable.)
Then after 13. . . . NxB 14. P–
N5 N–Q2 15. K–N1! Q–B5 16.
R–Q3! White has a slight advantage, as in Shamkovich–
Quinteros, Lone Pine 1975.

| 13. . . . | Q–B5! |
| 14. QxQ? | |

By allowing Black's Rook to
reach an active location on his
QB5, White starts going from
bad to worse. Also unsatisfactory is 14. Q–B3? because

of 14. . . . P–N5 15. PxP QxP
16. P–N5 RxN! and Black has
more than sufficient compensation for the Exchange. As
Vasiukov points out, White
should continue with the consistent 14. P–N5. Then after 14.
. . . QxQ 15. N/4xQ N–N5 16.
B–B3 N–K6 17. QR–N1 fol-
lowed by 18. B–B2, White is
just a shade worse.

| 14. . . . | RxQ |
| 15. B–B3?! | |

Again the wrong move. Here
is the last chance to protect his
weaknesses with 15. BxN NxB
16. P–R3!, as **IM** Kaplan
recommended.

| 15. . . . | N–B4! |

Attacking the KP three times,
and there is no satisfactory way
to protect it. 16. KR–K1 allows
16. . . . N/3xKP! 17. BxB
NxN, and 16. BxN fails to the
simple 16. . . . BxB 17. N/4–
K2 NxP.

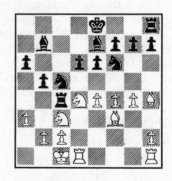

16. B–K2

Black's Rook only looks trapped, and Black has a pretty combination in store. The beginning of the combination is simple enough, but the main point is quite unusual.

16. . . .   N/3xKP!
17. NxN?

Savon is already short of time and recaptures without much thought. The move would be O.K. *if* Black did not have the shot on move 18. Imperative is 17. BxB NxN 18. PxN KxB 19. BxR BxR 20. BxNP, although Black's superior pawn formation guarantees him a clear advantage after 20. . . . B–N2.

17. . . .   BxN
18. BxB   N–N6ch!!

Only so! After the routine 18. . . . KxB?! 19. BxR BxR 20. BxNP Black is only a shade better because White's pawn formation is normal not, as in the previous note, inferior.

As Mecking tells it, Savon had an unhappy facial expression during the last few moves, and after the last Black move the expression changed to shock, from the clear realization that White now is completely busted. When he played his 14th move White apparently hadn't noticed this check.

19. K–N1

At least equally hopeless is 19. NxN RxPch 20. K–N1 RxBch 21. K–R1 BxR, etc.

19. . . .   RxN
20. BxQP   BxR
21. PxN   RxRch
22. BxR   K–Q2

Black's combination yields the Exchange and the superior pawn formation. The win should be only a matter of normal technique, but Mecking's active way of realizing his advantage is impressive.

23. B–K5   P–B3
24. B–QB3   B–K5ch
25. K–R2?!

The King is not only unsafe here, but also misplaced, for it allows Black's Rook to penetrate White's position. The centralizing 25. K–B1 is correct.

25. . . .   K–B3
26. P–QR4   R–Q1
27. B–K2   P–K4!

Giving White the unenviable option either of allowing Black to create a passed KP or of permitting Black's Rook the full use of the seventh and eighth ranks. It doesn't matter what White plays any more: his position is hopeless and already fully resignable.

28. BPxP   BPxP
29. BxP   R–Q7
30. B–B1   R–Q8
31. PxPch?!

Opening the QR-file allows immediate mate, though the end is also imminent after 31. B–R3 P–N4, etc.

31. . . .	**PxP**
32. B–R3	**P–N5**
33. BxP	**R–Q2!**

White resigns

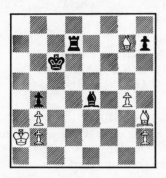

Next comes 34. . . . . R–R2 mate!

GAME 38

White: L. Ljubojevic (Yugoslavia)

Black: V. Savon (U.S.S.R.)

Played at Petropolis (Brazil) Interzonal Tournament, August 6, 1973, Round 10.

Caro-Kann Defense

A strange game. White employs something like a King's Indian Reversed formation and makes demonstrations on the Queenside. Black on the other hand expands in the center and the Kingside. Chances are roughly in balance when White forces or allows a promising Exchange sacrifice by Black.

But by now Black is short of time and does nothing with his opportunities. White consolidates his material advantage and wins rather effortlessly. White does not so much win as Black loses.

1. P–K4   P–QB3

Late in the 19th century M. Kann from Vienna and H. Caro from Berlin recommended this defense, which soon thereafter received the name of the inventors. The defense has never achieved raging popularity but always has had a steady respectability. After the usual 2. P–Q4 P–Q4 Black's QBP supports the challenge to White's KP, and then after 3. N–QB3 Black plays 3. . . . PxP. The resulting positions are fairly straightforward; White has a slight space advantage, Black a solid position free of fundamental weaknesses. Though Black's winning chances often are slight, his prospects for an honorable draw are excellent.

2. P–Q3

The Yugoslav GM invariably prefers this modest move to the usual 2. P–Q4. He likes Old Indian/King's Indian Reversed formations with the extra move for White and the hope that Black's first move will not turn out to be particularly useful. In theory White's plan should be harmless but in practice Ljubojevic has scored many successes.

| 2. . . . | P–Q4 |
| 3. N–Q2 | P–KN3?! |

By far the most common response, but I don't think that it is fully satisfactory because the fianchettoed KB has little meaningful scope. A steadier route to equality is the symmetrical 3. . . . PxP! 4. PxP P–K4 5. KN–B3 Q–B2.

4. KN–B3

The usual plan for White is the KB fianchetto by means of 4. P–KN3, but Ljubojevic specializes in the text, which is followed by developing the KB on its original diagonal.

| 4. . . . | B–N2 |
| 5. P–B3 | |

For much of the subsequent play the QBP can just as well remain home and thus the immediate 5. B–K2! is more accurate, as Ljubojevic played with great success in the middle 1970s. Black's soundest response then is 5. . . . N–B3.

| 5. . . . | P–K4 |

Here, too, 5. . . . N–B3 may be better.

6. P–QR4

Instead of this immediate Queenside demonstration the developmental 6. B–K2 N–K2 7. O–O is more logical. Then after the premature 7. . . . B–

N5?! (correct is 7. . . . O–O), White gains the advantage with 8. PxP! BxN (8. . . . PxP? 9. NxP!) 9. BxB PxP 10. P–B4, as in Ljubojevic–Pomar, Las Palmas 1975.

6. . . .	N–K2
7. P–R5	O–O
8. B–K2	P–KR3
9. O–O	P–KB4

The battle lines are drawn distinctly: Black will attack on the Kingside; White will try to do something on the Queenside. The position is very unbalanced, but objectively the chances should be equivalent.

10. P–QN3	K–R2
11. B–R3	R–N1
12. R–K1	P–KN4

Black's central and Kingside pawn mass looks very imposing so that White decides to reduce it slightly. This, however, brings Black's QB into play.

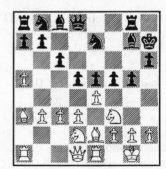

| 13. PxBP | BxP |
| 14. N–B1 | N–Q2 |

Trying to bring the QN into the game is logical enough,

though at the moment regrouping the Kingside forces is a bit more effective. For this 14. . . . N–N3! 15. N–N3 B–K3 is in order. Savon then gives the following interesting variation: 16. B–KB1 N–Q2 17. N–R5 B–R1 18. N–Q4! PxN 19. RxB PxP 20. P–Q4, followed by 21. B–Q3 and the obscure position still yields equal chances.

15. N–N3   B–N3
16. P–R6

Weakening Black's QBP and removing White's QRP from the range of Black's Queen.

16. . . .   P–N3
17. P–Q4!

Black's strong center must be challenged, and this and the next moves are quite in order. White's pieces are much too passively placed to expect anything more than equality from the "attacking" 17. P–R4. After 17. . . . P–N5 18. P–R5 (18. N–R2?! P–R4 19. P–B3 B–B3 gives White *less* than equality) 18. . . . PxN 19. PxBch NxP 20. BxP N–B3, Black's active position ensures him good prospects.

17. . . .   P–K5
18. N–Q2   N–B3
19. P–B3   R–K1!

Black's pawn on K5 exerts strong cramping effect on White; thus it is in Black's interest to retain, if possible, his presence there.

20. PxP   PxP
21. N–B4   N/2–Q4
22. B–N2?!

The QBP has to be protected, of course, but this is both awkward and passive. Logical and correct is 22. Q–B1! with about equal chances.

22. . . .   Q–B2!
23. N–K5   RxN!

Forced and forcing. For the Exchange, Black receives a pawn and strong attacking chances on the Kingside.

24. PxR   QxP
25. R–QB1   N–B5
26. B–R1   Q–K2
27. P–N4   R–Q1
28. Q–N3

Up to here Black has played excellently but has used up almost all of his time; in what follows he becomes completely unrecognizable. Quite strong now is 28. . . . P–R4! and 29. . . . P–R5 to continue the attack. White has to defend accurately to hold on. Also rea-

sonable is the "positional" 28.
. . . N/3–Q4.

28. . . .   N–Q6??

This is something like chess madness. Black exchanges his active Knight for White's KB (and thereby goes against the general principle that the attacking side should hold on to his pieces), exposes his KP, allows White's Rooks to become active, and even permits an exchange of his own Rook.

29. BxN   RxB
30. QR–Q1   Q–Q2?

The Queen is poorly placed here. Correct is 30. . . . RxR and 31. . . . P–R4. Black then has at least some practical chances for an attack.

31. Q–B2   N–N5?

Loses two tempos. At the moment 31. . . . P–R4? is refuted by 32. NxKP! BxN 33. RxB! RxRch 34. R–K1ch!. Black's only try is 31. . . . RxR 32. QxR Q–K3, again aiming for 33. . . . P–R4.

32. Q–K2   N–B3
33. P–B4

All of White's pieces now are trained on Black's center and KP. The latter's days, and thus Black's, are numbered.

33. . . .   RxR
34. RxR   Q–K2
35. BxN!

This and the following move are a pretty and effective tactical

way to win the KP. Black has obviously been left without enough pieces to cover the required ground, so it is not surprising that White has a winning combination at his disposal.

35. . . .   BxB
36. NxP!   BxN?!

White's response is so obvious that the text is equivalent to choosing to die with one's boots on. If Black doesn't want to resign then he should play 36. . . . QxN 37. QxQ BxQ 38. R–Q7ch K–N3 39. RxP P–N4, even though White does have a forced win with 40. P–B5 B–QB6 41. R–K7 B–Q4 42. R–Q7! (42. P–R7?! BxQNP!! 43. P–R8=Q BxBPch followed by 44. . . . BxR is not clear) 42. . . . BxQNP 43. RxB! PxR 44. P–B6 and one of White's pawns will queen.

37. R–K1   B–Q5ch
38. K–R1   BxPch
39. KxB

Black overstepped the time limit and lost.

White has a decisive material and positional superiority. Black's loss on time here, in lieu of resignation, is just a formality.

GAME 39

White: V. Savon (U.S.S.R.)

Black: V. Hort (Czechoslovakia)

Played at Petropolis (Brazil) Interzonal Tournament, August 11, 1973, Round 13.

Pirc Defense

A fighting opening leads to a fighting middlegame with balanced chances. Then inexplicably White sacrifices (throws away?) his center pawns for nothing perceivable. Black accepts the gifts, consolidates efficiently, and realizes his advantage in good style.

1. P–K4	P–Q3
2. P–Q4	N–KB3
3. N–QB3	P–KN3

This is the basic position in the Pirc Defense, named for Yugoslav GM Vasja Pirc, who was the first top master to demonstrate the playability of Black's system. It is a relatively new opening, having been taken seriously only after the Second World War and thus has had a "professional" life of about thirty years. The Pirc can be looked on as a KP counterpart of the King's Indian. The key difference between the King's Indian and the Pirc is that in positions of the former White's QBP is on the fourth rank rather than back home on QB2. Therefore, in the King's Indian White has a more imposing center (albeit one more subject to successful counterplay), whereas in the Pirc White is a move ahead in developing his pieces.

4. P–B4

In the King's Indian this would be the fourth pawn on the fourth rank and would risk a shaky center situation. In the Pirc the move is considered the active positional continuation. A noncommittal and popular strategic plan is 4. N–B3, followed by 5. B–K2 and 6. O–O. A sharp fight follows 4. B–KN5 (see Game 59, Mestel–Tukmakov, Hastings 1972/73).

4. . . .	B–N2
5. N–B3	P–B4

This counter to White's center prior to Black's castling can lead to great complications. The faint-at-heart prefer the safer 5. . . . O–O, after which 6. B–Q3 gives White a slight plus.

6. B–N5ch

The alternative is 6. PxP Q–R4 7. B–Q3 QxP 8. Q–K2 O–O 9. B–K3. In either case White can hope to obtain the usual first-move advantage.

6. . . .   B–Q2
7. BxBch?!

But this is completely harmless since Black can efficiently recapture with the KN. Correct is 7. P–K5 N–N5 when White has three logical ways to go for a slight advantage: 8. P–K6, 8. P–KR3, and 8. BxBch QxB 9. P–Q5.

7. . . .   KNxB!

Only so! After the inferior 7. . . . QxB?! 8. PxP! PxP 9. O–O N–B3 10. P–K5 QxQ 11. RxQ N–KN5 12. P–KR3 N–R3 13. B–K3, White's space advantage gave him a comfortable endgame plus in Hort–Böhm, U.S. Open Championship 1975.

8. P–Q5   N–R3
9. O–O   O–O
10. P–B5

With the idea of opening the diagonal for the QB, but it carries the significant strategic disadvantage of handing Black's K4-square over to Black permanently. Savon obviously was not satisfied with the move because a few months later, against Korchnoi at the 1973 U.S.S.R. Championship, he played 10. Q–K2. But after 10. . . . N–B2! 11. R–Q1?! (11. P–QR4 is better) 11. . . . P–QN4! 12. NxP NxN 13. QxN R–N1 14. Q–K2 BxP 15. BxB RxB, Black's chances in the sharp fight turned

out superior to White's. The fault I think lies with 7. BxBch?!.

10. . . .   Q–N3

The Queen gets in the way more than it helps in the Queenside play. More accurate is 10. . . . N–B2! with the idea 11. . . . P–QN4, as in the previous note.

11. K–R1   N–B2
12. N–K2

The idea behind this maneuver is unclear. Much more in the spirit of White's tenth move is 12. Q–K1! followed by 13. Q–R4.

12. . . .   P–B5
13. N–N3   P–QR4
14. R–QN1   P–B6?!

And here more accurate is 14. . . . P–R5 first. When playing the text Black didn't pay sufficient attention to White's 16th and 17th moves.

15. P–QN3   P–R5

Otherwise White plays 16. P–QR4, and Black's advanced QBP can turn out to be quite weak.

16. B–N5!   N–B3
17. NPxP

An interesting position. Opening the QN-file gives White's Rook pressure against the QNP. In addition Black's 16th move has made the protection of his QBP difficult. It appears that White will wind up a pawn ahead, and the important question remaining is whether Black will have sufficient compensation.

17.	. . .	Q–R2
18.	N–Q4	QR–N1
19.	N/4–K2!	QxP
20.	NxP	Q–R4
21.	B–Q2	KR–B1

So White has won the QBP and is a pawn ahead. Black does have some pressure along the QB-file, and White's QRP, QBP, and KP are inherently somewhat weak. White cannot clearly or simply do anything with his extra pawn; nevertheless, Black's compensation for the pawn should not be, theoretically, quite sufficient.

22. PxP   BPxP

The positional capture is 22. . . . RPxP; i.e., toward the center. There is really nothing wrong with that, but Black, cognizant of being a pawn down, prefers to unbalance things and hopes to have some potential play along the KB-file

in case the QB-file turns out unpromising.

23. Q–B3

Doesn't seem like a comfortable square for the Queen. 23. P–QR4! instead is good to gain some extra space on the Queenside and neutralize the possible positional threat of . . . P–QN4.

23. . . .   Q–R3
24. P–K5??

This throws away both of White's central pawns for no reason. It is not that White overlooked some special or deep response, since all of Black's moves are normal and obvious. The only explanation is the collapse of his chess nerves: White felt that he had to do something, and what's more logical than a central advance? 24. P–QR4! is still the correct and indicated move.

24. . . .   PxP
25. QR–K1?!

White continues to play "thematically." Protecting the QP with 25. KR–Q1 is better.

25. . . .   R–B1
26. Q–Q1?!

Can White have overlooked that 26. RxP allows 26. . . . N/3xP? The passive Queen retreat also can't be right. 26. Q–Q3, aiming for an endgame in which Black's extra pawn is a doubled KP, is the logical way to head for a draw.

26. . . .   N/2xP

Thank you.

27. NxN   NxN
28. Q–N1?!

This, too, is inexact because White's Rook will be misplaced on KB1. The accurate move order is 28. RxRch! RxR 29. Q–N1.

28. . . .   RxRch!
29. RxR?!

Here 29. NxR is better.

29. . . .   R–QB1!
30. Q–N3

White needs to get the Knight into the game, but here 30. N–K4? fails to 30. . . . RxP!— showing up the error in White's 28th move.

30. . . .   Q–B5!
31. QxP

The endgame after 31. QxQ RxQ 32. R–B1 P–K5 is equally hopeless for White since Black will win the QBP and then remain up two pawns.

31. . . .   P–K5!

Black first achieves total domination of the board. He sees that the Queenside pawns won't run away.

32. Q–N3   P–K6!
33. B–R5   P–K3!
34. R–K1   QxP
35. Q–N7   Q–B3
36. Q–N3

A time-pressure reflex which hastens the end. The exchange of Queens, however, would only prolong the game without affecting the outcome. White's QRP would go lost, and Black's two passed KPs would be strong enough to win.

36. . . .   N–B5
37. R–KN1   B–Q5
38. Q–Q1   Q–Q4

White overstepped the time limit and lost.

Losing on time is just a formality here, too. There is no way for White to cope with the coming 39. . . . P–K7.

Chapter 15

Smyslov, Vassily

Born on March 24, 1921, in Moscow, Smyslov has been living there ever since. He came to the attention of the chess world by placing third in the very strong Groningen 1946 International Tournament, the first strong post–World War II tournament. This opened the doors to participation in the 1948 match tournament for the World Championship, in which Smyslov finished second behind Botvinnik. By winning the 1953 Candidates tournament he got the chance to challenge Botvinnik in 1954 and played a 12:12 tie. Again in 1956 Smyslov became the Challenger, and in 1957 he defeated Botvinnik 12½–9½ to become World Champion. The triumph was short-lived, however, since Botvinnik exercised his right of a return match (taken away from the Champion starting in 1963) and in 1958 regained the title 12½–10½. Since then Smyslov has not come particularly close to challenging again for the World Championship.

In all other chess results he has remained very close to the top, however. He played on every Soviet Olympiad team from 1952 through 1972 (except 1966), participated in eighteen U.S.S.R. Championships (winning in 1949), and won at least twenty-two first places (including ties) in international tournaments. His latest successes include winning Szolnok 1975 and finishing, undefeated, third in the very strong Leningrad 1977 tournament. Smyslov took part in the 1945 and 1946 radio matches against the U.S.A. as well as in the "in person" matches of 1954 and 1955. At Lone Pine 1976 he finished in a nine-way tie for second place, receiving $1,511.

A book of his best games appeared in Russian in 1952 and in an updated English edition in 1958. Smyslov is coauthor with Levenfish of the acclaimed *Rook Endings*, first published in 1957.

His 1977 FIDE rating is 2595.

GAME 40

White: W. Uhlmann
    (East Germany)

Black: V. Smyslov
    (U.S.S.R.)

Played at Hastings (England) International Tournament, January 3, 1973, Round 7.

English Opening

A model game when played: a modern opening with a piquant tactical shot leads to a strategically superior middlegame, in which positional advantages are transformed by means of beautiful combinations into a direct, decisive mating attack. The passage of time has shown White's opening idea not to be quite correct; nevertheless, this does not decrease Uhlmann's creative and sporting achievements.

1.	P–QB4	P–K4
2.	N–QB3	N–QB3
3.	N–B3	N–B3
4.	P–KN3	B–N5

This subvariation of the English Four Knights has been exceedingly popular in the 1970s. The reason is clear: a strategically unbalanced, complicated, full-play position results, in which both sides have excellent winning chances, but neither totters at the edge of an abyss. The major points of the text are: *(1)* Black gets ready to castle and then will be able to use the KR for central purposes on K1; and *(2)* the exchange of the KB will increase Black's central influence and most likely give White doubled pawns. The strategic disadvantages of Black's plan may be that Black's advanced center (particularly if the KP advances to K5) can be liquidated to White's advantage and that White's Bishop pair can exert strong pressure. The course of the game allows White to demonstrate both of these factors.

5.	B–N2	O–O
6.	O–O	

This noncommittal move is the standard choice here, but 6. N–Q5 is also playable. We'll see that in Game 43, Smyslov–Mecking, Petropolis Interzonal 1973.

6. . . .   P–K5

This immediate advance is very demanding of Black. More flexible and a shade more accurate is 6. . . . R–K1.

7. N–KN5

Looks great since the triple attack on the KP forces Black's reply. But it has been established that the Knight's location on KN5 has more disadvantages than advantages. Thus the modest retreat 7. N–K1! is at present viewed as the only method to gain a slight advantage. A recent example is

Petrosian–Rogoff, 1976 Biel Interzonal, which went 7. . . . BxN 8. QPxB P–KR3 9. N–B2 P–Q3 10. N–K3 R–K1 11. Q–B2 P–N3, and now instead of 12. B–Q2? N–K4! with at least equality for Black (and a draw in 19), White can keep a slight plus with either 12. P–N3 or 12. P–B4.

7. . . .   BxN
8. NPxB

8. QPxB is pointless here since the KN has no good retreat square.

8. . . .   R–K1
9. P–B3?!

Works well in this game, but objectively it is not sound because White's King position is weakened too much. Black's KP must be attacked, but hindsight tells us that the correct way is 9. P–Q3!. After 9. . . . PxP 10. PxP P–Q3 the chances are even.

9. . . .   PxP
10. NxBP/3   P–Q4!

Quickly striking at White's center, while developing his own pieces, is the thematic response.

11. PxP   NxP?

This capture is the losing move. After the debacle here, Smyslov made a searching analysis of the position after White's 11th move and concluded that after 11. . . . QxP! Black is fine. His judgment was rewarded the next time he was

Black in this position; G. Sigurjonsson–Smyslov, Reykjavik 1974, continued 12. N–Q4 (12. P–Q4 Q–KR4 also favors Black) 12. . . . Q–KR4 13. NxN PxN 14. P–K3 B–N5 15. Q–R4 R–K3 (perhaps stronger is the immediate 15. . . . B–K7!?) 16. R–N1? B–K7 with advantage to Black, who won on move 24. Uhlmann had not noticed this game and allowed Makarichev of the U.S.S.R. to play the same variation at the 1975 IBM tournament at Amsterdam. He did try to improve by playing 15. B–B3, but after 15. . . . Q–N3! 16. BxB NxB 17. Q–K2 QR–Q1 18. B–R3 P–KR4, Black had a clear advantage because of play in the center and against White's weakened Kingside. Makarichev won in 61 moves, and ever since Uhlmann has switched to 7. N–K1!.

12. P–K4!!

This tactical shot allows White to build a strong center and a strong attacking position along the KB-file. These two factors and the Bishop pair give White a strategically won position, whose exploitation Uhlmann demonstrates with fine tactics. The KP is en prise but can't be taken: 12. . . . RxP?! 13. N–N5! R–K2 14. Q–R5! is devastating. Unsatisfactory also is 12. . . . N–B3 because of 13. P–K5! NxP 14. NxN RxN 15. P–Q4 R–K1 16. B–N5 with an irreparable weakening of Black's

Kingside to follow. Not that what happens in the game is much better for Black.

**12. . . .   N–N3
13. P–Q4!**

Thanks to tactics, the building of White's center continues. 13. . . . RxP? 14. N–N5 is even worse for Black than on the previous move.

**13. . . .   B–N5
14. P–KR3   B–R4
15. P–K5   N–Q4
16. B–Q2   Q–Q2
17. P–N4!**

White's center is secure, his minor piece development complete. Thus it is time to start active play where the attacking chances lie, the Kingside.

**17. . . .   B–N3
18. N–N5   N–R4?!**

Black is anxious to start something himself, but this gives White the tempo he needs to seriously weaken Black's Kingside. The minor evil is 18. . . . P–KR3 19. N–K4.

**19. P–KR4!   P–KR3
20. P–R5   PxN**

About equivalent is 20. . . . BxP 21. PxB PxN 22. Q–B3! followed by 23. BxP.

**21. PxB   PxP
22. Q–B3   P–B3
23. BxP**

White's advantages are multiple: central space, protected passed KP, two Bishops in an open position, attacking chances against Black's weakened Kingside, superior pawn formation, etc. Even so, Uhlmann's crisp and decisive exploitation of these factors is noteworthy.

**23. . . .   N–B5
24. Q–R3   Q–K3?!**

Allowing White to double Rooks on the KB-file speeds Black's demise. 24. . . . R–KB1, is better, though after 25. B–K4 Black's prospects are obviously bleak.

**25. R–B2   R–KB1
26. B–B3!!**

This move and the idea behind it are the real crusher. Since Black has no defense against it anyway, he may as well take the BP.

**26. . . .   NxBP
27. QR–KB1!**

The threat is 28. R–R2!, and there is nothing to be done about it but sacrifice the Exchange for some temporary relief. Uhlmann gives the following clear line after 27. . . . Q–Q2: 28. R–R2 QxQPch 29. K–R1 RxB 30. Q–R7ch K–B2 31. RxRch K–K3 32. QxPch, etc.

27. . . .	RxB
28. QxR!	N–N4
29. K–N2!	

Frees the KR-file for a Rook check and thus prepares the coming beautiful combination. Black does not notice it, but he has no defense anyway. For instance, if 29. . . . Q–Q4 30. QxQ PxQ 31. P–K6 followed by 32. P–K7 and 33. R–B8ch, or if 29. . . . Q–K1 30. P–K6!! NxP (30. . . . QxP allows 31. Q–B8ch!! as in the game) 31. Q–B7ch QxQ 32. PxQch K–B1 33. R–K1! with the unstoppable threat 34. B–K7 mate!

| 29. . . . | NxQP |
| 30. Q–B8ch!! | Black resigns |

An electrifying finish: 30. . . . RxQ 31. RxRch K–R2 32. R–KR1 mate!. It's curious how

Black's doubled KNPs hem in his King.

GAME 41

White: V. Smyslov
(U.S.S.R.)

Black: B. Larsen
(Denmark)

Played at Hastings (England) International Tournament, January 4, 1973, Round 8.

Sicilian Defense
(Closed Variation)

Smyslov sees that his attempt to enter a standard line in the Closed Variation is foiled and reacts to the changed circumstances with a lot of originality and little strategic logic. In short order Black has a significant space advantage. When White voluntarily opens a line against his own King, this adds to Black's prospects. Black achieves pressure on the King-side and then opens the Queen-side. Under normal circumstances White would be hard pressed to guard all his weaknesses, but in time pressure he completely falls apart and offers no resistance whatsoever.

| 1. P–K4 | P–QB4 |
| 2. N–QB3 | |

Smyslov has had many successes on the White side of the

Closed Variation and employs it periodically. The usual lines start with 2. . . . N–QB3 3. P–KN3 P–KN3 4. B–N2 B–N2 5. P–Q3 P–Q3, etc. Characteristically, Larsen chooses a less common continuation.

2. . . .   P–K3
3. Q–K2?!

This brute attempt at preventing Black's . . . P–Q4 will fail, and K2 is hardly the square to which the Queen should go on move 3. Logical are either 3. P–KN3 to stay in the Closed Variation or 3. N–B3 and 4. P–Q4 to transpose back into open lines.

3. . . .   N–QB3
4. N–B3   KN–K2!
5. P–KN3   P–Q4
6. B–N2

6. PxP PxP opens the Black QB's diagonal forcing White to worry about . . . B–KN5 followed by . . . N–Q5.

6. . . .   P–Q5
7. N–Q1?!

The Knight will have no future here. Correct is 7. N–N1 followed by 8. P–Q3. The QN can then be brought back into the game via Q2.

7. . . .   P–K4!
8. O–O   P–B3
9. P–N3?!

In this early part White's play is much too passive. A fianchettoed QB will have nothing to do,

and the QN doesn't have much future there either. 9. N–K1 is better, and if then 9. . . . B–K3, White can exchange Black's "good" QB with 10. B–R3! BxB 11. Q–R5ch and 12. QxB.

9. . . .   B–N5
10. N–N2   Q–Q2
11. P–QR4   P–KN4

Black obviously has a large space advantage in the center and on the Kingside. White's position is so passive and cramped that he is in no position to attack any of Black's central or Kingside points. Already Black's advantage is unquestionable.

12. P–R3   B–K3

White's tactical point was 12. . . . BxP?! 13. NxKP! NxN 14. Q–R5ch followed by capturing the QB. Black can keep the pin with 12. . . . B–R4 but now that White has weakened his Kingside prefers to place his Bishop centrally.

13. P–R4

Otherwise 13. . . . P–N5 is very unpleasant.

13. . . .   P–KR3
14. N–Q3   N–B1!

At the moment there is nothing wrong with 14. . . . P–N3. But Black does not want White to have anything to attack with P–QR5. After Black castles Queenside, this factor has some importance.

15.	N–R2	R–KN1
16.	P–KB4?	

Opening the KN-file against his own King has to be completely wrong. I suppose White played it out of frustration with his uncomfortable position. Correct is 16. PxP RPxP 17. P–KB3 to try to set up a semiblockade with 18. N–KN4.

16.	. . .	NPxBP
17.	PxP	Q–N2
18.	P–B5	B–B2
19.	K–R1	N–Q3!

With the help of tactics (20. NxBP NxBP!) the Knight returns to the game to prepare . . . P–QB5, which will gain additional space while weakening White's Queenside pawn formation. Strategically Black has a won position: he has strong pressure on the Kingside, clear central superiority, and play on the Queenside. In practice the game has still to be won, but at this level of play, the only significant question remaining is

where the decisive action will take place.

20.	R–KN1	P–B5!
21.	PxP	NxQBP
22.	B–N2	O–O–O
23.	B–KB3	Q–R2
24.	RxR	QxR
25.	R–KN1	Q–R2
26.	B–B1	P–KR4
27.	N–N2	N–N3!
28.	Q–N5	N–Q2!
29.	N–Q3	B–Q3
30.	P–R5	P–R3
31.	Q–R4	R–N1!

Black has prevented a weakening of his King position and has retained all minor pieces so that White's pawn weaknesses can be attacked. However, Black welcomes the exchange of Rooks since the semiblockaded nature of the position prevents his Rook from being an effective attacking power, whereas White's Rook can be useful defensively.

32.	B–R3	RxRch
33.	KxR	BxB
34.	QxB	Q–R3
35.	N–KB1	B–B5!

Black's attack comes from both the Kingside and the Queenside. There is no way for White to hold all his weaknesses, but affected by time pressure, he does manage to lose the fastest possible way.

36. K–B2?!

Usually King centralization is the right method in the endgame, but the King is more exposed here than back home on KN1. The punishment is immediate.

36. . . .   BxN!
37. QxB

After 37. PxB White's Queen is separated from his King.

37. . . .   Q–B5
38. N–N3   QxRP
39. BxP   N–B4
40. Q–R3?

A time-pressure blunder, which loses a piece. After the mandatory 40. Q–KB3, Black has the pleasant choice between taking the QRP with 40. . . . NxRP or going for more with 40. . . . N–N5.

40. . . .   NxPch
White resigns

After 41. K–N2 NxN 42. QxN QxB Black's up a Knight and pawn.

GAME 42

White: V. Smyslov (U.S.S.R.)

Black: W. Browne (U.S.A.)

Played at Hastings (England) International Tournament, January 7, 1973, Round 11.

Queen Pawn Opening

After achieving approximate equality out of the opening, Black overlooks a simple combination and drops a pawn. But Smyslov, instead of consolidating his advantage, very uncharacteristically allows a Rook and Knight to be trapped on the seventh rank. His efforts to extricate them are the worst, and he ensures the end by a ridiculous Queen sacrifice. Black takes advantage of every offered chance, but White is solely responsible for the outcome of the game.

1. P–Q4   N–KB3
2. P–KN3   P–B4
3. PxP

White's second move was unusual, and this capture is even more so. Smyslov likes positions which are clear, not cluttered, and his move is in the clearing tradition. Whether it can lead to an opening advantage for White is, however, questionable.

3. . . .   N–R3

Black prepares for a somewhat esoteric recapture. The normal 3. . . . P–K3! is simpler and probably better.

4. B–N2	**NxP**
5. P–QB4	**P–KN3**
6. N–QB3	**B–N2**
7. N–R3	**0–0**
8. 0–0	**P–Q3**
9. N–B4	**P–QR3**

White's P–QB4 has given him a bit more central influence. Therefore Black plans to neutralize it by means of . . . P–QN4. Once that is achieved Black will have full equality.

10. B–K3	**R–N1**
11. R–B1	**N–N5!**

First, though, White's QB must be chased away. The immediate 11. . . . P–QN4? loses the Exchange after 12. PxP PxP 13. P–QN4 N–K3 14. B–R7.

12. B–Q2	**P–QN4**
13. PxP	**PxP**
14. P–QN4	**N–K3**
15. N/4–Q5	

Black has good symmetrical equality and would retain it with the developmental 15. . . . B–Q2. Instead he overlooks White's simple, pretty threat.

15. . . .	**N–K4?**
16. NxP!	

Black's QNP is gone since 16. . . . RxN? runs into 17. RxB QxR?? 18. NxPch, winning the Queen. Therefore Black must rush to develop his QB.

16. . . .	**B–QR3**
17. N/N–B7?	

Normally Smyslov likes clear positions, especially if they are inherently favorable. Thus, White could be expected to play here 17. P–QR4! BxN 18. PxB RxP 19. Q–R4 with a marvelous position: fine, active piece deployment, the two Bishops, and a strong passed QNP. The adventurous text only muddies the positional waters.

17. . . .	**NxN**
18. RxN	

Possible is 18. NxN B–B5 19. N–Q5 BxRP, but Black is obviously much better off than in the previous note. Thus Smyslov decides to jump in the mud with both feet.

18. . . .	**P–K3**
19. R–R7	**B–N4**
20. N–B7	

Placing both Rook and Knight in precarious positions from which they do not escape. Theoretically the move is playable, but 20. N–K3 is considerably safer. Black then has some compensation for the pawn, but White is in no noticeable danger.

20. . . .   B–QB3
21. Q–B2?

And this is a very serious waste of time. Correct is 21. P–N5!, and whether Black captures the QNP or plays 21. . . . BxB 22. KxB N–B5 23. B–N4! White is still somewhat better (23. . . . R–B1 24. P–N6!).

21. . . .   R–N3!
22. P–N5

White finally starts to recognize the danger, but it's almost too late.

22. . . .   Q–N1!
23. R–R3?!

23. R–R6 has to be better even though after 23. . . . RxR! 24. NxR QxP Black's active position gives him the advantage.

23. . . .   BxB
24. KxB   R–B1
25. R–B1

25. R–QB3? is refuted by 25. . . . N–Q2.

25. . . .   RxP

Black has recaptured the pawn and has a significant advantage.

26. NxR??

Sacrificing the Queen for nothing is an act of madness. Hastings was not a successful tournament for Smyslov, and the course of this game graphically illustrates why. 26. R–N3! is imperative with some chances for successful resistance. White's Knight does remain clumsily placed, but it is not certain that Black can win it.

26. . . .   RxQ
27. RxR   QxN
28. R–B8ch   B–B1
29. R/3–R8

29. B–R6 allows 29. . . . Q–N2ch, whereas after the text Black can win White's Bishop with 29. . . . Q–Q4ch. Could Smyslov have overlooked these elementary possibilities?

29. . . .   K–N2!?

Tempting White to save the piece and run into a mating attack. White decides to oblige.

30. B–B3   B–K2
31. P–B4?!   QxPch
32. K–N1   K–R3!
33. PxN   B–N4
                  White resigns

Mate is imminent with 34.
. . . B–K6ch coming up.

GAME 43

White: V. Smyslov
(U.S.S.R.)

Black: H. Mecking
(Brazil)

Played at Petropolis (Brazil)
Interzonal Tournament, August
7, 1973, Round 11.

English Opening

The young Brazilian GM
handles the strategic opening
better than his experienced opponent, and thanks to some
thematic tactics he carries a
clear advantage into the middlegame. Some positionally and
tactically sharp play extends the
middlegame advantage into the
endgame. Then a strategic
sacrifice leads to a situation in
which the combination of
Black's Rook and pawns over-
whelms White's minor pieces. A
perfect, and impressive, game by
Mecking.

1.	P–QB4	P–K4
2.	N–QB3	N–KB3
3.	N–B3	N–B3
4.	P–KN3	B–N5
5.	B–N2	O–O
6.	N–Q5!?	

As we mentioned in con-
nection with Game 40, the usual
move is 6. O–O. The less common text, however, seems to be
at least equally good.

6. . . .　　　P–K5!

With this and the next move
Black deflects the White KN
and places his KB actively. This
is the most exact way to go for
dynamic equality.

7. N–R4

Of course not 7. NxB?? PxN
8. NxN PxB and Black wins.

7. . . .	B–B4
8. O–O	R–K1
9. P–Q3	PxP
10. QxP	N–K4
11. Q–B2	

The last moves are easy to
understand: White breaks the
grip of Black's P–K5 and Black
activates his pieces toward the
center. The text is preferable to
11. Q–QB3?!, which after 11.
. . . NxN 12. PxN P–Q3 13. P–
QN4 B–N3 14. B–N2 Q–N4
led to good play for Black in
Kane–Popovych, Marshall
Chess Club Championship, New
York 1976.

11. . . .   P–B3!?

The fighting approach to the opening, though the passive 11. . . . NxN 12. PxN P–Q3 also seems playable.

12. N–QB3??

A completely incomprehensible retreat, leaving a valuable central pawn hanging. Smyslov apparently overlooked some rather simple tactical or strategic point. With the routine 12. NxNch or 12. N–K3 White can retain approximate equality. Strongest, however, is the zwischenzug 12. B–K3!, with White reaching a slight plus even after Black's best defense: 12. . . . PxN! 13. BxB P–Q3 14. B–Q4 PxP 15. KR–Q1! N–B3!, as in Gheorghiu–Szmetan, Torremolinos 1976.

12. . . .   NxP

Thank you.

13. N–R4?!

Leads to a practically hopeless position for White. Imperative is 13. N–K4 NxN 14. BxN P–Q4! 15. BxRPch K–R1. Black's center and active piece deployment give him the advantage, but material is even and White has chances to resist. Smyslov correctly evaluated this position as favorable for Black, but what he winds up with after the text is infinitely worse!

13. . . .   B–B1
14. QxN   P–QN4

15. Q–Q4   PxN
16. P–K4

The weakness of the KP doesn't allow White to recapture the QRP. Equally unpromising is 16. P–K3 because of 16. . . . Q–R4.

16. . . .   B–R3
17. R–K1   Q–N3!

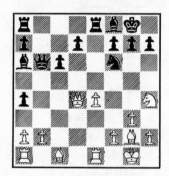

A winning position for Black: he not only is a pawn ahead but also has the initiative. Obviously undiscussable is 18. QxQ? PxQ with Black having a perfect pawn chain. There is no time for 18. QxRP because of 18. . . . N–N5 19. Q–B2 B–B4. Therefore White's next is his best try, but Black finds a sparkling rejoinder.

18. B–K3   B–N5!
19. QxQ

What else? 19. Q–Q1 Q–R4 is obviously pointless for White, while 19. KR–Q1 is parried by 19. . . . QxQ! 20. RxQ B–B4 21. RxRP B–N4 22. R–R5 BxB 23. PxB NxP.

19. . . .	PxQ
20. KR–Q1	B–K7
21. R–Q4	P–B4!

Sharpest and most accurate. After 21. . . . B–B4 22. R–Q2 BxB 23. RxB the opposite-color Bishops give White some hope for a draw.

22. RxB

About equivalent to 22. R–Q6 R–K3 when White has no compensation for his missing pawn.

22. . . .	PxR
23. P–K5	N–N5
24. BxR	NxB
25. R–K1	B–B5
26. B–K4	N–Q4
27. P–QR3	PxP
28. PxP	N–B6

Here, too, White obviously has no compensation for the pawn, and Black must win in due course. Even so with 29. P–B4 White can make things more difficult. The erroneous text allows Black a pretty liquidating combination.

29. B–B3?	P–B3!
30. R–QB1	RxP!
31. K–N2	

The end is immediate after 31. RxN? R–K8ch 32. K–N2 B–B8ch 33. K–N1 B–R6 mate.

| 31. . . . | R–QB4! |
| 32. RxN | B–B8ch |

33. KxB	RxR
34. B–Q5ch	K–B1
35. K–K2	RxRP

The end of the forced play has led to this situation: with a Rook and three pawns for two minor pieces Black has a decisive material and positional superiority. White could resign in good conscience.

36. K–Q2	P–QN4
37. N–B5	P–N5
38. N–K3	P–N6
39. K–B3	R–R7
40. K–N4	RxP

Black simplifies by trading his Queenside for White's Kingside and receives another pawn in the bargain.

41. KxP	P–N7
42. B–R2	RxP
43. K–N3	R–R6
44. N–B1	R–R8
45. N–Q2	R–KN8
White resigns	

After 46. KxP RxP Black has four passed pawns and an assured win.

Chapter 16

Spassky, Boris

Of all the Soviet masters, probably the one best known to the American on the street is Boris Spassky. The reason is of course his 1972 match with Robert Fischer, a match which drew world-wide interest. Fischer's 12½–8½ win took the World Champion title away from Spassky, who had himself only gained it in 1969 from Petrosian by a score of 12½–10½.

Born in Leningrad on January 30, 1937, Spassky came to the attention of the chess world as a teenager. At Antwerp 1955 he became the World Junior Champion and shortly thereafter he obtained the grandmaster title when he qualified for the Candidates Tournament at the Göteborg 1955 Interzonal. His first serious crack at the World Championship came in 1966 when he became Petrosian's Challenger, but he lost the closely contested match by 12½–11½. Then three years later he was victorious. Spassky is the most experienced match player in the world. He has defeated Keres, Geller (twice), Tal, Larsen, Korchnoi, R. Byrne, Hort, and Portisch, while losing to Fischer, Karpov and Korchnoi. In 1961 and 1973 Spassky won the U.S.S.R. Championship. He has been member of five winning Olympiad teams, five winning European Championship teams, and four winning student teams. First prizes in international tournaments range from Moscow 1959 to Amsterdam 1971. He won the 2nd Piatigorsky Cup at Santa Monica 1966 in a photo finish with Robert Fischer and the San Juan 1969 International Tournament.

Though by schooling a journalist, Spassky has done very little chess writing and has not written any books. He lived in Moscow after he became World Champion; prior to that time he lived in Leningrad. After marrying for the third time (a French-Russian girl) he obtained a visa to reside in France during 1976/77.

His 1977 FIDE rating is 2610.

GAME 44

White: H. J. Hecht
(West Germany)

Black: B. Spassky
(U.S.S.R.)

Played at the West German International Championship, Dortmund, May 18, 1973, Round 2.

Sicilian Defense

White does not really get much out of the opening, and in the early middlegame he would acquiesce to a draw. But Spassky wants more, and to unbalance the position he weakens his central pawn chain. Hecht quickly seizes the offered chance, applies pressure against the weakest spot in the chain, and gets a favorable endgame. Spassky does not defend it well, and Hecht wins in good style. The game is a good practical demonstration of how to beat the Russians.

1. P–K4   P–QB4

Spassky's primary weapon against the KP is 1. . . . P–K4. His choice of the Sicilian shows that he's determined to win.

2. N–KB3   N–QB3
3. B–N5

As in Game 24, Kuzmin–Larsen, Leningrad 1973, in which Black now played 3. . . . N–B3. Spassky selects a more common continuation, in which the fianchettoed KB controls Black's key Q5- and K4-squares and at the same time helps prepare Black for quick Kingside castling.

3. . . .   P–KN3
4. O–O   B–N2
5. R–K1   N–B3
6. N–B3

A more common plan is 6. P–B3 followed by 7. P–Q4. The text move presages a more closed contest.

6. . . .   O–O
7. BxN

In Round 3, Spassky–Kunsztowicz, White tried 7. P–K5 N–K1 8. BxN, but after 8. . . . QPxB! 9. P–KR3 N–B2 10. P–Q3 N–K3 11. N–K4 P–N3 12. B–Q2 Q–Q4 Black had good equality and the game ended a draw in 29.

7. . . .   NPxB

An unbalancing, thematic (toward the center) recapture. From the standpoint of clearer equality, 7. . . . QPxB!, as in the previous note, is simpler.

8. P–KR3   P–Q3
9. P–K5   N–Q2

Or 9. . . . N–K1. White stands somewhat better after 9. . . . N–Q4?! 10. PxP PxP 11. NxN PxN 12. P–Q4.

10. PxP   PxP
11. P–Q3   R–N1

12. B–N5!	P–B3
13. B–B4	N–K4
14. R–N1	

Black has somewhat greater space control at the cost of a weakened Queenside pawn formation and a certain innate looseness of his position. Black should therefore play aggressively so as not to give White time to build on Black's weaknesses. Hecht gives this line for Black: 14. . . . R–N5! 15. NxN BPxN 16. B–K3 R–KR5!? with approximately even chances. As played, Black achieves no play —and it is therefore impossible to win. When Spassky tries anyway, he gets punished.

14. . . .	R–N2
15. N–K4	N–B2
16. B–Q2!	

The Bishop must find a more useful and safer location. 16. Q–Q2?! is faulty because of 16. . . . P–N4! 17. B–R2 P–KR3 and Black is ready to really push White back starting with 18. . . . P–B4.

16. . . .	R–K1?!

Overlooking the following small combination. More accurate is 16. . . . R–K2. Now White is able to temporarily disjoin the cooperation of Black's pieces.

17. B–R5!	Q–Q2

Of course not 17. . . . QxB? 18. NxBPch BxN 19. RxRch followed by 20. RxB.

18. B–B3	R–K3
19. Q–Q2	Q–Q1
20. B–R5	Q–B1
21. B–B3	

To play for a win, White's last two moves were pointless. Hecht blames them on the inability to properly concentrate because of the sound of rock-and-roll music from a nearby park. This turns out to be a blessing in disguise since Spassky now decides on an unmotivated central push. There is little question that a draw is to be had with 21. . . . Q–Q1 22. B–B3, etc. But Spassky wants more—and comes up with less.

21. . . .	P–Q4?

Weakens the forward QBP permanently. White is very effective in immediately starting to line up against it.

22. N–N3	Q–Q3
23. P–N3!	B–R3

24. RxR	BxR
25. Q–K2	B–Q2
26. R–K1	B–KB1

Preventing the incursion of White's Queen and protecting the QBP.

27. B–N2!	B–B1
28. Q–Q2	K–N2
29. B–R3	

Already White has the strong threat 30. P–Q4!.

29. . . .	Q–Q1
30. Q–B3	R–N4
31. P–Q4!	Q–R4
32. QxQ	RxQ
33. BxP	BxB
34. PxB	K–B1

White has efficiently transformed his middlegame edge into a pleasant endgame advantage: Black will be weak on the dark squares, will have a rather impotent QB, will have problems in placing his Rook soundly, and will have difficulties in protecting the QBP. Overall, White has some winning chances and no risk of a loss—an excellent practical situation. With his last move Black prevents White's Rook from getting to his seventh or eighth ranks.

35. N–Q4   N–Q1!

A good defensive move, whereby Black protects his QBP and the important K3-square. The immediate 35. . . . RxBP? is faulty because of the sur-

prising 36. R–K6! and White will win a pawn.

36. N/3–K2	RxBP
37. N–B4	B–Q2?!

Prepares the following move, but the Rook does not find a happy home there. Preferable therefore is 37. . . . K–B2, keeping White's Knight out of the K6 hole. Hecht gives this probable continuation: 38. P–KB3 R–B6 39. R–K2 B–R3 40. R–Q2 P–N4 41. N/B–K2 BxN 42. NxB R–K6 43. K–B2 R–K1 44. R–Q4 followed by P–QB4 and a slight plus for White.

38. P–KB3	R–R4
39. P–QR4	P–QB4?

A very serious weakening of the central pawns and for what purpose? Black chases White's Knights where they want to go! The simple 39. . . . K–B2 is imperative, with White only slightly better.

40. N/Q– K6ch	NxN
41. NxNch	K–N1

Instead 41. . . . BxN?! 42. RxB K–B2 43. R–B6 leads to a miserable R + P endgame, whereas 41. . . . K–B2? leads to a direct loss after 42. N–Q8ch K–B1 43. N–N7.

42. N–B7

The sealed move and not the best one. Subsequent analysis showed that the Knight was a powerhouse on K6 and there was no need to move it. 42. P–KN4! is the strongest move (taking Black's KB4-square away from his Bishop). Black is then practically in zugzwang.

42. . . .   P–Q5?

Spassky has no luck with his pawn moves in this game. Correct is 42. . . . P–B5 43. P–QN4 (43. R–Q1?! B–B4! gives Black counterplay) 43. . . . RxP 44. NxP R–R3 45. R–K7 and White is significantly better, but Black may not yet be definitely lost.

43. N–K6!

Spassky overlooked this paradoxical looking retreat in his home analysis and now spent half an hour looking for a satisfactory response. Sacrificing a pawn to free his Rook is the best practical chance. Ultimately hopeless is further pas-

sivity with 43. . . . B–B3 44. K–B2 B–Q4 because of 45. N–B7 B–B2 46. N–K6! and Black is in a complete bind.

43. . . .   P–B5!?
44. NxP   K–B2
45. K–B2   P–R4
46. P–R4   R–Q4
47. K–K3

With 47. . . . R–K4ch 48. K–B2 R–Q4 Black can now reestablish the status quo. The definitive winning line is therefore 47. R–Q1 B–B4 48. PxP R–R4 49. NxB PxB 50. K–K3 RxP 51. K–Q4 and a won R + P endgame (as given by Hecht).

47. . . .   P–N4
48. P–N3   R–K4ch
49. K–B2   BPxP
50. BPxP   RxR?

Why did Spassky think the resulting pawn-down minor-piece endgame offered drawing chances? To hope to cope with White's Queenside pawns Black will obviously need the services of an active Rook. A reasonable defensive move therefore is 50. . . . R–QB4.

51. KxR   K–K2
52. K–Q2   K–Q3
53. K–Q3   K–K4
54. P–R5   P–R3
55. P–QN4

White prepares to create a passed pawn with a properly timed P–QN5 break, and there will be nothing that Black can do about it. The attempt to get immediate counterplay by 55. . . . PxP 56. PxP K–B5 is foiled by the "zwischen-check" 56. P–B4ch!: 56. . . . K–Q4 57. PxP B–R6 58. N–N3 B–B8ch 59. K–K3 B–N4 60. N–Q2 P–B4 61. N–B3 K–B5 62. N–Q4! KxP 63. NxP KxP 64. N–Q6! and White will win on the King-side (analysis by Hecht)! Nevertheless this variation offers Black more hope than the game continuation.

55. . . .	K–Q4?!
56. K–B3!	PxP
57. PxP	K–K4
58. K–B4!	K–Q3

White's P–N5 cannot be prevented, and Black is completely lost. If 58. . . . K–B5 instead, White wins with 59. K–B5 K–N6 60. K–Q6 B–B1 61. K–B7! B–R6 62. P–N5!.

59. P–N5	PxPch
60. NxPch	K–K4
61. K–B5!	B–B1
62. K–N6!	B–R6

Or 62. . . . K–B5 63. N–Q6!.

| 63. P–R6 | B–N7 |
| 64. P–B4ch! | |

White is, of course, interested in queening the QRP for nothing rather than allow Black's Bishop to sacrifice itself for it. With the elegant text move, White deflects Black's King from White's Q6, and White's Knight can then start to block Black's Bishop from the QRP.

64. . . .   KxP

Equally hopeless is the defensive 64. . . . K–K3. White plays 65. N–Q4ch, then N–K2, N–N3, and P–R7 and either wins the KRP or queens his QRP.

65. N–Q6

There is no way for Black's Bishop to cope with the QRP; e.g., 65. . . . B–R1 66. K–R7 B–N7 67. K–N8 followed by 68. N–N7, etc.

65. . . .	P–B4
66. N–N7!	K–N6
67. P–R7	P–B5
68. P–R8=Q	P–B6
69. Q–QN8ch	Black resigns

GAME 45

White: B. Spassky
(U.S.S.R.)

Black: J. H. Donner
(Netherlands)

Played at Amsterdam (Netherlands) IBM International Tournament, July 1973, Round 9.

Sicilian Defense (Najdorf Variation)

Spassky allows a sharp variation with which he could be expected to be familiar. But just as the independent thinking should start, he tries an unbelievably unsound combination. Donner gains two pieces for a Rook and wins very easily.

1. P–K4	P–QB4
2. N–KB3	P–Q3
3. P–Q4	PxP
4. NxP	N–KB3
5. N–QB3	P–QR3
6. B–N5	

The sharpest continuation, showing that Spassky is going for the win. This game follows the course of Game 30 through move 12.

6. . . .	P–K3
7. P–B4	QN–Q2
8. Q–B3	Q–B2
9. O–O–O	P–N4
10. B–Q3	

Spassky himself successfully resurrected this move for his 1972 Fischer match and thus it is reasonable to assume that he continually keeps abreast of its ramifications. This game shows otherwise.

10. . . .	B–N2
11. KR–K1	P–R3
12. Q–R3	O–O–O

Up to now like Game 30, Timman–Polugaevsky, Hilversum 1973, in which White was successful with 13. BxN! NxB 14. N–Q5!. Donner was of course familiar with that game, but although it had been played over a month earlier, Spassky was still unaware of it. After some deliberation he played

13. P–B5?!

Inferior to 13. BxN and calamitous as a preparation for what follows.

13. . . .   P–K4

Now White has nothing better than 14. BxN NxB 15. N–N3 though after 15. . . . B–K2 Black has at least full equality. Instead he continues with his combination/hallucination . . .

14. N–K6??

With the plan 14. . . . PxN? 15. PxP N–B4 16. BxN PxB??

17. P–K7ch, but he overlooks the simple . . .

14. . . .   PxB!

. . . whereby Black gains the decisive material superiority of two pieces for a Rook in a position in which White doesn't have a chance for anything. Since 15. NxQ RxQ 16. PxR KxN is now absolutely hopeless, White has to stay in the middle-game.

15. QxR	**PxN**
16. PxP	**N–B4**
17. Q–R3	**P–KN5**
18. Q–N3	**Q–K2**

Black will smoothly recover the pawn and then start to exploit his material superiority.

19. P–N4

Realizing that he must be lost, White embarks on an essentially suicidal opening of the Queenside. 19. N–Q5 QxP 20. P–B4!? has to be a shade better.

19. . . .	**NxBch**
20. QxN	**QxP**
21. P–QR4	**PxP**

21. . . . Q–B5 is safe and sound, but Black feels that opening the position will redound to the advantage of his Bishops.

22. N–Q5	**K–N1**
23. K–N2	**NxN**
24. PxN	**Q–Q2**
25. P–B4	**B–K2**

26. K–R3	**R–KB1**
27. R–KB1	**RxR**
28. RxR	**B–KB3**

Black's KB is now well placed and his KP is passed. White therefore hurries for one last try at Black's King.

29. R–QN1   B–B1

With the threat of 30. . . . Q–B4. If now White plays 30. P–B5, then 30. . . . Q–N4 puts a stop to everything.

30. P–N5	**PxP**
31. RxPch	**K–B2**
32. Q–Q2	

White's attack is only of cosmetic strength since there is nothing to back it up.

32. . . .	**K–Q1!**
33. R–N6	**Q–QB2**
34. R–B6	**Q–N1**
35. Q–R5ch	**K–K2**
White resigns	

White's "attack" is over and now it's Black's turn; e.g., 36. R–N6 Q–B2 37. Q–N4 B–Q2 38. R–N7 Q–B1 39. R–N6 Q–B4, etc.

Chapter 17

Suetin, Alexei

By profession a mechanical engineer, Alexei Suetin has worked as a chess master and writer/journalist for many years. Born on November 16, 1926, in Kirovograd he has lived in many areas of the Soviet Union and since 1968 has been residing in Moscow.

Suetin became an international grandmaster in 1965, and that is essentially the starting point for his international career. His successes are many, starting with first at Sarajevo 1965 and 1st–3rd at Copenhagen 1965, through cowinner of Hastings 1967/68 and cowinner at Brno 1975, and lately winning Lublin 1976. Generally his international results have been better than his results at home, though he has been champion of White Russia seven times and has taken part in ten U.S.S.R. Championships.

Suetin has been a very busy author of chess books and has written on both general and specific opening theory as well as on various facets of the middlegame at both the basic and advanced levels. In 1969 a book of his best games was published. His work is readily available in Russian, English, and German. East Germany in particular has published much of his work in the 1970s.

Suetin's 1977 FIDE rating is 2525.

GAME 46

White: A. Suetin
(U.S.S.R.)

Black: L. Portisch
(Hungary)

Played at Ljubljana-Portoroz (Yugoslavia) International Tournament, April 1973.

French Defense (Tarrasch Variation)

Suetin handles the opening soundly and enters the middlegame with a slight advantage. He manages the middlegame quite well and achieves a clearly superior double-Rook endgame. But in time pressure in the endgame he falls apart completely. First he throws away his advantage, then botches an equal position, and by adjournment stands significantly worse in a single-Rook endgame. Upon resumption of play he puts up good resistance in the beginning but falters later on and fails to take advantage of a good drawing opportunity. A good endgame effort by Portisch, though White must take the blame for the loss rather than Black the credit.

1. P–K4   P–K3

The French is an unbalanced, steady, though somewhat cramped approach to meeting the aggressive 1. P–K4. Black plans to neutralize White's active KP by a . . . P–Q4 and ensures that he can recapture with his KP in case White plays PxP.

2. P–Q4   P–Q4
3. N–Q2

White's KP is challenged and he must decide what to do about it. The exchange 3. PxP is harmless and 3. P–K5—the Advance Variation—is playable though currently out of fashion. That leaves 3. N–QB3 and the text as workable alternatives. The most aggressive choice is 3. N–QB3, but since that allows the Winawer Variation (3. . . . B–N5) with resultant great complications, many players prefer the more modest text. Originated by Tarrasch, it has two clear advantages over 3. N–QB3: the pin on the QN is prevented and the QBP can be used for central support with P–QB3. The disadvantages are that the QN applies no pressure against Black's center and that the QB is blocked in.

3. . . .   N–KB3

One of three theoretically significant moves. The Guimard Variation, 3. . . . N–QB3, immediately applies pressure to the QP but blocks off the QBP. Most popular currently is 3. . . . P–QB4, an excellent move to go for equality but the positions resulting after 4. KPxP KPxP or 4. . . . QxP are almost unwinnable for Black. The text is something in between 3. . . . P–QB4 and 3. . . . N–QB3: Black has a more unbalanced position than after the former and a strategically more flexible one than after the latter.

4. P–K5   KN–Q2
5. B–Q3

More modern and currently about equal in popularity is the center-strengthening 5. P–KB4.

5. . . .   P–QB4
6. P–QB3   N–QB3
7. N–K2   PxP
8. PxP   P–B3

In this type of position the thematic approaches for Black are to try to undermine White's center with . . . P–QB4 and . . . P–KB3. Instead of the text 8. . . . Q–N3 9. N–KB3 P–B3 and 8. . . . N–N3 are also playable and popular.

9. PxP

The attempt to attack with 9. N–B4? boomerangs: 9. . . . NxQP! 10. Q–R5ch K–K2 11. N–N6ch PxN 12. QxR NxP and Black has a slight material and a significant central advantage.

9. . . .   NxBP

About equivalent is 9. . . . QxP. In either case Black will try to get in . . . P–K4.

10. N–KB3   B–Q3
11. B–KB4

The exchange of the dark-square Bishops is in White's strategic interest since this will weaken the dark squares in Black's position and leave White with the significantly superior Bishop. However the exchange is not so easy to bring about. Therefore, 11. O–O! is more accurate and only after 11. . . . O–O 12. B–KB4. If Black tries to prevent this by 11. . . . Q–B2 then White retains the superior chances with 12. N–B3 P–QR3 13. B–KN5.

11. . . .   O–O?!

Giving White what he wants. Correct is 11. . . . Q–R4ch!, and if 12. B–Q2 Q–B2 and Black is a tempo ahead of the previous

note. If instead 12. Q–Q2, Black gets an essentially equal endgame after 12. . . . QxQch 13. BxQ O–O 14. O–O B–Q2, as in Parma–Tatai, Madonna di Campiglio 1974 (draw in 20).

12. BxB   QxB
13. O–O   P–K4

This is the only way to free Black's position, and Black must hurry with it before White has a chance to prevent it.

14. PxP   NxP
15. NxN   QxN
16. Q–Q2   B–Q2
17. QR–K1

Modern master practice has shown that this type of position invariably favors White. Black's QP, though passed, is isolated and readily blockadeable on White's Q4 and is much more a weakness than a strength. White's Bishop has much more attacking scope than Black's. Overall Black has no prospects for active play and has to defend accurately to prevent White's pieces from penetrating.

Theoretically Black is just a shade worse, but in practice his task is unpleasant.

17. . . .	K–R1
18. B–N1!	N–N5
19. N–N3	Q–Q3
20. P–B3!	N–B3
21. R–Q1	Q–B4ch
22. Q–B2!	P–QN3
23. R–B1!	Q–Q3

With his thoughtful 17th to 23rd moves, White has pushed Black's Queen and Knight around and simultaneously improved the position of his own forces. Black's Queen is an excellent defender; it is better to keep it than allow the prospectless endgame after 23. . . . QxQch?! 24. RxQ.

| 24. Q–Q4 | QR–K1 |
| 25. B–Q3 | K–N1 |

Black anticipates the coming endgame and thus brings his King back closer to the center.

| 26. N–K4! | Q–K4?! |

26. . . . NxN allows the strong 27 PxN!; nevertheless, the coming endgame is very bleak for Black, and Suetin therefore feels that Black should stick to the middlegame with 26. . . . Q–K2!, whose immediate tactical point is that Black need not fear 27. NxNch RxN 28. QxPch since 28. . . . B–K3 recovers the pawn.

| 27. NxNch | RxN |
| 28. QxQ | RxQ |

| 29. R–B7 | B–B4 |
| 30. BxB | R/3xB |

Up to here White has played perfect chess and after the obvious 31. RxRP would have an extra pawn and excellent winning chances. Then 31. . . . R–K7 is refuted by 32. P–KN4! followed by 33. R–B2, and Black would therefore have to look for counterchances by means of 31. . . . P–Q5.

31. K–B2?!

Influenced by time pressure, White completely loses the bearings of the position over the next ten moves. The centralizing King move does keep out Black's Rook, but 31. RxRP wins a pawn for nothing!

31. . . .	R–B2!
32. R–B8ch	R–B1
33. RxRch	KxR
34. R–K1	

With the idea of a winning K + P endgame after 34. . . . RxR? 35. KxR K–K2 36. K–Q2 K–Q3 37. K–Q3 since White's Kingside pawn majority will yield him the outside passed pawn. But since Black doesn't have to exchange, to grab the QB-file immediately with 34. R–B1! is more efficient. Black then still has a very hard defensive road ahead.

| 34. . . . | R–R4! |
| 35. R–QB1? | |

There is no reason to give Black the KRP. Correct is 35. P–KR3! and only then 36. R–QB1. Since Black's King remains cut off, the penetration of White's Rook is assured. White would still have a clear advantage.

35. . . .	RxP
36. R–B8ch	K–K2
37. R–B7ch	K–Q3
38. RxNP	

Considerably simpler for drawing purposes is 38. RxRP!. White continues to play to win mostly out of inertia.

38. . . .	P–QR4
39. K–N1??	

Chasing the Rook where it wants to go (on KR3 it protects the QNP and can swing over to QB3), and giving up the center to Black's King and QP. Correct is 39. K–K3 with approximate equality.

39. . . .	R–R3
40. R–N8	K–K4!
41. R–QB8	K–Q5

From a clearly inferior endgame, Black has achieved a clearly superior one. Material is equal, but Black's active King and passed QP give him a tangible positional advantage. Black now threatens 42. . . . K–Q6 followed by 43. . . . P–Q5, 44. . . . K–Q7, etc. White correctly tries to prevent that as long as possible.

42. R–B3!	P–N4
43. K–B2	P–N5

The important factors in the position are Black's Rook, King, and QP, and the move by the QNP costs Black a tempo. Immediately activating the Rook with 43. . . . R–R8! is stronger.

44. R–B7	K–Q6
45. P–B4!	

White's only hope for counterplay is the passed KBP.

45. . . .	K–K5
46. R–R7	P–Q5
47. RxQRP	R–QB3!

Rook activity is always very important in R + P endgames, and the text is considerably stronger than 47. . . . KxP?! 48. R–QN5!.

48. R–R7	R–B7ch
49. K–N3	RxP
50. R–K7ch	K–Q4

Black doesn't want to block his QP with 50. . . . K–Q6, but the game course shows that that must happen anyway.

51. RxP   RxP
52. R–QN7   K–B5

A static evaluation gives White, with connected passed pawns, the superior pawn formation. But the dynamics all favor Black: his pawns are further advanced and his King is able to assist the pawns' advance.

53. R–B7ch   K–Q6
54. R–QN7   K–B6

The King must do the protecting since 54. . . . R–N7? allows the KBP to run: 55. P–B5!, etc.

55. R–B7ch   K–Q7
56. R–QN7   P–Q6!

The QNP can't be protected so that Black gives it up to mobilize the QP's advance.

57. P–B5   K–K7!

57. . . . K–B6?! is fruitless since after 58. K–B3! White's King can help to stop the QP: 58. . . . P–Q7 59. K–K2!.

58. RxP   P–Q7
59. R–N1!

The only way to stop the QP. Immediately losing is 59. R–K4ch? K–Q6 60. R–K8 R–R5! 61. R–Q8ch R–Q5.

59. . . .   R–R5!

In order to win the coming R vs. 2P endgame, Black must prevent White's King from assisting in the advance of the BP and NP for as long as possible; i.e., until Black's King can get back in time. Only drawing is 59. . . . P–Q8=Q? 60. RxQ KxR 61. K–B4! RxP 62. P–B6, etc.

60. R–KR1!   R–K5?!

Here too 60. . . . P–Q8=Q? gives White a draw after 61. RxQ KxR 62. P–B6! R–R3 63. P–B7 R–KB3 64. K–R4 RxP 65. P–N4, etc. Correct, however, is 60. . . . R–QB5! 61. R–QN1 R–B8 62. R–N2 R–B8! 63. K–N4 K–K6 64. RxP KxR and compared to the above line, Black's King and Rook are effectively placed and can stop the pawn(s).

61. R–R1   K–Q6
62. R–Q1?

White allows a variation of the previous line, and this is quite hopeless. The only chance is 62. P–B6!? R–K8 63. P–B7! RxR 64. P–B8=Q P–Q8=Q 65. Q–Q6ch, and White has perpetual check according to Suetin.

62. . . .   R–K8!
63. RxPch   KxR
64. K–B4   K–Q6
65. P–B6   K–Q5!

Black's King gets back very quickly, and the end is in sight.

66.	K–B5	K–Q4
67.	P–N4	R–B8ch
68.	K–N6	K–K3
69.	P–N5	R–B4
70.	K–R6	K–B2

White resigns

The pawns have been stopped and 71. K–R5 R–B5! 72. K–R6 R–KR5 is mate!

GAME 47

White: A. Suetin
(U.S.S.R.)

Black: J. Smejkal
(Czechoslovakia)

Played at Ljubljana-Portoroz (Yugoslavia) International Tournament, April 1973.

Dutch Defense (Leningrad Variation)
(By transposition)

Uncharacteristically, Suetin opens with the QBP and soon doesn't really know what to do. He allows the doubling of pawns for nebulous chances along the QN-file, fears to undertake anything in the center, and finds himself contained all across the board. Black has a strong grip on the center and after judicious preparation starts a positional Kingside attack. White is so disgusted at his position that he resigns while he still has material equality.

1. P–QB4?!

The losing moment! Objectively, of course, there is nothing wrong with the English, but Suetin is an inveterate KP man and will not feel at ease in the coming strategic waters. On the other hand, Smejkal is a fine positional player and feels at home on both sides of this opening, as Games 6 and 14, for example, demonstrate.

1. . . .   P–KB4

An offer to enter the Dutch Defense by means of 2. P–Q4. The text (and the Dutch Defense) has the strategic point of acting on the important K5 central square and preparing an attack along the KB-file (occurring in this game on move 32!). The disadvantages are that the move does nothing to further development and carries with it a slight weakening of the Kingside.

2.	N–QB3	N–KB3
3.	P–KN3	P–KN3

4. B–N2   B–N2
5. P–Q4

This two-square advance of the QP transposes the game into the Leningrad Variation (characterized by the fianchetto of Black's KB rather than its development on K2) of the Dutch Defense. A formation with 5. P–Q3 retains the characteristics of the pure English.

5. ...   O–O
6. N–B3   P–Q3
7. O–O   P–B3
8. R–N1?!

Already White shows himself to be unfamiliar with the specifics of the opening. The correct and theoretical move is 8. P–Q5!, which leads to a slight plus for White.

8. ...   N–K5!

Now after 9. NxN?! PxN 10. N–N5 Black has 10. ... P–Q4.

9. B–B4   P–KR3
10. Q–B2   NxN
11. PxN?!

The doubling of the QBPs gives White an inferior pawn formation without any noticeable compensation. The hoped for pressure along the QN-file comes to nothing since White has no way to weaken Black's QNP and QBP. Correct is the modest 11. QxN with approximate equality.

11. ...   P–KN4!

With White in no attacking shape of any kind, Black can afford to expand his Kingside influence with a gain of time.

12. B–B1   P–K4

And now Black has excellent influence in the center also.

13. B–QR3   R–B2
14. KR–Q1

White's edge in development is a mirage because he is too passive to be able to undertake anything of value. Thus 14. PxP?! (opening the position) leads to nothing but a further weakening of the pawn formation (isolated, doubled QBPs) after 14. ... PxP 15. KR–Q1 Q–K1.

14. ...   P–K5!
15. N–Q2   Q–B2
16. P–K3   N–Q2

A position containing significantly more opportunities for Black than for White. Black has superior central influence and characteristic chances for an attack on the Kingside. White's doubled pawns are a fundamental weakness, and his chances for play are nowhere in sight. If White continues to do nothing Black will complete his development with . . . N–B3, . . . B–K3, . . . QR–KB1 and then be ready for a decisive thrust on the Kingside. White must, therefore, undertake something.

17. P–B3!

The direct elimination of Black's advanced KP is White's best course. 17. P–N4?! is too risky because of 17. . . . N–B3! 18. PxP P–Q4 when Black's KP is safe whereas White has a seriously weakened Kingside.

17. . . .   PxP
18. BxBP   N–B3
19. Q–Q3?!

White's position needs breathing room and thus 19. P–K4! is correct, after which White is only slightly worse.

19. . . .   B–K3
20. R–KB1?

Here was the last chance for 20. P–K4!.

20. . . .   P–Q4!

Fine strategic play by Black. He voluntarily allows White to liquidate his doubled pawn but gets a complete grip on the important K5 and QB5 central squares in return. This will mean that White will be without chances for active play and that Black will be able to prepare the thematic attack on the Kingside at his relative leisure.

21. PxP   PxP!
22. QR–B1   R–QB1!
23. B–K2   Q–R4
24. B–QN4   Q–R5!

Surely not 24. . . . QxP??, losing the Queen after 25. R–R1 Q–N7 26. KR–N1.

25. Q–B2   Q–K1!

Black wants to keep the Queen for attack and is not about to lighten White's load by an exchange.

26. Q–Q3   P–R3
27. B–Q1   B–Q2!

The Bishop on K3 is like a glorified pawn, and Black obviously wants to bring it to a more useful location.

28. B–N3   P–N3!
29. KR–K1?!

Black's last is not so much to protect the QB4-square as to prepare the QRP advance, which will cause a complete misplacement of White's forces. Therefore White has to play 29. P–QR3!. After 29. . . . P–QR4 30. B–Q6 P–R5 31. B–R2 P–N4 the bind on White's position continues, but at least White's pieces have reasonable locations.

29. . . .   P–QR4
30. B–R3   P–R5
31. B–Q1   B–N4
32. Q–N1   P–B5!

At last Black starts his Kingside attack; White's disorganized army is in no condition to resist.

33. NPxP   PxP
34. N–B3   N–K5
    White resigns

White still has material equality but resigned here in disgust at the helplessness of his position. A probable continuation is 35. B–N4 (to protect the QBP) 35. . . . R–QB3 36. Q–N2 (36. R–B2 allows 36. . . . B–Q6) 36. . . . R–N3ch 37. K–R1 PxP 38. RxP N–N6ch 39. PxN QxR, etc.

GAME 48

White: A. Suetin
          (U.S.S.R.)

Black: B. Ivkov
          (Yugoslavia)

Played at Ljubljana-Portoroz (Yugoslavia) International Tournament, April 1973.

Ruy Lopez (Steinitz Deferred Variation)

White plays an interesting opening novelty and when Black does not defend correctly achieves a significant advantage. He gains a pawn for nothing and could safely consolidate his material plus. Instead, in a moment of chess blindness, he plays a faulty combination. Black wins a piece and thereafter the game. The swing from a winning to a losing position is immediate and drastic.

1. P–K4   P–K4
2. N–KB3   N–QB3
3. B–N5   P–QR3
4. B–R4   P–Q3
5. O–O   B–Q2
6. P–Q4

In Game 3 White played 6. R–K1 instead. The text is the more common choice, though ultimately the same position is usually reached. Not in this game, however!

6. . . .   N–B3
7. P–B4!?

An interesting and theoretically successful novelty. White's usual plans are 7. P–B3 and 7. R–K1; also good is the less frequent 7. BxN BxB 8. R–K1. The idea of the text is to gain an immediate spatial advantage on the Queenside. Black must react resolutely to thwart White's plans.

7. . . .   B–K2?!

This routine move allows White to accomplish his objective. The correct way was demonstrated subsequently in Suetin–Knaak, Polonica Zdroj 1974: 7. . . . PxP! 8. NxP P–QN4! 9. B–N3 NxN 10. QxN

B–K2 11. N–B3 O–O 12. R–K1 P–N5 13. N–Q5 NxN 14. BPxN P–QR4 with full equality for Black.

8. P–Q5!   N–R2

A more useful retreat square is QN1, and after 9. BxBch Black has 9. . . . QNxB, thereby controlling the QB4-square.

9. BxBch   QxB
10. N–B3   P–B4?!

Black wants to make it more difficult for White to get in P–QN4 but allows something considerably worse. The normal 10. . . . O–O is preferable.

11. PxP e.p.   QxP?!

Unfortunately 11. . . . PxP? allows 12. P–B5! and a permanent weakening of Black's Queenside pawn formation. Therefore Black must acquiesce to allowing White complete control of White's important Q5 central square. Even so the text is difficult to comprehend. Why not get the QN back into the game with 11. . . . NxBP?

12. B–N5!

Immediately going after the Q5-square.

12. . . .   QxBP?!

Until he gets the wondrous gift from White, Black seems overly fatalistic about his ultimate chances for resistance. It is difficult to believe that as fine a positional player as Ivkov doesn't realize that the QBP

capture is unsafe. The minor evil is 12. . . . O–O.

13. BxN   BxB

After 13. . . . PxB White has the pleasant choice between 14. N–Q5 and 14. N–KR4 followed by 15. N–B5.

14. QxP

Black's backward QP is gone, but now his KP is weak, his King caught in the center, and White's Knight ready to ensconce itself on Q5.

14. . . .   N–B1
15. Q–R3   N–K2?!

This makes a bad situation even worse. Black has to get his King to safety and protect the KP with 15. . . . B–K2 16. Q–R5 P–B3 17. KR–Q1 O–O, although White keeps a pleasant and significant advantage after 18. QR–B1.

16. QR–B1   R–QB1

16. . . . O–O? loses to 17. N–Q5.

17. NxP!

The tactical punishment for Black's strategic errors. The Knight is inviolate since 17. . . . BxN?? allows 18. N–Q5 QxQR 19. QxN mate!

17. . . .   Q–K3
18. Q–R4ch??

Instantaneously transforming a won position into a lost one. After the modest retreat 18. N–Q3, Black has nothing better than 18. . . . BxN 19. RxB RxR 20. QxR O–O, after which White plays 21. Q–N4 and remains a sound pawn up.

18. . . .   P–QN4
19. NxNP

Intending 19. . . . PxN?? 20. QxPch K–B1 21. N–Q7ch K–N1 22. RxRch! NxR 23. R–B1 and White wins. As Suetin tells it he was horror-stricken when he noticed, as he was playing this move, that it's legal for Black now to castle.

19. . . .   O–O!

Now both of White's Knights are en prise and one must go lost.

20. RxR   NxR
21. N–B4   PxN
22. QxP   QxP

White has two connected passed pawns for the piece, but the pawns cannot be quickly mobilized, whereas Black's forces rapidly come into play. White's situation is hopeless.

23. P–QN3   Q–K7
24. P–QR4   R–Q1!

Threatening an immediate end with 25. . . . R–Q8.

25. P–R3   B–Q5
26. Q–KB5   P–N3
27. Q–B4   Q–K3
28. Q–B3   N–Q3!
29. N–R5?!

29. NxN QxN ensures that White's Queenside pawns won't be able to advance, but allowing the Black Knight to live guarantees an accelerated end.

29. . . .   N–K5
30. Q–K2   BxPch!
31. RxB   R–Q7

Moving the attacked Queen away loses the Rook, and 32. QxR NxQ 33. RxN Q–K8ch or 32 QxN QxQ 33. RxR Q–K8ch leads to loss of the Queen and Rook. So . . .

32. N–B4   RxQ
White resigns

33. RxR P–B4, etc., is obviously hopeless for White.

Chapter 18

Taimanov, Mark

Mark Taimanov is one of those few grandmasters who has been able to pursue two professional careers with distinction. Born in Kharkov on February 7, 1926, he showed exceptional talent as a youngster in both chess and music. Taimanov was graduated from the Leningrad Music Conservatory and is recognized as a fine concert pianist.

His chess career reached world-class level in 1952 when he tied for 2nd–3rd in the Stockholm Interzonal and tied with Botvinnik for the U.S.S.R. Championship (though he subsequently lost the play-off match by 2½–3½). In 1956 he won the Championship outright. Taimanov holds the current record for participation in U.S.S.R. Championships, twenty-three. He has been on one winning Olympiad team, one winning student team, and four winning European Championship teams. Overall he has won eighteen first places (including ties) in international tournaments. Taimanov took part in the 1953 and 1971 Candidates events. At the latter he experienced the darkest moment in his chess life: he lost to Fischer by 0:6. His comment about this was, "Well, I still have my music!" Taimanov participated in the U.S.A. matches of 1954 and 1955.

Taimanov is among the few Soviet grandmasters who are members of the Communist party. He is well known for a series of opening books, which are published in East Germany. *The Nimzo-Indian Defense* and *Overseas Meetings* have appeared in Russian.

His 1977 FIDE rating is 2530.

GAME 49

White: E. Ungureanu
(Rumania)

Black: M. Taimanov
(U.S.S.R.)

Played at Bucharest (Rumania) International Tournament, Mach 1973.

King's Indian Defense (Normal Variation)

Taimanov tries an off-beat line in the King's Indian, but his opponent's strong and consistent strategy quickly demonstrates that it is White who gains from Black's experimentation. He puts Black in a bind on the Kingside, establishes control of key squares in the center and Queenside, and achieves control of the Queen file. This soon leads to gain of decisive material, and the rest is a mop-up operation.

1.	N–KB3	N–KB3
2.	P–B4	P–KN3
3.	N–B3	B–N2
4.	P–K4	O–O
5.	P–Q4	P–Q3

Because Taimanov does not usually play the King's Indian when he expects his opponent to play the main lines, he must have something particular in mind.

6.	B–K2	P–B3

We have reached the Normal Variation by transposition. Black's "normal" move is now 6. . . . P–K4 (see Game 21).

7.	O–O	P–QR3?!

So this is Black's off-beat plan! It is superior to the ridiculous 7. . . . Q–N3? of Game 23 but inferior to the usual 7. . . . P–K4. The idea behind the text is to start action on the flank by means of . . . P–QN4.

8. P–QR4!

Immediately putting a stop to Black's plans. 8. B–N5 is not bad either, and after 8. . . . P–N4 9. P–K5 N–K1 10. R–K1 White was better in Uhlmann–Doda, Polonica Zdroj 1967.

8. . . .	P–QR4

Forced because of the threat of 9. P–R5. But Black's QRP has taken two moves to reach QR4, and thus it is White's turn to move again. The Queenside weaknesses are about equivalent, but White has gained without cost a tempo for development.

9.	P–R3	N–R3
10.	B–K3	N–Q2
11.	Q–Q2!	

This and the following moves are unquestionably White's most active approach. Also good is 11. N–Q2, and after 11. . . . P–K4 12. P–Q5 White had a

slight advantage in Bobotsov–
Sakharov, Sochi 1966.

11. . . .   R–K1?!

Neither this nor the next
preparatory move adds punch,
and as a result White can build
a more active position. Correct
is the immediate 11. . . . P–K4.

12. QR–Q1   Q–B2?!
13. N–KR2!   P–K4
14. P–B4!   PxQP
15. BxP

A marvelous position for
White has been reached soon
after the opening. White's development is complete, and he
has a significant superiority in
the center, good pressure against
Black's weak QP, and excellent
attacking chances against
Black's Kingside. Black has no
prospects for active play and
hasn't even developed his
Queenside.

15. . . .   P–B3

The exchange of Bishops ir-
reparably weakens Black's
Kingside; e.g., 15. . . . BxBch?!

16. QxB N/2–B4 (or 16. . . .
N/3–B4 17. N–N4!) 17. P–
B5!, in either case with an ex-
ceedingly strong attack for
White.

16. N–N4   N/3–B4
17. Q–B2   N–K3
18. B–K3   N/3–B1?

Black's position is very
cramped and therefore nearly
critical. Exact maneuvers are required, and so imperative is 18.
. . . N–Q1! followed by 19. . . .
N–B2, which allows the Knight
to protect the QP and the important KR3-square. After the
inexact text move, Black is
caught in a bind from which he
never recovers.

19. P–KB5!   N–K4

Even worse is 19. . . . PxP?
20. N–R6ch! BxN 21. BxB PxP
22. NxP and Black's Kingside
soon crumbles.

20. NxN   QPxP

20. . . . RxN? loses to 21. B–
B4 and 20. . . . BPxN? to 21.
P–B6.

21. P–B5!   R–Q1
22. N–N1!

Black's Kingside is immobile,
the Queenside still undeveloped,
and there are lots of weaknesses
in his camp. White prepares to
send his Knight to QB4 and
from there to Q6, QN6, or
QR5, depending on the situation. Black is strategically lost;
but giving White's Knight the

K4-square a move later amounts to driving another nail into his own coffin.

22. . . .	K-R1
23. N-Q2	PxP?!
24. PxP	B-Q2
25. N-K4!	

25. N-B4 isn't bad, but the text completely paralyzes Black.

25. . . .	B-K1
26. B-QB4	R-Q2
27. RxR!	NxR?!

Overlooking White's plan. Some resistance can be mounted with 27. . . . QxR.

28. B-R2!

Threatening 29. Q-N3 followed by mate on KN8. There is no defense to this threat.

28. . . .	P-N4
29. Q-N3	B-R4
30. P-N4	

Since the attacked Bishop can't afford to retreat, White wins a clear piece.

30. . . .	PxP
31. Q-B4	Q-N2
32. PxB	P-R3
33. R-B2	

Black is totally busted, and only White's time pressure gives Black the nerve to continue the game.

33. . . .	Q-N5
34. R-Q2	P-R6
35. PxP	QxRP
36. K-B2	R-QN1

If 36. . . . R-Q1 37. RxN! anyway.

37. RxN

Now Black is two pieces down in a hopeless situation. If 37. . . . R-N7ch 38. R-Q2. Still he braves it to move 40.

37. . . .	Q-N7ch
38. N-Q2	R-KB1
39. R-KB7	R-Q1
40. R-Q7	R-KB1
41. Q-KN4	Black resigns

GAME 50

White: R. Byrne
(U.S.A.)

Black: M. Taimanov
(U.S.S.R.)

Played at Leningrad (U.S.-S.R.) Interzonal Tournament, June 16, 1973, Round 10.

Sicilian Defense
(Taimanov Variation)

Both players handle the opening creatively, with White perhaps emerging with a tiny edge. The middlegame is, however, all Byrne's. Some deep strategy backed by ultrasharp tactics leads to White's decisively gaining material. A time-pressure slip by White affords Black the opportunity to gain a problem draw in an endgame in which he has Rook and pawns against White's Queen and pawn. After missing this opportunity he is quickly extinguished. Overall an excellent effort by Byrne, showing the creative and sporting form which enabled him to reach the Candidates matches.

1.	P–K4	P–QB4
2.	N–KB3	N–QB3
3.	N–B3	P–QR3
4.	P–Q4	

Instead 4. P–KN3 P–Q3 transposes into our Game 3. Byrne prefers the normal waters that result after the text.

4.	. . .	PxP
5.	NxP	P–K3

With some transposition of moves we've reached one of the positions of the Taimanov Variation. Black establishes some central presence and plans perhaps to start something soon on the Queenside. The whole approach in the Taimanov is to have a fluid, if not to say ambiguous, situation. Such an approach forces White to start independent thinking early on. The slight disadvantage to

Black's approach is that his moves are often not those most logical for central development.

6. P–KN3

The fianchetto of the KB is strategically sound. Other good moves are 6. B–K2 and 6. B–K3.

6. . . . KN–K2

Somewhat esoteric looking, though with the reasonable plan of conveniently exchanging Knights with 7. . . . NxN 8. QxN N–B3. More common is 6. . . . Q–B2.

7. N–N3

Preventing the above plan is White's most common response. Worth considering, however, is 7. B–K3 since then 7. . . . NxN 8. QxN N–B3 allows White to bind down Black's Queenside with 9. Q–N6!.

7. . . . P–QN4?!

This immediate Queenside demonstration has quickly gone out of master practice since it carries no concrete threats, loses time, and weakens the Queenside without significant benefit. Also not quite successful is the further attempt to exchange Knights with 7. . . . N–R4, since after 8. Q–R5! White obtains a very active position. The modern move is the developmental 7. . . . P–Q3 followed by 8. . . . B–Q2 (9.

QxP?? loses the Queen after 9. . . . N–Q4).

8. B–N2	P–Q3
9. P–B4	B–N2
10. B–K3	P–N3

A plan that succeeds in this game. Even so, the more modest development 10. . . . N–N3 11. O–O B–K2 is somewhat sounder.

| 11. Q–Q2 | Q–B2 |
| 12. Q–B2 | |

After this Black has enough time to consolidate. The only way to seriously question Black's setup is the active 12. O–O–O! R–Q1 13. Q–B2! R–Q2 14. P–K5! and Black is exposed to a dangerous attack.

12. . . .	B–N2
13. O–O	O–O
14. QR–Q1	KR–K1
15. R–Q2	N–B1!

Black has approximate equality after this fine multi-purpose move, whereby Black protects the QP, allows his Queen to help protect the King-side in case of a P–KB5 by White, and allows the KR pressure on the King file in case it is opened. White has no immediate active course available; e.g., 16. P–B5 N–K4!, 16. P–K5 N–Q1!, or 16. KR–Q1 N–R4 17. NxN QxN 18. P–QR3 P–N5 and Black is the one attacking! Therefore White quite soundly takes time out for a preventive move on the Queen-side.

16. P–QR3!   R–N1!

Black strives to get lines opened on the Queenside, his thematic attacking side.

17. KR–Q1	P–N5
18. PxP	NxP
19. B–Q4!	

Black's KB is an excellent defensive and offensive piece, and it is in White's interest to exchange it.

19. . . .	BxB
20. QxB	B–R1
21. B–B1	

Keeping a watch on Black's QRP at the cost of some weakening of his own KP. A good alternative is 21. Q–B2 with the plan 22. P–B5.

21. . . .   P–K4

Possible is 21. . . . NxP 22. RxN RxN, but it appears that after 23. BxP White's passed QNP gives him a slight plus.

| 22. PxP | RxP |
| 23. Q–B2!? | |

Both a good move and a trap. It works like a charm.

23. . . .   BxP?

Taimanov felt that Byrne had simply left a pawn en prise. This seems like a naive approach against a world-class GM. Correct is 23. . . . Q–K2 or the sharper 23. . . . P–B4!? in either case with approximate equality.

24. NxB   RxN
25. P–B3   N–B3??

When one doesn't search he can't be expected to find anything. Black is still ignorant of White's threat(s). The surprising 25. . . . N–B7! is imperative even though White still has a clear advantage after 26. B–Q3 N–K6 27. BxR NxR 28. RxN RxN 29. B–Q5 R–N1 30. R–KB1 since he recovers his pawn and retains the superior position.

26. N–B5!!

This should mean the end for Black. The dual threats 27. NxR and 27. NxP force the capture and then . . .

26. . . .   PxN
27. R–Q7

. . . wins the Queen because of the threat of 28. QxPch.

27. . . .   QxR
28. RxQ   R–K2
29. R–Q1?!

White's position is quite won, but in incipient time pressure he starts taking things too lightly. Easily winning is 29. RxR N/1xR 30. BxP. Instead White wants to retain his Rook for attacking purposes; in practice only Black can gain from thus complicating the position.

29. . . .   N/1–R2
30. BxP   N–K4
31. B–B1?!

And this makes things even more uncertain. Winning by force is 31. QxP! RxP!? 32. R–Q8ch! (in time pressure White considered only 32. QxR?? whereupon Black draws with 32. . . . N–B6ch) 32. . . . K–N2 33. QxR N–B6ch 34. K–B1 NxPch 35. K–K1 N–B6ch 36. K–Q1—White's King now has access to this square.

31. . . .   P–B5
32. B–N2?!

Allowing Black access to his Q6 and a surprising chance for a draw. After 32. R–Q5! White should still win—slowly but surely.

32. . . .   N–Q6
33. Q–Q4   N–N4!
34. QxP   NxNP
35. Q–B4   QR–K1
36. R–N1   N–Q6?

Leads to additional material loss. In time pressure and seeing, in effect, nothing over the last part of the game, it is not at all surprising that Taimanov misses the problem draw available with 36. . . . NxP!! 37. RxN R–K8ch! 38. B–B1 (38. K–B2?? N–Q8ch) 38. . . . N–K7ch 39. RxN R/1xR 40. Q–B4! RxBch!! 41. KxR RxP. Black does have a significant material disadvantage, but the presence of pawns on only one side of the board does not allow White a winning maneuver; e.g., 42. P–N4 R–R5! 43. Q–B8ch K–N2 44. Q–B3ch K–N1 45. Q–KN3 P–N4 followed by . . . R–R3 (Zuckerman), and how is White to make progress?

37. Q–Q2   N–R6
38. R–R1

The Knights are in an untenable situation. If now 38. . . . N–K8 39. RxN/3 R–K7, White scores with 40. R–R8!.

38. . . .   R–K8ch
39. RxR   NxR
40. Q–Q7   R–K7
41. B–Q5   K–N2
Black resigns

Black sealed his 41st move but then resigned without con-

tinuing the game. After 42. QxPch K–R3 43. Q–B8ch K–R4 44. B–B3ch he loses his house.

GAME 51

White: M. Taimanov
(U.S.S.R.)

Black: J. Smejkal
(Czechoslovakia)

Played at Leningrad (U.S.-S.R.) Interzonal Tournament, June 23, 1973, Round 15.

King's Indian Defense (Yugoslav/Panno Variation)

By a deft move order, Smejkal is able to catch Taimanov in a variation which Taimanov does not normally play as White. The results are not long in coming: White falls into an opening trap and loses a pawn for nothing. Smejkal takes the pawn and brings home the point in a matter-of-technique endgame.

1. P–QB4   N–KB3
2. N–QB3   P–B4
3. N–B3   N–B3
4. P–KN3

An invitation to the Tarrasch/Reti complexes after 4. . . . P–K3 5. B–N2 P–Q4 or the English after 4. . . . P–Q4.

4. . . .   P–KN3

Black prefers a symmetrical approach, showing himself to be ready for the Yugoslav Variation of the King's Indian.

5. B–N2   B–N2
6. O–O   O–O
7. P–Q4

7. P–Q3 is harmless; thus the text transposes into a normal QP opening, the Yugoslav Variation of the King's Indian Defense. Objectively it's O.K. for White, but as White Taimanov invariably plays the Normal Variation against the King's Indian. He's not familiar with the Yugoslav.

7. . . .   P–Q3

The pure Yugoslav. 7. . . . PxP leads to the Semi-Yugoslav (see the next game!).

8. P–Q5

The full-play approach. The exchanging 8. PxP PxP leads to a minute plus for White after either 9. B–K3 or 9. B–B4.

8. . . .   N–QR4
9. N–Q2

At first glance this may look awkward, but over twenty years of master experience has shown it to be the only satisfactory way to defend the QBP.

9. . . .   P–QR3

With this Black voluntarily enters a variation possible in the Panno (see Game 60), in which White continues with 8. P–Q5 N–QR4 9. N–Q2 and Black plays 9. . . . P–B4. With the text Black aims for quick action along the QN-file with . . . P–QN4. The alternatives 9. . . . P–K4 and 9. . . . P–K3 keep the game in the pure Yugoslav.

10. Q–B2   R–N1
11. P–N3   P–QN4
12. B–N2

The two most common plans for Black now are 12. . . . P–K3 and 12. . . . P–K4. But Smejkal has a better idea: speculating on White's lack of expertise in the variation he decides on a more trap-ridden plan.

12. . . .   PxP
13. PxP   B–R3!?

With the obvious threat 14. . . . BxN followed by 15. . . . NxBP. White has two good responses: the dynamic 14. P–B4! and the strategic 14. N/3–N1!, in both cases with a slight ad-

vantage. But isn't there a
sound, simple method like

14. P–K3??

NO, because of . . .

14. . . .   B–B4!
15. P–K4

White must lose a pawn no
matter what he does; e.g., 15.
Q–B1 B–Q6 followed by 16.
. . . NxBP or 15. N3–K4 NxN
16. BxN BxB 17. NxB NxP.

15. . . .   BxN
16. N–Q1

No better is 16. PxB NxBP
17. N–Q1 NxB 18. NxN B–R3
and White's a pawn down for
nothing, as in Foguelman–
Panno, Buenos Aires 1968.

16. . . .   B–Q2!
17. BxN   PxB
18. QxB   NxP
19. Q–B3   N–N3

Black is up a sound protected
passed QBP, and White has no
compensation for it. Black's
doubled KBP is no problem
since White can't attack it, and
the Black Kingside is fully defensible. This allows Black to
work on his strength—the
Queenside—and Smejkal does a
workmanlike job there. White
does not get the slightest chance
anywhere.

20. R–K1   N–R5
21. Q–Q2   K–N2
22. R–QB1   R–N5!

23. N–K3   B–N4!
24. N–B2

24. N–N4?! is foiled by 24.
. . . P–B4! since 25. PxP?? is
not feasible because of the
hanging Knight.

24. . . .   R–N7
25. P–QR3   P–B5

The QBP is safe both here
and later on B6, and it restricts
White's piece deployment. Thus,
for this middlegame position,
passed pawns should be pushed.

26. Q–Q4   Q–N3
27. QxQ

The endgame is hopeless, the
middlegame untenable.

27. . . .   NxQ
28. B–B1   R–B1
29. N–Q4   R–B4
30. K–N2   P–B6!
31. NxB   PxN
32. B–Q3   R–R7
33. R–QR1   R–Q7!
34. R/K–Q1   RxR
35. RxR   N–B5
36. R–QR1

White's on his last legs. After
36. BxN RxB 37. K–B3 R–R5
White loses another pawn.

36. . . .   N–N7
37. B–B2   P–B4!

The undermining of the QP
will soon lead to its gain, and
then at the very least Black
will have connected passed QB
and Q pawns. White could resign here with a clear conscience.

38.	K–B3	N–B5
39.	K–K2	PxP
40.	BxP	P–B4
41.	B–Q3	N–N7
42.	R–QB1	K–B3
43.	P–B4	RxP
44.	B–N1	

The pawn-down K + P endgame after 44. RxP RxB 45.

RxR NxR 46. KxN K–K3 is hopeless.

44.	. . .	R–Q7ch
45.	K–B3	N–Q8
46.	P–N4	PxPch
47.	K–N3	

47. KxP P–B7, etc.

47.	. . .	P–Q4
White resigns		

Enough is enough. Taimanov was under no illusions after his blunder on move 14 and, realizing the hopelessness of his position, played the rest of the game at virtual blitz tempo, using only 2 hours and 5 minutes for it all. Smejkal, wanting to make the win sure, spent a whole hour more.

Chapter 19

Tal, Mikhail

From 1957 to 1960 when he was sweeping everything in sight, Mikhail Tal was referred to as "The Terror from Riga." Born in Riga, Latvia, on November 9, 1936, he has lived there most of his life. Though by profession a journalist, he has been a chess player all his adult life.

Tal's attempt to reach the top occurred very early and culminated in total success. In 1957 he became U.S.S.R. Champion and repeated again in 1958. He won the Portoroz Interzonal in 1958 and the Candidates Tournament in 1959, thereby becoming Botvinnik's Challenger in 1960. And at the age of twenty-three he became World Champion by defeating Botvinnik 12½–8½. This, however, was the high point, the pleasure short-lived. The very next year Botvinnik regained the title in a return match by a score of 13–8. True, Tal was ill both before and during the match, but an obvious underestimation of his opponent was also a contributing factor.

Since 1961 Tal has remained a world-class player but has never come very close to regaining the world championship. There has been no lack of other successes, however: Champion of U.S.S.R. in 1967, 1972, 1974; Olympiad team member in 1966, 1972, 1974; and European team member 1970, 1973, 1977. International successes have continued apace, too, the latest being a clear first at Tallinn 1977 and a tie for first at Leningrad 1977.

Tal is the author of an excellent and exhaustive book on his 1960 World Championship match. His autobiography, *The Life and Games of Mikhail Tal*, was published in English in 1976 and has received excellent reviews.

Tal's 1977 FIDE rating is 2620.

GAME 52

White: M. Tal
(U.S.S.R.)

Black: E. Torre
(Philippines)

Played at Leningrad (U.S.-S.R.) Interzonal Tournament, June 4, 1973, Round 2.

King's Indian Defense (Semi-Yugoslav Variation)

Tal considers that he must beat the youthful Philippine master but obtains little advantage out of a closed opening. A balanced middlegame leads quickly to a balanced endgame, and at exactly this moment Tal's psychological need to win reasserts itself. He eschews normal good moves and to unbalance the position puts his pieces on ridiculous squares. Torre penetrates Tal's camp, wins a pawn, and brings home the full point in a well-played, though not too difficult R + P endgame. One more example in which unmotivated playing to win leads straight to a loss.

1. N–KB3

Tal is one of the great, creative attacking players of all time. He also has a very broad opening repertoire and frequently plays the strategic text. In this game the choice works

out badly. White obtains no attacking chances at all, and neither does he achieve a position offering winning chances.

1.	. . .	N–KB3
2.	P–B4	P–KN3
3.	N–B3	B–N2
4.	P–KN3	O–O
5.	B–N2	P–B4
6.	P–Q4	

White must play this soon; otherwise the position becomes quite symmetrical. By transposition the game has entered the Yugoslav Variation of the King's Indian Defense.

6. . . .   PxP

This central capture leads to the Semi-Yugoslav. The normal Yugoslav follows 6. . . . P–Q3 (see the previous game).

| 7. | NxP | N–B3 |
| 8. | O–O | NxN |

The slight strategic problem with the Semi-Yugoslav is that Black has to give up more central space to White in order to complete the normal development of his Queenside; e.g., 8. . . . P–Q3?! is a dubious pawn sacrifice.

9.	QxN	P–Q3
10.	Q–Q3	P–QR3
11.	B–K3	

A good active developing move, with the point that 11. . . . R–N1?! is met by 12. B–R7! R–R1 13. B–Q4!. Also playable for White are 11. P–K4 and 11. B–Q2.

11. . . .	N–N5
12. B–Q4	N–K4
13. Q–Q1!	R–N1!

Black's correct approach is to aim immediately for counterplay with . . . P–QN4. Instead, 13. . . . B–K3? proves to be an unsound pawn sacrifice after 14. BxP R–N1 15. BxP RxP 16. N–Q5, and 13. . . . NxP?? loses the Knight after 14. BxB KxB 15. Q–Q4ch N–K4 16. P–B4.

14. R–B1

The usual move, but worth considering is the preventive 14. P–QR4!?. It was successfully used in Shamkovich–Zuckerman, New York International 1977, in which after 14. . . . B–K3 15. N–Q5 P–N3 16. P–N3 P–QR4 17. P–K4 N–Q2 18. BxB KxB 19. P–B4 White's central superiority gave him a small though steady edge.

| 14. . . . | B–K3 |
| 15. N–Q5 | |

15. P–N3 has often been recommended but has not so far been tried in actual practice.

| 15. . . . | P–QN4 |
| 16. PxP | |

White gets nothing from 16. P–B5 BxN! 17. BxB P–K3 18. B–N2 P–Q4.

| 16. . . . | BxN |

Played regularly, though 16. . . . PxP also seems to be O.K.

since after 17. N–B7 Black has 17. . . . BxP!?.

| 17. BxB | PxP! |

This seems stronger than 17. . . . RxP 18. B–N2 Q–R4 19. P–QR3, and White had a slight advantage in Tukmakov–Smejkal, Erevan 1976.

18. Q–Q2?!

White not only does nothing about Black's plan but also makes sure that Black can execute it with gain of time. White has two logical approaches. He can play 18. P–N3 or the sharper 18. P–B4!?. Then after 18. . . . N–N5 White retains some edge with 19. B–KB3 BxBch 20. QxB N–B3 21. R–B6 (Zaitsev), but 18. . . . N–Q2! 19. B–R7 R–B1 20. Q–Q2 N–B4! 21. P–QN4 Q–B2! is quite equal, Ribli–Gheorghiu, Las Palmas 1973.

18. . . .	P–K3!
19. B–N2	N–B5
20. Q–B3	BxB
21. QxB	P–Q4

| 22. P–N3 | Q–N3! |
| 23. KR–Q1 | |

Leads to a completely un-winnable endgame. If White truly wants to win, then he should keep the Queens on the board.

23. . . .	QxQ
24. RxQ	N–Q3
25. R–B6	KR–Q1

Black can also play actively with 25. . . . N–B4 26. R–QN4 R–R1 27. R–B2 KR–B1!, but having full respect for his opponent he prefers a safer route.

26. P–K3?!

It's not clear what this has to do with the game. A normal continuation is 26. R–Q1 QR–B1 27. R/1–QB1 with equality. Larsen has correctly pointed out that because White's Bishop is inactive, White's safest route to a draw is 26. P–K4.

| 26. . . . | QR–B1 |
| 27. R–N6?? | |

Truly incomprehensible; moreover, Tal spent a considerable amount of time both on this and his previous move. White allows Black to walk right in, and for what purpose? The obvious 27. RxR RxR 28. B–B1 is correct, and there is no reason for the game not to end in a draw.

27. . . .	R–B8ch
28. B–B1	N–K5!
29. K–N2	

29. RxNP loses the Exchange after 29. . . . N–B6 30. R–N7 N–K7ch. Not that what happens is any better. With the text White hopes for 29. . . . R–B7?! 30. B–Q3! RxBPch 31. K–N1 R–Q7 32. BxN and White is safe. But the following zwischenzug spoils White's dreams.

| 29. . . . | P–K4! |
| 30. R–N4 | R–B7! |

Material loss now is unavoidable. The only remaining question is whether White can save himself after all the exchanges are completed and the number of Black pawns has been greatly reduced.

31. P–QR4	PxP
32. PxP	RxPch
33. K–N1	R–R7
34. R–N8	

Since White has no realistic prospects of pushing his QRP he tries to get at Black's central pawns.

34. . . .	RxR
35. RxRch	K–N2
36. R–N5	N–B6
37. R–B5	N–Q8

Black heads for a R + P endgame, in which he will be up a pawn and will have various positional pluses. The next few moves are forced.

38. RxP	NxP
39. RxP	NxB
40. KxN	RxKRP!

The position Black had in mind. Using the technique seen later in the game, he plans to create two connected passed pawns on the Kingside. Meanwhile, the active location of Black's Rook and the passive location of White's King mean that White's QRP is no threat.

41. R–K7?!

The sealed move and nothing but a waste of time. With the immediate 41. R–K2! R–R8ch 42. K–B2 R–R8 43 R–K4 White's King could at least get off the back rank.

41. . . .   R–R7
42. R–K4

A sad retreat, but 42. R–R7 immobilizes White's Rook and allows Black's King readily to get to White's Kingside.

42. . . .   P–R4
43. R–R4   P–B3
44. K–N1   K–B2
45. K–B1   K–K3
46. R–K4ch   K–B4
47. R–B4ch   K–K4
48. R–R4   R–Q7!

With the threat 49. . . . R–Q5! since Black's King is close enough to the QRP. Therefore White's Rook must move away, and Black's NP can advance.

49. R–QN4   P–N4
50. R–N3   R–QR7
51. R–N4   K–B4
52. K–N1   K–N3
53. R–QB4   P–N5

Black is building for a properly timed . . . P–R5, which will make his KBP and KNP connected and passed.

54. R–N4   P–B4!
55. R–N8

Otherwise 55. . . . K–N4 and 56. . . . P–R5.

55. . . .   P–R5!

Ensuring that Black will get connected passed pawns is the clearest method of winning.

56. PxP   RxP
57. K–N2   R–R6
58. R–N8ch

If 58. R–N6ch K–R4 59. R–KB6, then 59. . . . R–KB6 spells the end.

58. . . .   K–B2
59. R–N5   K–B3
60. R–N8   R–R6
61. R–KR8   K–K4
62. P–R5

Leads to the loss of the pawn, but otherwise 62. . . . K–B5 is decisive.

62. . . .	K–B3!
63. P–R6	K–N3
64. R–N8ch	KxP
65. K–B2	

Equivalent to resignation. But no better is 65. R–R8ch K–N4 66. RxR PxRch 67. KxP K–B5! 68. K–N2 K–K6! with a routine K + P endgame win.

65. . . .	R–R6
66. K–N2	K–R4
67. K–B2	K–R5

White resigns

The threat is 68. . . . R–R7ch followed by 69. . . . K–N6, and 68. R–R8ch allows Black's King to go to KN4 and thence to KB5.

GAME 53

White: G. Estevez
    (Cuba)

Black: M. Tal
    (U.S.S.R.)

Played at Leningrad (U.S.-S.R.) Interzonal Tournament, June 5, 1973, Round 3.

Sicilian Defense (Scheveningen Variation)

Tal allows his opponent the kind of attacking position that Tal himself would like to have. While Estevez meaningfully improves the position of his pieces, Tal flutters to and fro with little consistency of thought. He gets his Rook caught in the center of the board, and while both players are in time pressure Estevez finally administers mate. The kind of game in which Tal, not his opponent, would seem to be playing the White pieces.

1. P–K4	P–QB4
2. N–KB3	P–K3
3. P–Q4	PxP
4. NxP	N–KB3
5. N–QB3	P–Q3

Tal has chosen the Scheveningen Variation, a relatively safe way to handle the unbalancing Sicilian Defense. Black establishes a modest but clear central presence and plans to mobilize his Kingside forces before initiating Queenside activity.

6. B–K2

White's normal positional continuation. Sharper are Keres's 6. P–KN4!? and 6. B–QB4.

6. . . .   P–QR3

Now in many lines we get something like a cross between the Najdorf and the Scheveningen. There is no immediate need for this move; the usual Scheveningen proceeds with 6. . . . B–K2 (see Game 58, Westerinen–Tukmakov, Hastings 1972/73).

7. P–QR4

There is even less need for this precaution since Black is surely not threatening . . . P–QN4. The normal good moves are 7. O–O and 7. P–B4.

7. . . .   Q–B2

It's also too early for the Queen to head here since the QB-file may be more useful for the QR, especially if Black chooses a setup with . . . QN–Q2. 7. . . . B–K2 or 7. . . . N–B3 is preferable.

8. B–K3   P–QN3

Here, too, Black has an easier time equalizing with 8. . . . N–B3.

9. P–B4   B–N2
10. B–B3   QN–Q2
11. Q–K2   B–K2

11. . . . P–N3?! is too dangerous because of 12. P–K5! PxP 13. PxP NxP 14. BxB QxB 15. B–N5!: 15. . . . N/3–Q2 16. N–K4! or 15. . . . N/4–Q2 16. NxP!. And 11. . . . N–B4 12. B–B2 will probably transpose into the game continuation.

12. O–O   O–O
13. K–R1   N–B4
14. B–B2

White has harmoniously developed his pieces and is ready to proceed with the central advance 15. P–K5!. Black has two reasonable choices, the blockading 14. . . . P–K4, which allows 15. PxP PxP 16. N–B5 with some advantage to White, or the text move.

14. . . .   P–Q4

In theory a desirable move, but it will lead to an isolated QP. Black is O.K. after 15. P–K5 N/3–K5 16. BxN NxB 17. NxN PxN, but White plays better.

15. PxP!   NxQP
16. BxN!   PxB

Black's QB will remain rather dead for the rest of the game, but 16. . . . BxB 17. NxB PxN suffers from the disadvantage of giving Black an isolated pawn and no prospects of active play.

17. Q–N4!

White's KN has access to KB5, and thus White will have a strong attacking formation. Black must show that he can equalize.

17. . . .   B–KB3
18. N–B5   N–K3

It's logical to overprotect the crucial KN2-square. 18. . . . N–K5?! is very dangerous because of 19. B–R4!.

19. B–R4!

Removing the strong Black Bishop is the right idea for both tactical and strategic reasons.

19. . . .   BxB
20. QxB   KR–K1?!

Black prevents N–K7ch and places his Rook on an open file. After the loss in the previous round to Torre, Tal is anxious to win against the young Cuban, especially since Estevez lost his first two games and is the lowest-rated participant. 20. . . . QR–Q1? is worse than the text because of 21 R–B3!, and now 21. . . . P–Q5 (with the idea 22. R–R3? BxPch!) is refuted by 22. N–K7ch K–R1 23. QxPch!! KxQ 24. R–R3 mate. However, Black does not really have time for the text and should continue with the immediate 20. . . . P–Q5!. After 21. N–Q5! BxN 22. N–K7ch K–R1 23. NxB Q–B4 24. P–B4 PxP e.p. 25. NxBP, White has

only a slight advantage, according to Estevez.

21. QR–Q1!   Q–B4
22. Q–N3!   K–R1
23. N–K2!   Q–KB1?!

Moving backward is hardly in Tal's style and in general cannot lead to good results. Perhaps he has to risk 23. . . . QxP 24. N/2–Q4 Q–B2! (24. . . . QxP?? 25. R–QN1 followed by 26. NxN). Then 25. R–B1 Q–Q2 26. NxN PxN 27. QxPch QxQ 28. NxQ allows White to recover his pawn, but after 28. . . . R–K2! Black has no worries. Therefore White would have to continue with 25. R–B3! and a very strong attack. But at least Black would have a pawn for his worries. In the game he has nothing to compensate for his suffering.

24. N/2–Q4   N–B4
25. Q–R4   R–K5?!

The Rook occupies an untenable position here. 25. . . . N–K5 is more in the spirit of his previous move.

26. N–KN3   Q–K2?

Retreating the Rook is unpleasant because of 27. P–B5, but leaving it exposed in the center is worse.

27. Q–N4!

Now Black is hopelessly lost, since 27. . . . R–K6 fails to 28. N(either)–B5.

27.	. . .	B–B1
28.	Q–R5	P–N3
29.	Q–R6!	

White is interested in much bigger game than the QP. If now 29. . . . R–K6, then 30. P–B5 is the killer. So Tal tries tactics, but Estevez is right on the ball.

| 29. | . . . | B–N5 |
| 30. | NxR | QxN?? |

Allowing his Queen to be trapped in the middle of the board is unforgivable. Not much better is 30. . . . BxR?! because of 31. N–B5! Q–B1 (31. . . . PxN 32. N–B6) 32. N–N5! QxQ 33. NxBPch K–N1 34. N/5xQch K–N2 35. RxB and White is a safe piece ahead. 30. . . . NxN is the best there is, though after 31. QR–K1 Black is theoretically quite lost.

31. KR–K1

The end.

31.	. . .	BxR
32.	RxQ	NxR
33.	P–B5	

White is up a decisive amount of material and has a killing Kingside attack. Only both sides' severe time pressure causes the game to be continued.

33.	. . .	R–K1
34.	PxP	PxP
35.	N–K6!	R–KN1
36.	Q–B4	

With the threat 37. Q–K5ch followed by mate on KN7. Tal "prefers" a different end.

| 36. | . . . | P–KR4 |
| 37. | Q–R6 mate! | |

An excellent game by Estevez, played in the active style characteristic of a Tal.

GAME 54

White: M. Tal
(U.S.S.R.)

Black: R. Hübner
(West Germany)

Played at Leningrad (U.S.-S.R.) Interzonal Tournament, scheduled for June 7 but because of Tal's illness actually played on June 10, 1973, Round 4.

Sicilian Defense
(New Taimanov
Variation)

Smarting from the previous two losses, Tal is gung ho for a

victory and plays sharply for a mating attack. But Hübner's defense is perfect, and the best that White has is to reach for an even endgame. Tal disdains that and is soon forced to accept a middlegame in which his opponent not only gets the material edge of two Rooks and a pawn for a Queen but also retains the overall superior chances. When White plays inexactly he gets hit by an unstoppable attack against *his* Kingside. A fine example of the hunted's suddenly changing roles and becoming the hunter.

1. P–K4	P–QB4
2. N–KB3	P–K3
3. P–Q4	PxP
4. NxP	P–QR3
5. N–QB3	

By transposition the same New Taimanov position has been reached as in Game 18, Keres–Popov, Dortmund 1973. Master practice of the middle 1970s has shown that the flexible 5. B–Q3! is more unpleasant for Black, for it leaves open the possibility of P–QB4, which would strengthen White's central control.

5. . . .	Q–B2
6. B–K2	

This is more promising than the 6. P–KN3 of Game 18.

6. . . .	P–QN4!?

An interesting psychological moment: Hübner realizes that

Tal is hungry for a win, and he therefore chooses a most enterprising plan in the hope that Tal will overpress an attack. The risk, of course, is that Black can be killed by a sharp attack, but Hübner has concluded that Tal's play in this tournament is too unsure to present much real danger. The normal steady move is 6. . . . N–KB3, and after 7. O–O Black usually switches to the Scheveningen with 7. . . . P–Q3.

7. P–QR3?!	

Since there is no immediate threat to the KP, this move is essentially a loss of time. Either 7. O–O or 7. P–B4 are more useful.

7. . . .	B–N2
8. P–B4	N–QB3
9. B–K3	NxN
10. QxN	N–K2!

Hübner is handling the opening creatively and well. Black has good space on the Queenside, and the KN heads to QB3 to dislodge White's Queen from its active post.

11. R–Q1	R–Q1?!

However, this move is neither necessary nor beneficial. The Rook may not be well placed here (a B–QN6 by White would catch Black's Q and R in a scissor) and can well find a better home on QB1. The obvious 11. . . . N–B3 equalizes after both 12. Q–N6 QxQ 13. BxQ P–B3 and 12. Q–Q2 P–Q3.

12. O–O   N–B3
13. Q–Q2

Because of Black's misplaced QR, 13. Q–N6 now leads to a slight endgame plus for White. However, the text is also O.K.

13. . . .   B–K2
14. Q–K1

The fancy 14. N–Q5?! leads to nothing but equality after 14. . . . PxN 15. PxP Q–Q3.

14. . . .   P–Q3

Unfortunately 14. . . . O–O is met by the annoying 15. Q–B2!—see the comment to Black's 11th move. With the text, Black frees the Q2-square for his Rook.

15. P–B5!?

Tal grabs at the first opportunity at a direct attack and already envisions the followup Exchange sacrifice. Black must allow it since 15. . . . N–K4?! 16. Q–N3 B–KB3 17. PxP PxP 18. B–R5ch gives White an attack at no cost.

Nevertheless the text is somewhat premature. The attack after 15. Q–B2! R–Q2 16. B–N6 Q–N1 17. R–Q3! followed by 18. R–R3 is more easily sustainable as Hübner's second at Leningrad, GM Hecht, recommended.

15. . . .   O–O
16. P–B6

The only logical followup since Black otherwise continues with . . . N–K4 and . . . B–KB3 and stands better because of the control of the K4-square.

16. . . .   BxP
17. RxB   PxR
18. Q–R4

White must go for a direct attack since there is no time for 18. R–Q3? on account of 18. . . . N–K4! 19. B–R6 N–N3 20. R–N3 Q–B4ch 21. K–R1 K–R1 22. BxR RxB and White has no compensation for his missing pawn.

18. . . .   Q–K2

The KBP must be protected. Losing is 18. . . . N–K4? 19. QxBP N–N3 20. N–Q5!! PxN 21. B–R6 with mate to follow.

19. R–Q3?!

With a cute threat (19. . . . K–R1?? 20. B–Q4!! and White wins), but Hübner's perfect defense stamps the move as not fully satisfactory. Correct is the obvious 19. B–R6 K–R1 20. R–Q3 P–B4! (Black has no time for 20. . . . R–KN1?? 21. R–R3 P–B4 because of 22. B–N5! and White wins), and now best play leads to an even ending after 21. QxQ NxQ 22. BxR RxB 23. RxP N–B1! 24. R–Q7 BxP 25. NxB PxN 26. K–B2! N–N3 27. R–R7 N–R5!.

19. . . .   P–B4
20. B–N5   P–B3
21. B–R6   PxP!

Ensuring a fine center and an extra pawn, and showing admirable coolness under fire.

22. R–N3ch   K–R1
23. B–N7ch

White can regain some of the sacrificed material but not all of it. Black now winds up with two Rooks and a pawn for his Queen, a definite material advantage. Yet the inherent looseness of the position allows White's Queen much freedom of action, and thus White's prospects are only slightly inferior. The text is much better than 23. BxR? RxB 24. NxP N–K4 when Black has both a material and positional advantage.

23. . . .   QxB
24. RxQ   KxR
25. NxKP

Worse is 25. Q–N4ch K–R1 26. QxKP/6 N–K4! and Black's remaining KP is farther advanced than in the game and quite secure on K5.

25. . . .   N–K4
26. N–N3   N–N3?!

Hübner considers this inaccurate since the Knight stood quite well and removing it to here only serves to chase the White Queen toward the Queenside, where White's *real* attacking chances lie. The accurate plan is 26. . . . K–R1! and only after 27. Q–R6 N–N3.

27. Q–Q4   K–R1
28. N–R5   N–K4!

28. . . . R–Q2? clearly is bad because of 29. NxP P–K4 30. Q–KN4 when Black has lost a pawn for nothing. White also gets too much play after 28. . . . P–K4?! 29. Q–N6 R–Q2 30. P–B4! PxP 31. BxP P–Q4 32. BxRP BxB 33. QxB P–Q5 34. Q–B6 R–K2 35. Q–Q6.

29. Q–KR4?

Heading in the wrong direction again. Tal dreams of his opponent's King, but his chances lie on the Queenside! White can try either of these plans: 29. N–B4 B–B1 30. P–QR4 or 29. Q–N6 R–Q2 30. P–QR4, and in either case White has good play and stands almost equal.

29. . . .   R–Q2!
30. NxP?

Taking the KBP here opens the gates for Black's Rooks. The Knight should have been left where it was in favor of starting action on the Queenside with 30. P–R4.

30. . . .   R–N2!

Black has the attack now, and it is decisive. Check the following lines:

(1) 31. P–KN4 B–B6;

(2) 31. P–KN3 R/2–KB2 32. N–K4 R–B8ch 33. K–N2 R/8–B7ch;

(3) 31. N–N4 BxP! 32. KxB NxN 33. BxN RxBch! 34. QxR R–KN1 with a won K + P ending.

Tal's move is equally hopeless.

31.	Q–R6	R–B2
32.	K–B1	N–N5!
33.	B–R5	RxPch
34.	BxN	RxB

White resigns

The coming 35. . . . R–N3 will win White's Knight and leave Black with a huge material superiority.

GAME 55

White: J. Rukavina
(Yugoslavia)

Black: M. Tal
(U.S.S.R.)

Played at Leningrad (U.S.-S.R.) Interzonal Tournament, June 25, 1973, Round 16.

King's Indian Defense

Tal decides that to play for a win he must produce a series of unusual, antipositional, confusing opening moves. It soon turns out, however, that the only one confused is Tal himself. Rukavina takes note of all of Black's weaknesses, lines up on them, and is about to start the harvest when after adjournment Tal resigns. White demonstrates perfectly that the best way to handle unusual, antipositional moves is with good positional play.

1.	N–KB3	N–KB3
2.	P–KN3	P–KN3
3.	P–N3	

White's choice of a double fianchetto against the King's Indian setup is a slightly passive but positionally sound plan.

3. . . .   P–QR4?!

It's somewhat outlandish to move the QRP out so quickly, but the move is probably playable if Black follows up consistently. However, Tal is much more interested in creating confusion rather than achieving consistency, and the text therefore works out poorly.

4. B–QN2   B–N2
5. B–N2   P–Q3?!

The point behind 3. . . . P–QR4 should be to play on the light squares. Thus a logical plan is 5. . . . O–O 6. O–O P–Q4 with an opportune . . . P–R5 to follow. Transposing into the King's Indian with the text means that Black's 3rd move was a waste of time and weakened the Queenside.

6. P–Q4   P–B3
7. O–O   O–O
8. QN–Q2   P–R5
9. P–QR3   QN–Q2?!

A sensible light-square policy still consists of 9. . . . PxP 10. PxP P–Q4!.

10. R–N1   Q–B2
11. R–K1

An immediate 11. P–K4! is more than playable. However, White's moves are deliberately slow and safe in the correct expectation that Black will hang himself.

11. . . .   P–K4?!

Leads to new weaknesses; e.g., Black's Q3. The minor evil is 11. . . . P–Q4!.

12. P–K4   R–K1
13. P–R3   P–QN4?

Impatient, Black creates a very serious new weakness on the Queenside: either the QNP or the QBP will now be weak. The only sensible way to develop the QB is by means of 13. . . . P–N3.

14. P–QN4!

A strategically won position for White. His development is complete, and his pieces, though apparently modestly placed, are well trained toward the center. White will soon get in P–QB4, thereby opening the holes in Black's Queenside.

14. . . .   N–N3
15. PxP!

Ensuring that White's dark-square Bishop will be the superior one and making Black's KP a new weakness in Black's position.

15. . . .   PxP
16. B–KB1!   B–QR3
17. P–B4!   NxBP

Not capturing allows 18. PxP making Black's QNP a permanent weakness.

18.	NxN	PxN
19.	Q–B2	P–B6

Forcing the exchange of the light-square Bishops is no accomplishment at all, but Black has no satisfactory continuation. To attempt pawn exchanges with 19. . . . P–B4 is zapped by 20. P–N5! BxP 21. BxKP!.

20.	QxBP	BxB
21.	KxB	Q–N2
22.	Q–B4	N–Q2
23.	KR–Q1	N–N3
24.	Q–K2	

White's basic strategy should be quite clear, to pile up against the isolated QBP. Pleasant adjuncts to this are pressure along the Queen file and against the KP. Rukavina is already starting to feel the time shortage, and thus his play is not the most efficient in realizing his advantages. Thus 24. Q–B2! is simpler, and after 24. . . . Q–R3ch 25. K–N2. Nevertheless Black's prospects are nonexistent, so Tal isn't able to generate an ounce of counterplay, anyway.

24.	. . .	P–R3
25.	QR–B1	R–K3
26.	N–K1!	

Aiming for Q3 and then QB5.

26.	. . .	N–Q2
27.	Q–Q3	N–B1
28.	Q–B2	P–R4
29.	N–Q3	N–Q2

30.	Q–K2	B–B1
31.	R–B2!	

A flexible move with three possible uses: doubling on the QB-file, doubling on the Q-file, and bringing the Bishop to the excellent K3 central location.

31.	. . .	Q–N4
32.	B–B1	R–Q3
33.	B–K3	R–Q1
34.	N–N2!	

White's Bishop prevents a Black's . . . P–QB4; thus White can offer the exchange of Queens and of a pair of Rooks. No matter what course Black chooses, positionally he remains quite lost.

34.	. . .	N–B3
35.	RxR	BxR
36.	P–B3	B–K2
37.	QxQ	

There was, of course, no need to exchange Queens in this manner and remove the pressure on the QBP. But in time pressure the text looked good and safe to White. The control of the QB-file will allow White to attack Black's QNP, and Black's KP also remains weak. Thus White still retains a winning position. More thematic, however, is 37. Q–B4! followed by 38. K–B2.

37.	. . .	PxQ
38.	K–K2	N–Q2
39.	N–Q3	B–Q3
40.	R–B6	B–N1
41.	N–B5	Black resigns

Black can't prevent material loss and will continue to have the inferior position. Tal actually sealed 41. . . . N–B1 but resigned without continuing the game. Indeed, White mops up starting with 42. R–N6.

Chapter 20

Tukmakov, Vladimir

Vladimir Tukmakov was born on March 15, 1946, in Odessa (Ukraine) and still lives there. By education he is an engineer, but like his compatriots he has worked only as a professional master. His series of significant successes started in 1970 when he finished second to Korchnoi in the U.S.S.R. Championship and an excellent second to Fischer at Buenos Aires. The only reason Tukmakov didn't become a grandmaster then is that he hadn't yet been an international master. It took another grandmaster result—at Moscow 1971—before Tukmakov obtained his title.

Throughout his career Tukmakov's results have been erratic. Thus a fine second place in the U.S.S.R. Championship in 1972 was followed by a disastrous 16th (out of 18) at the 1973 Leningrad Interzonal. On the other hand, a poor 10th–11th (out of 15) at Odessa 1976 was followed in 1977 by a decisive win at Decin. His potential is fine as is his 1977 FIDE rating of 2540.

GAME 56

White: W. Hartston
(England)

Black: V. Tukmakov
(U.S.S.R.)

Played at Hastings (England) International Tournament, December 27, 1972, Round 1.

Sicilian Defense
(Velimirovic Attack)

White obtains a slight edge out of the opening but by undertaking a premature attacking sortie allows Black central counterplay. Black, however, fails to follow up correctly, and White achieves a strong attacking formation. Black defends poorly and White quickly obtains a winning position.

1.	P–K4	P–QB4
2.	N–KB3	N–QB3
3.	P–Q4	PxP
4.	NxP	N–B3
5.	N–QB3	P–Q3
6.	B–QB4	

This move is usually credited to Soviet master Sozin, who played it a few times—mostly unsuccessfully—from 1929 to 1931. It was however Bobby Fischer who showed the world how to handle the variation, and this was Fischer's main line from the late 1950s through the 1972 match against Spassky. Thanks to Fischer's innovations the move received at least equal prominence with the Richter-Rauzer Attack (6. B–KN5).

6.	. . .	P–K3
7.	B–K3	P–QR3
8.	Q–K2	

Fischer's "attack" consisted of castling Kingside and an early P–KB4. The text is an idea of the creative and dangerous attacking master of Yugoslavia, GM Velimirovic. White is going to castle Queenside and then unleash a pawn storm against Black's Kingside. Bobby tried this plan only once: unsuccessfully against Larsen at the 1970 Palma de Majorca Interzonal.

| 8. . . . | N–QR4?! |

This premature acentral jump allows White a very successful regrouping at no risk whatever. Black should postpone the move until White has castled Queenside and Black has achieved some development. Correct therefore is either 8. . . . B–K2 or 8. . . . Q–B2.

9. B–Q3!

Exactly! White now will castle on the Kingside and achieve strong pressure against Black's center. The QN will be quite obviously out of the way.

| 9. . . . | Q–B2 |

After 9. . . . B–K2 also comes 10. P–B4, and 9. . . . P–QN4?! allows the surprising 10. P–QN4! with advantage to White: 10. . . . N–N2 (10. . . . Q–B2? 11. N/3xP!) 11. O–O P–K4 12. N–N3 Q–B2 13. B–Q2 B–Q2 14. P–QR4 as in Mestrovic-Polugaevsky, Varna 1972.

| 10. | P–B4 | P–QN4 |
| 11. | O–O | B–N2 |

11. . . . P–N5 12. N–Q1 weakens Black's Queenside and achieves nothing. Now, however, White must prevent 12. . . . P–N5.

12.	P–QR3	B–K2
13.	QR–Q1	R–QB1
14.	K–R1	O–O
15.	B–B1	

White has achieved very harmonious development, every one of his pieces is well placed and his King is safe enough on KR1. His immediate threat is 16. P–K5, and Black must work to prevent it.

15. ...   N–B5
16. R–B3?

This KR sortie only serves to misplace the Rook. The key central plan is P–K5; therefore, the correct move is 16. P–QN3!. Then Black has no time for pawn grabbing with 16. ... NxRP? because 17. BxN QxN 18. P–K5 N–K1 19. BxRPch! KxB 20. R–Q3 followed by 21. R–R3ch and 22. Q–R5 leads to a winning attack. Therefore Black would have to retreat with 16. ... N–N3, when with 17. B–N2 White safeguards his Queenside and reestablishes 18. P–K5 as the threat. After 17. B–N2 White has a pleasant, risk-free advantage.

16. ...   P–N3!

Safeguards his KR2 and by controlling KB4 prepares the

following central thrust. Black already is better.

17. R–R3

Hardly an attractive location for the Rook, but something had to be done to give the KN a reasonable retreat square.

17. ...   P–K4!
18. N–B3

18. PxP PxP opens the diagonal of Black's KB, so that White prefers to sacrifice his KBP.

18. ...   PxP
19. R–B1!

Of course not 19. BxP? because of 19. ... NxNP. With the text White hopes for some action on the Kingside. After his erroneous 16th move, White chooses the best practical alternatives.

19. ...   Q–B4?

Overlooking the response. 19. ... N–R4? is much too risky because of the sacrifice 20. RxN!. In order is the positional 19. ... N–K6! 20. BxN PxB 21. QxP P–KR4! with Black having some advantage: his King is safe, he has a nice two-Bishop game, and White's KB looks like an overgrown pawn.

20. P–QN4   Q–N3
21. BxP

White has won back his pawn under reasonable circumstances,

and chances are roughly even. Now it is quite dangerous for Black to go after the QRP since after 21. . . . NxRP? 22. B–K3 Q–B2 23. B–Q4 White has a very strong attack. 21. . . . KR–K1! is correct to apply pressure to the KP. Then after 22. B–N5 Black has 22. . . . N–Q2, and 22. P–K5?! is met by 22. . . . B–B1.

21. . . .   N–N5?

In principle it is good to establish control over Black's K4, but Black overlooks the obvious reply.

22. BxN   PxB

If 22. . . . RxB? 23. N–Q2 and White threatens both 24. NxR and 24. QxN.

23. N–Q2   P–KR4

The Knight has to stand its ground. Worse is 23. . . . N–K4?! 24. BxN PxB 25. NxP Q–Q5 26. N–R5 since 26. . . . RxN is refuted by 27. R–Q1! (Hartston).

24. NxP   RxN?

This "combination" leads to a hopeless situation in short order. It is imperative to retain the KN and continue 24. . . . Q–Q5!. White retains the edge with 25. N–R5, but Black is not without chances.

**25. QxR   N–B7ch
26. RxN   QxR**

**27. R–B3   QxP
28. B–R6**

Black's Queen has no checks, and his Rook can't move. Black is quite lost.

**28. . . .   P–Q4
29. Q–Q4**

Not bad, but immediately winning is 29. Q–B7!: 29. . . . PxP 30. QxKB! or 29. . . . R–K1 30. Q–Q7.

**29. . . .   P–B3
30. BxR**

Good enough to win, but with the zwischenzug 30. R–B2! White retains the KP.

**30. . . .   PxP
31. R–B1   KxB
32. N–Q5   BxN
33. QxB   Q–K7
34. Q–Q1**

White's material advantage is sufficient to win in an endgame, and the looseness of Black's King position means that Black has no practical chances in the middlegame. White needs to do little more than safely reach the time control at move 40.

34.	. . .	Q–N7
35.	Q–B1	Q–R7
36.	Q–R6ch	K–B2
37.	Q–R7ch	K–B1
38.	QxNP	QxP
39.	QxKP	K–B2

After 39. . . . QxP White can choose to win either with 40. QxQ or 40. RxPch.

| 40. | Q–R7ch | K–B1 |
| 41. | Q–R8ch | Black resigns |

GAME 57

White: V. Tukmakov (U.S.S.R.)

Black: M. Stean (England)

Played at Hastings (England) International Tournament, December 28, 1972, Round 2.

Sicilian Defense (Accelerated Dragon Variation)
(By transposition)

A game of ups and downs. An unbalanced opening leads to a middlegame of equal chances. When Black is careless for a moment, White gains a very strong attack with a creative piece sacrifice. Black defends inexactly, and White first misses a forced win and then a chance

for a superior position. Suddenly almost all White's pieces are en prise, and he cannot prevent Black from getting a material advantage and repulsing White's attack. Once the advantage is his, Stean plays exactly and with full confidence.

1.	N–KB3	P–QB4
2.	P–B4	P–KN3
3.	P–Q4	PxP
4.	NxP	N–QB3
5.	N–B2	B–N2
6.	P–K4	

By the kind of transposition common in master chess, a position has arisen which is completely different than that we would have been expecting from the first moves. Instead of a Reti-English, we have a KP opening, specifically the Accelerated Dragon Variation of the Sicilian Defense, which White has met with the Maroczy Bind. The normal move order is 1. P–K4 P–QB4 2. N–KB3 N–QB3 3. P–Q4 PxP 4. NxP P–KN3 5. P–QB4 B–N2 and now White has played 6. N–B2. This Knight retreat has a long history but is not currently given a high rating because it is antidevelopmental and acentral and it allows Black's KB to dominate his central diagonal. Best for White is 6. B–K3! with a slight but definite plus.

6.	. . .	N–B3
7.	N–B3	P–Q3
8.	B–K2	N–Q2!

Black plays the opening moves in exact order and thus achieves very strong pressure against White's center. After the routine 8. . . . O–O?! 9. B–K3 White is slightly better.

9. B–K3

Very double edged. Safer is 9. B–Q2, but the passivity of that move does not give White much hope for an opening advantage.

9. . . .   N–B4?!

But this is inaccurate. In order is the sharp 9. . . . BxNch! 10. PxB Q–R4 11. Q–Q2 N–B4 with equal chances for Black—we'll see this soon in the game.

10. Q–Q2?!

White reciprocates. Correct is 10. N–Q4! O–O 11. O–O with White slightly better after either 11. . . . NxN 12. BxN B–K3 13. BxB KxB 14. Q–Q4ch, as in Portisch–Gheorghiu, Teesside 1972, or 11. . . . B–Q2 12. Q–Q2 NxN 13. BxN, as in Portisch–Reshevsky, Palma de Majorca 1971.

10. . . .   Q–R4!

Now all is well for Black again because 11. N–Q4? loses to 11. . . . NxN! 12. BxN NxP!. Therefore White's response is forced.

11. P–B3   BxN!
12. PxB

An unbalanced position, but inherently quite satisfactory to Black. Of course, he does miss the Dragon Bishop, but in dying the Bishop ruined White's Queenside pawn formation. Black's Knights and Queen are exceedingly well placed to take advantage of this factor. Most accurate now is 12. . . . P–B3!, as in Polgar–Forintos, Kecskemet 1972, because the normal 13. O–O?! loses a pawn after 13. . . . N–R5 14. N–N4 NxP!. Also good is 12. . . . Q–R5 13. O–O B–K3 14. N–N4 R–QB1, as in Portisch–Deze, Vrsac 1971.

12. . . .   B–K3

Probably sufficient for equality but not as accurate as either of the above moves. Now, by playing 13. N–Q4!?, White could force Black to think. Instead he continues routinely with . . .

13. O–O   P–B3

Everything's fine again.

14. N–Q4   B–B2
15. N–N3   Q–R6

16. QR–N1	P–N3
17. N–Q4	R–QB1
18. B–R6	N–K4
19. R–N4	N–R3?!

This acentral retreat gives White the opportunity for a surprising combination. Correct instead is 19. . . . N–B3! with equality since neither side has anything better than to repeat the position with 20. N–N5 Q–R3 21. R4–N1 N–K4 22. R–N4 N–B3, etc.

20. N–N5	Q–R4
21. B–N7!	R–KN1
22. BxP!	PxB

This capture is forced because 22. . . . NxR? is much worse: 23. PxN Q–R3 24. NxQPch! PxN 25. QxP N–B3 26. P–N5 and White's attack is decisive.

23. NxPch	K–K2
24. N–N7!	Q–R6?

By being too greedy Black risks a certain loss. As Tukmakov points out it is necessary to get Black's Queen into the game with 24. . . . NxPch!. Then White can retain a slight edge with either 25. PxN Q–KN4ch 26. QxQ PxQ 27. R–R4 or 25. RxN Q–K4 26. R–R4 N–B4 27. NxN QxNch 28. Q–Q4. Of course, 24. . . . KR–Q1? is also unsatisfactory for Black because of 25. Q–N2!.

25. Q–Q6ch?!

White correctly smells victory but is too careless in the execution of his plan. The text allows Black's Queen to pin the Rook, and this presents some difficulties for White. Correct is to first chase Black's Queen away from protecting the Q3-square with 25. R–N3! Q–R5 and then 26. Q–Q6ch K–K1 27. QxP wins by force since there is no way to protect the K4 Knight, and it can't move away because of 28. N–Q6ch.

25. . . .	K–K1
26. RxP!	

26. QxP is playable, but after 26. . . . QxBP! the KN is protected and White's QR remains en prise. Apparently White can't get more than equality after 27. N–Q6ch when Black has the choice between 27. . . . K–B1 and 27. . . . K–Q2.

26. . . .	N–B4!

And not 26. . . . QxRP? 27. RxN QxB 28. QxP and White's attack can't be repulsed. After the text we get the critical position in the game.

27. R–N3??

Putting the Rook en prise leads to a material disadvantage too large for White to recover enough of. Tukmakov correctly gives 27. R–N5! as retaining White's advantage. Then 27. . . . N/K–Q2? loses to 28. NxN NxN 29. R–N7!. The best Black can achieve is an unfavorable endgamelike position with 27. . . . Q–R3 28. QxQ NxQ 29. N–Q6ch K–K2 30. NxRch RxN 31. R–R5 R–B3 32. P–B5!.

27. . . .	**QxP**
28. QxP	

Suddenly White has no satisfactory continuation. Thus 28. NxN fails to 28. . . . QxB, and there is no time for 29. R–N7 because of 29. . . . Q–K6ch 30. K–R1 QxN 31. R–K7ch K–B1!.

28. . . .	**N/B–Q2!**
29. N–Q6ch	**K–B1**
30. Q–N5	**QxR**
31. NxR	**K–N2**

The bloodbath is over and Black is a piece up. White's three-pawn compensation is inadequate because the doubled QBPs are indefensible and Black's QRP is a very strong passed pawn. Black handles the following part quite well, both defending and attacking. It is soon clear that White is fighting a lost cause.

32. N–K7	**R–K1**
33. R–Q1	**BxP**

34. N–B5ch	**K–R1**
35. N–Q4	**QxP**
36. P–R4	**BxB**
37. NxB	**Q–B4ch**
38. K–R1	**Q–K2**
39. Q–N3	**N–KB3**
40. N–B4	**P–QR4!**
41. R–R1	**R–R1**
42. N–Q5	**NxN**
43. PxN	**N–B2**
44. Q–B4	**Q–K4!**

White resigns

Both the middlegame after 45. Q–R4 QxP and the endgame after 45. QxQch NxQ are hopeless.

GAME 58

White: H. Westerinen (Finland)

Black: V. Tukmakov (U.S.S.R.)

Played at Hastings (England) International Tournament, January 9, 1973, Round 12.

Sicilian Defense (Scheveningen Variation)

After a perfectly played opening, White achieves a very strong Kingside attack in the middlegame. Nevertheless, one inaccuracy is sufficient to enable Black to escape into an approximately even endgame. By now both sides are in severe time pressure and the play becomes very inexact. First White allows Black the somewhat superior chances, and then Black, by underestimating a passed pawn, allows a combination which gains White a full Rook.

1.	P–K4	P–QB4
2.	N–KB3	P–K3
3.	P–Q4	PxP
4.	NxP	N–KB3
5.	N–QB3	P–Q3
6.	B–K2	B–K2
7.	O–O	N–B3

Compared to Game 53 in which Black played an early . . . P–QR3, Tukmakov here chooses to work first on his development.

8. B–K3   B–Q2?!

Posting the QB here is premature. More in the spirit of his previous play is 8. . . . O–O.

9. P–B4   O–O
10. N–N3!

By preventing the exchange of this Knight, White makes

Black's QB look rather impotent on Q2. If instead 10. Q–K1 NxN 11. BxN B–B3 and Black has good central influence.

10. . . .   P–QR3
11. P–QR4!   N–QR4?!

White was of course threatening to fix Black's Queenside with 12. P–R5, and the text was a popular method in the early 1970s to prevent that. Nowadays 11. . . . P–QN3 is accepted as Black's best, though White does obtain strong attacking chances with P–KN4 either on move 12 or shortly thereafter.

12. P–K5!

This central thrust shows up the disadvantage of Black's last move. Impossible is 12. . . . PxP? 13. PxP N–K1 because 14. NxN wins a piece. Therefore Black's KN must retreat immediately.

12. . . .   N–K1
13. NxN   QxN
14. Q–Q2!   R–B1

The obvious 14. . . . B–QB3?! allows the tactical 15. P–QN4! when Black's Q and QB will be pushed back because 15. . . . QxNP? loses to 16. N–Q5!. The alternative to the text is 14. . . . Q–B2 with White, similarly to the game, retaining the advantage after 15. B–Q4.

15. B–Q4   B–QB3
16. Q–K3   N–B2

Black looks for counterplay with the help of tactics; e.g., 17. P–QN4? is parried by 17. . . . QxNP 18. KR–N1 Q–R4 19. B–N6 N–Q4!. Instead of the text, in Westerinen–Sanz, Torremolinos 1974, Black tried the retreat 16. . . . Q–B2, but after 17. B–Q3 P–KN3 18. P–B5! QPxP 19. BxKP B–Q3 20. BxB QxB 21. QR–Q1 N–B3 22. B–K2! Q–K2 23. PxKP QxP 24. Q–Q4 White had a clear advantage.

17. B–Q3

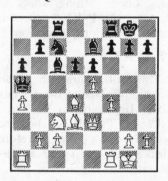

A position significantly favoring White: he has superiority in the center, both of his Bishops are trained on Black's King, and White's Queen and Knight can soon join in the attack. To stem the tide, Black's defensive efforts must be Herculean.

17. . . .   N–Q4
18. Q–R3   P–R3

The other pawn move, 18. . . . P–N3, loses after 19. PxP BxP 20. Q–R6 P–B3 21. BxNP! with a winning attack.

19. P–B5!?

Very much in Westerinen's aggressive attacking style—as sharp a move as possible at every turn! Less aggressive souls would have played 19. N–K4!, thereby bringing another piece against Black's King. In either case, it is questionable whether Black can hold the position.

19. . . .   Q–N5

Not satisfactory, but what is? Thus 19. . . . QPxP is met 20. PxP!, and now 20. . . . PxB? loses immediately to 21. Q–B5. And against the recommended 20. . . . P–B4 White has this promising sacrifice: 21. RxP! PxB 22. NxN! BxN 23. QR–KB1! and White seems sure to at least win back the piece with advantage.

20. N–K2   QPxP
21. PxP   P–B4

This should not be sufficient but at least has the practical advantage of bringing about complications. The only alternative loses simply: 21. . . . PxB 22. PxPch K–R1 23. Q–B5 N–B3 24. N–B4! P–KN4 25. N–N6ch K–N2 26. NxB, etc.

22. P–B4?

By being too materialistic White gives up all his advantage. Yugoslav GM Bukic has shown

that after 22. BxKP B–B4ch 23.
K–R1 N–K6 24. N–B4! NxR
25. RxN White's attack is
devastating.

22. . . .	PxB
23. PxN	BxQP
24. BxBP	P–Q6!

If now 25. BxP Q–N3ch followed by capture of the KP and
Black has a lovely two-Bishop
game. Therefore White allows
Black's QP to live and again
heads for Black's King.

25. N–B4	Q–Q5ch
26. K–R1	P–Q7
27. Q–N4	R–KB3!

The threatened 28. Q–N6 had
to be prevented.

28. N–R5	QxQ
29. NxRch	BxN
30. BxQ	R–B7

The QP gives Black full compensation for the Exchange. By
now both sides are in severe
time pressure and the play
shows it.

| 31. QR–Q1 | B–N6 |
| 32. R–B3?! | |

This turns out to be the win-
ning move because Black misses
White's diabolical plot. Never-
theless, the move risks White's
being left with the worst of it.
The accurate way is 32. R–B2!
R–B8 33. R/2xP BxR 34. RxB
RxR 35. BxR BxP with a fully

equal opposite-color-Bishop
endgame.

| 32. . . . | RxP |
| 33. P–K7 | |

The critical moment in the
game. Black can't play the obvious 33. . . . BxKP?? because
34. RxB! RxR 35. B–K6ch
wins the Rook. Correct is 33.
. . . BxRP! 34. R–Q3 BxP 35.
R/3xP with Black, who has
two connected passed pawns
for the Exchange, better, but
White has good drawing
chances. Instead, Black selects
the "logical," "automatic" . . .

| 33. . . . | K–B2?? |

. . . and loses exactly as after
the "obvious" 33. . . . BxKP??.

| 34. RxB! | RxR |
| 35. B–K6ch! | Black resigns |

The choice is between losing
the Rook and allowing a new
Queen after 35. . . . KxB 36.
P–K8=Qch, which is no choice
at all.

GAME 59

White: J. Mestel
  (England)

Black: V. Tukmakov
  (U.S.S.R.)

Played at Hastings (England) International Tournament, January 11, 1973, Round 14.

Pirc Defense

Immediately out of the opening Black stands well but very quickly loses his bearings. White achieves some advantage, and then Black inconceivably acquiesces to a completely lost endgame. White does make things rather difficult for himself all the way through but finally wins the game. Some positions are just so inherently lost that almost nothing can save them; this can be said about the course of this game from move 23 on.

1. P–K4	P–Q3
2. P–Q4	N–KB3
3. N–QB3	P–KN3
4. B–N5	

The quietest way to meet the Pirc is 4. N–B3 (Karpov's move!), an in-between method is 4. P–B4 (see Game 39), and White's sharpest approach is the text.

4. . . .	B–N2
5. P–B4	

White again selects the most ambitious move. Less hurried is 5. Q–Q2.

5. . . .	P–B3

But Black prefers not to respond in kind. Almost incalculable complications can result after 5. . . . P–KR3 6. B–R4 P–B4!?.

6. N–B3

Black shows very nicely that it is quite important for White to play the next few moves in the right order. The accurate way is 6. Q–Q2!, then 7. B–Q3, and thereafter 8. N–B3.

6. . . .	O–O
7. Q–Q2?!	

Black shows up this routine move. Required first is 7. B–Q3.

7. . . .	P–Q4!!

Instead the usual lines go 7. . . . P–N4 8. B–Q3 and White is O.K. Theoreticians have paid no attention to the text either before or after this game, but it is very strong. White does not have the normal response 8. P–K5 now because after 8. . . . N–K5 9. NxN PxN Black gains lots of time from the attack on the KN.

8. B–Q3	PxP
9. NxP	B–N5
10. P–B3	

White must allow the ruination of his Kingside pawn formation because 10. N–K5?!

QxP 11. BxN PxB 12. NxB P–KB4 is worse since Black regains the piece with clear advantage.

| 10. . . . | BxN |
| 11. PxB | Q–Q4?! |

This gives White the chance, by means of simple tactics, to get rid of the isolated, double-pawn liability. As Mestel recommends, 11. . . . P–K3! followed by 12. . . . QN–Q2 leads to a position slightly preferable for Black, since White has no compensation for the doubled KBPs.

| 12. P–B5! | QN–Q2 |

12. . . . QxBP?? drops the Queen after 13. NxNch, and 12. . . . PxP? 13. NxNch PxN 14. B–R6 is simply horrible.

| 13. PxP | RPxP |
| 14. O–O! | |

After White's fine last move the position is in dynamic equilibrium: the partial looseness in White's Kingside is balanced by some greater central influence and the two Bishops.

| 14. . . . | KR–Q1?! |

Starting here Black loses all resolve to do anything. It is unquestionably proper to start challenging White's center immediately with 14. . . . P–B4 or 14. . . . P–K4. In either case chances remain even.

15. Q–K3!	QR–B1
16. P–N4!	R–K1
17. P–KB4!	P–N3
18. P–B5!	

While White has been moving resolutely forward Black has had difficulty deciding what to do. Even so after the thematic 18. . . . P–B4! White's advantage is relatively small.

| 18. . . . | PxP?? |

But this is just madness. The best Black can hope for now is a completely chanceless endgame. What kind of choice is that for a practical game?

| 19. RxP | QxR |

After 19. . . . Q–K3 20. Q–N3! the risk is great that Black will be mated; e.g., 20. . . . NxN 21. BxN QxB 22. B–R6!.

20. NxNch	PxN
21. BxQ	RxQ
22. BxR	

A hopeless endgame for Black. White is effectively a pawn up, has the two Bishops in an open position, and has a very strong, mobile passed KRP.

22. . . .　　R–K1
23. R–K1?!

Up to here White has played with real gusto, but from now on he hardly knows what to do. The only reason he wins is that Black's position is totally lost. Instead of the incomprehensible text, 23. K–B2! followed by 24. R–KN1!, etc., is obvious, logical, and decisive.

23. . . .　　N–B1
24. B–KB2

24. K–B2!.

24. . . .　　N–K3
25. B–N3　　B–B1
26. K–B2　　P–N4
27. B–K4　　R–B1
28. B–B5　　R–K1
29. B–R4　　B–N2
30. B–K4　　R–QB1

With time somewhat short White repeats moves, but now he needs a plan. Black is still in a complete bind; therefore, it is logical to activate the King with 31. K–B3!, followed by 32. K–N4 and 33. K–B5. Black's re-

sistance would then be very short.

31. R–QN1?!

On the face of it, the move looks pointless. It turns out to have a plan behind it, even though the plan is rather clumsy.

31. . . .　　N–B5
32. R–N3　　N–Q4
33. R–R3　　B–R3?!

Why let in White's Rook? Surely 33. . . . R–B2 is better.

34. RxP　　NxBP
35. B–B3　　N–Q4
36. BxN　　PxB
37. BxP

White has now transformed the positional advantage into a material one. Black must embark on a counterattack, but that will leave his King insufficiently protected.

37. . . .　　R–B5
38. P–QR3　　R–B7ch
39. K–N3　　B–B8
40. R–R5?!

On the last move before time control, White misses the right plan. Correct is the immediate 40. P–KR4!, planning a mating net after 41. P–R5, 42. R–R8ch, 43. R–R8 mate!

40. . . .　　R–B6ch
41. K–N4　　BxP
42. P–R4!　　K–R2

Black is almost at the end of the rope. The end is immediate

after 42. ... BxP? 43. R–R8ch
K–R2 44. P–R5.

43. P–R5?

This automatic move allows a
surprising defense. Mestel subsequently demonstrated that
there was a forced win with 43.
R–R8! K–N3 (43. ... R–B3
44. K–B5) 44. R–R6! followed
by 45. P–R5ch! and 46. R–R8.
This way White prevents the
defensive maneuver available to
Black in the game.

43. ...	R–B3!
44. K–B5	B–N7!
45. RxP	

The problem is that 45. R–
R8?! allows 45. ... RxBch! 46.
KxR BxPch 47. KxP B–B6 followed by 48. ... BxP and a
theoretically drawn position results.

45. ...	R–B7
46. K–K5!	

There is no time for 46. RxP?
because of 46. ... R–B7ch 47.
K–K5 R–K7ch with a draw because 48. K–Q6? allows 48. ...
R–K3ch.

46. ...	R–R7
47. KxP!	RxPch
48. K–B4	R–R6

The B + P endgame result-
ing after 48. ... RxR?! 49.
KxR is lost: 49. ... K–N3 50.

B–R8! K–R2 51. B–K5 K–N3
52. K–B4, etc.

49. R–N6

And so White is still up a
pawn and has two passed pawns.
Black's best chance now is to
try to activate his King with 49.
... K–N3!?. As played, his
King remains shut off, and this
ensures the loss.

49. ...	R–B6?!
50. B–K5	P–B4
51. R–KB6	R–B6ch
52. K–N5	R–B6
53. K–B5	R–B6ch
54. K–Q5	R–QN6
55. B–Q6	R–KB6
56. K–K5	R–K6ch
57. K–Q5	R–KB6
58. P–N5!	

After saving time to reach the
time control on move 56, White
starts to use his passed pawns.
The end appears close, but
White actually wins quite
securely.

58. ...	R–QN6
59. K–B4	R–B6ch

Or 59. ... BxP 60. KxR!
BxR 61. P–N6 B–Q5 62. P–N7
B–R2 63. K–N4 followed by
64. K–N5 and 65. K–R6.

60. K–N4	R–Q6
61. B–K5!	BxP
62. BxB	RxBch
63. K–B5	

The cardinal difference in this position is that White's King can help his passed pawn's advance, whereas Black's King is shut off from his pawn. Therefore White wins very easily.

63. . . .	R–B5
64. P–N6	K–N2
65. R–B6	R–B8
66. P–N7	**Black resigns**

A probable continuation is 66. . . . R–B8ch (66. . . . R–QN8 67. R–QN6) 67. K–N6 R–N8ch 68. K–B7 RxPch (otherwise 69. R–QN6) 69. KxR and Black's KBP can never advance; e.g., 69. . . . P–B5 70. R–B4, etc.

GAME 60

White: M. Quinteros (Argentina)

Black: V. Tukmakov (U.S.S.R.)

Played at Leningrad (U.S.-S.R.) Interzonal Tournament June 9, 1973, Round 6.

King's Indian Defense (Panno Variation)

White carries a tiny edge out of the opening into the strategic middlegame. However, Black's careful defense does not allow White to increase his advantage. Late in the middle-game White decides to trade his Queen and pawn for two Rooks. But Black's active Queen keeps the game in balance. So it remains until Black blunders on move 39. and allows a Rook sacrifice which leads either to mate or the decisive loss of material. A shockingly sudden end to a game well played by both sides.

1. N–KB3	N–KB3
2. P–B4	P–KN3
3. P–Q4	B–N2
4. P–KN3	O–O
5. B–N2	P–Q3
6. N–B3	N–B3
7. O–O	P–QR3

White has selected a sound positional approach, the KB fianchetto, against the King's Indian. With his 6th and 7th moves Black entered the Panno Variation, named after the Argentine GM Oscar Panno. The Panno is a fighting, flexible, sound variation, whereby Black's QN applies pressure against the QP and Black gets ready to advance on the Queenside with a . . . P–QN4. Now with 8. P–Q5 N–QR4 9. N–

Q2 White could enter variations akin to the Yugoslav, which was discussed in conjunction with Game 51. Instead White prefers a more independent approach.

8. P–KR3

For the play to come, it is useful for White to prevent both . . . B–KN5 and . . . N–KN5.

8. . . .   R–N1
9. P–K4

This centrally active push leads to main-line variations. Korchnoi has had success with the flexible 9. B–K3 P–QN4 10. N–Q2!.

9. . . .   P–QN4

Black has no choice: he must be active. Inferior is 9. . . . N–Q2?! 10. B–K3 P–QN4 11. PxP PxP 12. Q–B1! P–K4 13. R–Q1 and the many weaknesses in Black's position led to a clear plus for White in Hübner–Naranja, Palma de Majorca 1970.

10. PxP

Sharpest play possible results after 10. P–K5! N–Q2! 11. PxNP RPxP 12. N–N5 PxP! 13. BxN PxP 14. N–N5 R–N3! with something like even chances in an unclear position, though Black won in Szekely–Weinstein, Budapest 1976.

10. . . .   PxP
11. B–K3!

Of course here 11. P–K5 N–Q2 can lead to the variation given above. White has also tried 11. R–K1, though 11. . . . P–K3!, as in Portisch–Adorjan, Budapest 1975, allows Black eventually to equalize.

The text has not been played either before or since this game, but it seems to allow White to retain a slight advantage. The Bishop is developed immediately to an excellent central square, and White gets ready for rapid play along the QB-file.

11. . . .   P–N5
12. N–K2!   P–K4

Not 12. . . . NxKP?? 13. Q–B2 and White's Queen skewers both unprotected Knights.

13. PxP!   PxP
14. Q–B2

A position slightly though pleasantly in White's favor. He is devoid of weaknesses himself and has play against various weak spots on Black's Queenside.

14. . . .   B–N2!

The only correct defense. Wrong is 14. . . . B–Q2? 15. KR–Q1 Q–B1 16. QR–B1, and there is no satisfactory defense to the threat 17. RxB! followed by 18. QxN.

15.	KR–Q1	Q–B1
16.	N–Q2!	R–K1
17.	N–N3	B–QR1
18.	N–B5	

So White's first strategic achievement is full control of the important QB5-square. Black also must be careful to guard his weak QNP and QBP.

18.	. . .	B–B1
19.	N–B1!	

The Knight heads for QN3 where it will reinforce QB5 and also keep watch over the Q4-square.

19.	. . .	B–Q3
20.	N/1–N3	N–Q2
21.	R–Q2	NxN
22.	NxN	N–Q1!

Here and following, Black defends very accurately. The text brings the Knight to a good defensive post and allows the QB to start participating in the play. White, on his part, starts to activate his hitherto passive KB.

23.	B–B1!	B–B3
24.	K–R2	R–R1

Black cannot yet afford to offer the exchange of the light-square Bishops because after 24. . . . B–N4? 25. BxB RxB 26.

Q–B4! his position is too holey; e.g., 26. . . . R–N1 27. N–R6 winning at least a pawn, or 26. . . . Q–N1? 27. N–Q7 followed by 28. N–B6ch.

25.	B–QB4	N–N2!
26.	N–N3	B–Q2
27.	P–KR4	B–K3!
28.	BxB	QxB
29.	Q–B6	N–R4
30.	NxN	RxN

With some judicious exchanges Black has succeeded in lightening his defensive load. White still has a minute advantage because of the superior Bishop and the weakness of Black's Queenside pawns. However, since White's QRP is under attack, White decides to exchange it for Black's QNP and thereby creates a passed QRP for himself.

31.	P–R4	PxP e.p.
32.	PxP	R/1–R1

White's QRP only looks to be en prise; it is actually quite safe since attempts to capture it fail. Thus 32. . . . RxP?? loses a piece after 33. RxB!, and 32. . . . BxP? loses the Exchange to 33. QxQ RxQ 34. R/2–R2 R/3–R3 35. B–Q2! R–R5 36. B–B1.

33.	P–R4	R/4–R3

Black can't afford to go after the QNP with 33. . . . Q–N6?! because of 34. B–R6! since then 34. . . . R/4–R3 35. Q–Q7 RxP? allows White a mating attack: 36. RxB! PxR 37. QxQP!!.

34. Q–N7   K–N2

Instead 34. . . . RxP 35. QxRch RxQ 36. RxRch K–N2 leads to the game type of position with Black a tempo behind. With the text he hopes to do better.

35. R–Q5

The resulting exchanges are fine for Black. The only way to try to retain a slight advantage is 35. R/2–R2! followed by 36. P–R5. Even then it is not clear how White can strengthen his position.

35. . . .   RxP!
36. QxR   RxQ
37. RxR   Q–N5
38. R–R4   P–KB4!

Black's Queen is active and he has good play against White's weakened King position. The chances are balanced.

39. R–R7!

With the obvious threat 40. RxB, which Black decides to "prevent," much to his sorrow. Correct now is 39. . . . P–B5! with even chances since White has nothing better than 40. B–N6 K–R3! 41. BxP BxB 42. RxB PxPch 43. PxP QxKP 44. R–Q2! followed by 45 R/7–B2 with a stable position. Attempts to win achieve the opposite; e.g., 40. RxB PxB 41. RxBPch K–R3 42. R/6–Q7?? (42. PxB

transposes into a drawing line) 42. . . . QxR!! 43. RxQ P–K7! and Black gets a new Queen.

39. . . .   K–B3??

Black had ten minutes for the last two moves and so time shortage can't be blamed for this blunder. It's simply a reflection of Tukmakov's poor sporting form throughout the Interzonal.

40. RxBch!   Black resigns

He loses a piece since 40. . . . PxR 41. B–N5ch K–K3 allows 42. R–K7 mate.

GAME 61

White: R. Byrne (U.S.A.)

Black: V. Tukmakov (U.S.S.R.)

Played at Leningrad (U.S.-S.R.) Interzonal Tournament, June 13, 1973, Round 8.

Ruy Lopez (Breyer Variation)

Black plays the opening better than White and as a reward comes out a pawn ahead. But starting with the middle-game White shows more assurance than Black. Though still a pawn down, White is able to activate his pieces so as to get fair compensation for the missing button. In time pressure Black sees ghosts and promptly allows an elementary combination which nets White a full piece. An excellent example of how a player in top sporting form can recover from an unpleasant position, whereas the one in poor shape can do nothing with the offered chances.

1.	P–K4	P–K4
2.	N–KB3	N–QB3
3.	B–N5	P–QR3
4.	B–R4	N–B3
5.	O–O	B–K2
6.	R–K1	P–QN4
7.	B–N3	P–Q3
8.	P–B3	O–O
9.	P–KR3	N–N1
10.	P–Q4	QN–Q2
11.	QN–Q2!	

Up to here the game has followed the same course as Game 13, in which White played the impetuous 11. P–B4. The text is the usual and best choice. White already has a space ad-vantage; he now will complete his development and only then look for a more definitive plan. Black is clearly in no condition to attack White, so why shouldn't the first player strengthen his position before starting active operations?

11.	. . .	B–N2
12.	B–B2	

A good multipurpose move. By protecting the KP, the Bishop allows the QN to move to KB1 and makes way for the QNP to be used for Queenside play.

12.	. . .	R–K1

Black aims to safeguard his KP and possibly threaten White's after a timely . . . PxP. The alternative, often played by Gligoric, is to challenge White's center immediately with 12. . . . P–B4. At present this is less common because White can achieve a significant space advantage with 13. P–Q5, after which Black is hard pressed to find breathing room.

13. P–QN4

Karpov invariably prefers to play 13. N–B1 and 14. N–N3 first thereby usefully deploying the QN. The text is an active alternative.

13.	. . .	B–KB1

13. . . . P–Q4?! is premature because of 14. NxP NxN 15. PxN NxP 16. NxN PxN 17. Q–

N4 with good attacking chances for White in Kavalek–Robatsch, Sarajevo 1968.

14. B–N2

Not bad but a more consistent followup to the previous move is 14. P–QR4!, and after 14. . . . N–N3 15. P–R5 with space advantage for White, as in Fischer–Spassky, Match Game 10, 1972, for example.

14. . . .   N–N3!

Now it will be difficult for White to get his Queenside going. Inferior are both 14. . . . P–QR4?! 15. B–Q3! P–B3 16. P–R3 N–N3 17. R–QB1 KPxP 18. NxP KN–Q2 19. N/2–N3 with White better in Tal–Karpov, Leningrad Interzonal 1973 (played in this same round!), and 14. . . . P–N3?! 15. P–B4 KPxP 16. PxP PxP 17. NxP P–Q4 18. PxP RxRch 19. QxR BxQP 20. P–R3 P–B3 21. N–K4 and the better pawn formation and superior piece mobility give White a slight plus, as in Dueball–O'Kelly, West Germany 1971.

15. P–R3   KN–Q2

Possible also is the prophylactic 15. . . . P–R3. Then after 16. P–B4 NxBP!? 17. NxN PxN 18. PxP PxP 19. NxKP P–B4 20. NxQBP PxP!, as in Parma–Unzicker, Berlin 1971, Matanovic rates the position even.

16.	R–QB1	P–N3
17.	B–N1	B–R3
18.	R–B2	P–R4

White's pieces momentarily give the appearance of being in a hedgehog formation. However, White's pawns do control more space, and he can now snap out of his shell with 19. PxRP! RxP 20. P–B4! and thereby keep a tiny edge; e.g., 20. . . . NPxP 21. NxBP NxN 22. RxN.

19. P–B4?

The right plan all right but the wrong execution. Instead of having a secure QRP, White will now have a weak QNP, and this gives Black time to activate his pieces with great force.

19. . . .	RPxP!
20. RPxP	KPxP!
21. BxP	

21. NxP?! leads to the loss of the QBP for nothing after 21. . . . BxN.

| 21. . . . | PxP |
| 22. B–R2 | |

22. NxP leaves the KP hanging.

| 22. . . . | R–R5! |
| 23. Q–N1 | Q–R1! |

The pressure along the QR-file, against the QNP, and against the KP is very unpleasant for White. A defensive move such as 24. R–N2 is met strongly by 24. . . . Q–R3!, threatening 25. . . . R–R1. Therefore White decides to chuck a pawn and get some breathing room.

24. NxP   RxKP!

The complications after 24. . . . BxP?! 25. R/2–K2 are fine for White since 25. . . . BxQ? 26. RxRch QxR 27. RxQch N–B1 28. NxN! RxB 29. N–Q7 P–KB4 30. N–N5! leads to a winning Kingside attack despite the absence of Queens.

25. N–K3   P–QB4?!

The series of exchanges starting with this move accomplishes nothing for Black while serving to activate White's pieces. Much more annoying for White is for Black to keep the bind, by 25. . . . R–B5!, for example.

| 26. PxP | PxP |
| 27. B–B3 | |

It's possible that 27. BxP!? is playable, but by now both sides are in acute time pressure and on general principles the text looks like the correct move for White.

27. . . .	N–Q4
28. NxN	BxN
29. BxB	QxB

With White's pieces becoming active, Black can't interpolate 29. . . . RxRch? 30. QxR QxB because of 31. Q–K8ch B–B1 (31. . . . N–B1?? leaves the Rook hanging) 32. R–Q2 and White wins.

| 30. R–Q1 | Q–K3 |
| 31. R–N2! | |

The active location of White's pieces and the inherent looseness in Black's King position make it very doubtful whether Black can do anything with his extra QBP. White is threatening to play 32. R–N7 and, after the Knight moves, 33. R–N8. Therefore 31. . . . B–B5! is a worthwhile move for Black since then 32. P–N3? fails to 32. . . . QxP 33. PxB Q–N5ch 34. K–B1 QxN 35. R–N8ch N–B1 and Black's attack will come first. But in time pressure, Black sees ghosts rather than simple tactics and plays . . .

31. . . .	R–R1??
32. RxN	

Thank you. If now 32. . . . QxR 33. QxR, and whatever gets played, White will be up a piece. Only the mutual time pressure extends the game to move 40. Otherwise Black would resign on the spot.

32. . . .	R–K1
33. R–Q1	B–B5
34. R–N6	Q–B5
35. Q–N3	Q–K7
36. R–N7	P–B5
37. Q–N1	B–K6
38. R–KB1	B–B4
39. R–N8	P–R3
40. RxRch	RxR
41. Q–N5	Black resigns

GAME 62

White: V. Tukmakov (U.S.S.R.)

Black: J. Smejkal (Czechoslovakia)

Played at Leningrad (U.S.-S.R.) Interzonal Tournament, June 21, 1973, Round 13.

Grünfeld Defense

A game in which White is better in the first part, Black in the last. But whereas White can do nothing with his advantage, Black is able to win his superior endgame. White has a theoretical draw for a while, but bad form also means losing drawable endgames. This Rook and pawns endgame appeared in nearly all the chess magazines of the world.

1. P–Q4	N–KB3
2. P–QB4	P–KN3
3. N–QB3	P–Q4
4. N–B3	B–N2
5. Q–N3	

About thirty years ago this was the main line of the Grünfeld, but it is currently out of fashion. The present fashion is to look for flexible and strategic approaches, and the active text is too sharp and complicated. A strategic build-up with P–KN3 was discussed in connection with Game 2.

| 5. . . . | PxP |

The point of the Grünfeld is to launch an attack against White's center in the hope of eventually bringing it down. The active play after the text is therefore consistent. 5. . . . P–B3?! is self-cramping.

6. QxBP	O–O
7. P–K4	B–N5

This direct way to apply pressure against White's QP is originally an idea of Smyslov's. Currently more popular are the flexible 7. . . . P–QR3!? and 7. . . . P–B3!?.

| 8. B–K3 | KN–Q2 |

Part of the plan associated with 7. . . . B–N5: the KN will

go to QN3 to chase away White's Queen, and the QN will go to QB3 to attack the QP.

9. R–Q1

The main-line variations start with 9. Q–N3 N–N3 10. R–Q1 N–B3. The text gives both sides a chance to vary.

9. . . .   N–QB3

Black can enter the line above with 9. . . . N–N3 10. Q–N3 N–B3. Now White can try something else.

10. B–K2!

But here 10. Q–N3?! is inferior because of 10. . . . BxN! 11. PxB P–K4! and Black has at least equality.

10. . . .   BxN
11. PxB

This center-building recapture is generally the correct method in this variation. After 11. BxB?! P–K4! Black again stands well.

11. . . .   P–K4?!

But here this thematic push doesn't seem to work out well. Ambramov and Botvinnik recommend 11. . . . N–N3!? 12. Q–B5 P–B4! 13. P–Q5 N–K4 14. N–N5!? here, with approximately even chances in a very complex position.

12. PxP   N/3xP
13. Q–R4!   Q–B1
14. P–KR3

But the need for this defensive move (to keep Black's Knight from White's KN4 and Black's Queen from White's KR3) is unclear. Ambramov and Botvinnik recommend the immediate 14. P–B4! N–N3 15. Q–N3 with White judged to be better after either 15. . . . N–N5 16. B–B5 or 15. . . . N–B3 16. P–KR4! R–Q1 17. P–B5. This looks correct, but a practical test is needed to confirm this analysis.

14. . . .   N–N3
15. Q–N3   R–Q1
16. RxRch   QxR
17. O–O

This position is also somewhat advantageous for White. He has the two Bishops and the greater central influence and will have the more active Rook. Black's counterchances must rest with the White King's somewhat weakened position. However there seems to be no direct way of exploiting this factor; e.g., 17. . . . Q–R5 18. K–N2! (not 18. P–B4? because of 18.

... QxRP!) 18. ... B–R3 19.
N–N5!, and after 19. ... BxB
White can play 20. PxB with
advantage. Therefore with the
next move Black ensures a good
location for his new KN by preventing White's P–KB4.

17. ...	P–N4!?
18. N–N5	N–N3
19. R–Q1	Q–K2
20. P–QR4	N–KB5
21. B–KB1	B–K4
22. N–Q4	

The threat of 23. N–B5
forces the following exchange
all right, but Black is just able
to safeguard his weak spots.
Considerably stronger is the
direct 22. P–R5!, and after 22.
... N–Q2 23. NxRP, whereas
after 22. ... N–B1 White has
23. P–R6! PxP 24. N–Q4.

22. ...	BxN
23. RxB	R–N1
24. Q–Q1	

After 24. P–R5 Black has
24. ... N–Q2, but now Black
must prevent the serious threat
of 25. P–RS.

24. ...	P–QR4
25. R–Q2	R–K1
26. BxN/6	

White does win a pawn this
way at the cost of being left
with the significantly inferior
minor piece. Overall that turns
out to be no bargain for White.
More in the strategic spirit of
the opening are 26. Q–B2! and

26. Q–N3! with the threat 27.
Q–N5.

26. ...	PxB
27. R–Q7	Q–B3
28. RxNP	N–N3!
29. Q–Q7	R–Q1
30. Q–B5	

By now both players are out
of time and the next ten moves
take place at blitz tempo.

30. ...	QxQ
31. PxQ	N–R5
32. P–B6	

A move which looks more
terrifying than it is. 32. RxNP!
is simpler and good for full
equality.

| 32. ... | P–R3! |
| 33. B–K2? | |

"Developing" the Bishop
thusly is pointless. If White
wants to move the Bishop, then
33. B–B4 is correct probably
followed by 33. ... NxPch 34.
K–N2 N–K4 35. B–N3 R–Q3
36. R–K7 N–Q2 37. RxP K–R1
and 38. ... NxP and approximate equality. Also perfectly
playable is 33. RxNP R–Q8 34.
R–N5. Black then has a draw
by perpetual check starting with
34. ... NxPch 35. K–N2 N–
R5ch, etc., but he has no more
than that.

| 33. ... | R–Q3 |

Already Black is better. His
QNP is safe, and he'll regain
the missing pawn and be left
with the double advantage of

better pawn formation and superior minor piece.

34. P–B4!?

White doesn't want to be left in a very passive position after 34. R–B7 RxP 35. R–B3 R–B5 and thus prefers to sacrifice a pawn in such a way as to give Black isolated doubled pawns.

34. . . .   PxP
35. P–B3   RxP

White gets fine play after 35. . . . R–Q7?! 36. K–B1 RxP? (36. . . . R–Q3!) 37. B–B4.

36. R–Q7   R–B3
37. R–Q4   R–B7
38. K–B2   N–N3

After 38. . . . RxP 39. RxP it's difficult to see how Black can hope to advance the backward QNP.

39. P–N4   R–R7
40. PxP   PxP
41. K–B1

The sealed move. Black is obviously better, but the weakness of his pawn formation (four isolated pawns) makes ultimate success questionable.

41. . . .   K–N2
42. P–R4   P–R4
43. B–Q3   R–R6
44. K–B2   NxP
45. RxP   RxB

Home analysis apparently convinced Black that the coming R + P endgame offered better chances to win than keeping the minor pieces on after 45. . . . N–N3 46. R–Q4.

46. RxN   K–N3
47. R–QB4   R–R6
48. K–N3   K–N4!

Black must activate his King; otherwise there is no hope of making progress.

49. R–B5ch   P–B4
50. RxP   P–R5ch
51. K–N2   R–R7ch
52. K–R3   R–KB7
53. R–R8   RxPch

Not surprisingly Black has won back the pawn, but he is now left with the RP–BP combination which, if White's King and Rook are correctly placed, is a theoretical draw. Not that the draw is easy, many master games have been lost by the weaker side. Even so, White's simplest approach is to give up the QRP and achieve a theoretically drawn position. The way he plays, he eventually winds up with the worst of both worlds. The QRP will not do anything positive but will tie down White's Rook to its defense.

54. K–N2 R–N6ch
55. K–R2 R–R6
56. R–N8ch

Perhaps the fact that this is the last move before the time control explains this needless check. Improving White's King position with 56. K–N2! is the soundest approach.

56. . . . K–B5
57. R–KR8 K–N5
58. R–N8ch K–B6
59. R–QR8 P–B5
60. P–R5 K–B7
61. P–R6 P–B6
62. P–R7 R–R8

The only try. After 62. . . . K–B8?! 63. R–KB8 it's an instantaneous draw, and after 62. . . . R–R5?! 63. K–R3 Black is in zugzwang and again has nothing better than to allow 63. . . . K–B8 64. R–KB8 RxP 65. RxPch.

63. K–R3?!

This does not throw the draw away but does make White's task more difficult. As GM Flohr points out, here is the most opportune time to activate White's Rook with 63. R–QN8!. The following moves are then pretty much forced, and White's Rook can check Black's King away from the scene of action: 63. . . . RxP 64. R–N2ch K–K6 65. R–N3ch K–B5 66. R–N4ch

K–N4 67. R–N5ch K–N3 68. R–N6ch K–N2. Now White reverses gears and plays 69. R–N3! R–KB2 70. K–N1 P–B7ch (otherwise 71. K–B2) 71. K–B1 and will win the BP for a draw: 71. . . . K–N3 72. R–KR3 K–N4 73. R–R2, etc.

63. . . . R–R5

Black is trying to put White in zugzwang. Another try at winning is 63. . . . R–R8ch 64. K–N4 R–N8ch! 65. KxP R–N2. Then as Keres points out White can draw only with 66. K–R5! (66. R–QN8? loses to the simple 66. . . . RxP 67. R–N2ch K–N8 68. K–N3 P–B7! 69. RxP R–N2ch 70. K–B3 R–B2ch winning the Rook) 66. . . . K–N7 67. K–R6! since then 67. . . . P–B7? (67. . . . RxP is a draw) 68. KxR P–B8=Q 69. R–KN8! is good only for White.

64. K–R2 R–R6
65. K–R1??

It's only this horrible blunder that seals White's fate. There were still two(!) ways to draw: *(1)* 65. R–QN8, as in the note to White's 63rd move (after 65. . . . RxP we have the same position as there); and *(2)* 65. K–R3 K–B8 66. R–QN8!, as Keres pointed out. Again after 66. . . . RxP Black's King will have no satisfactory way to get out of checks.

65. . . . R–R7!

Now, because of the miserable location of White's King, Black has a forced win.

66. K–R2   K–B8ch

Because this occurs *with check*, White has no time for the "drawing" 67. R–KB8.

67. K–R1

67. K–R3 P–B7 68. KxP K–N7 leads to the variation shown in the note to White's 69th move.

67. . . .   P–B7
68. K–R2   P–R6!!

But not 68. . . . R–R6? 69. R–QN8! and again White's Rook will have enough checks to reach a drawn position.

69. K–R1

White can only choose between losing prosaically and losing poetically. The text leads to a normal finish, as does the immediate 69. R–QN8. The winning method for Black after 69. KxP is prettier. Then Black wins as shown in a 1890 study by Emanuel Lasker: 69. . . . K–N8 70. R–N8ch K–R8 71. R–KB8 R–R6ch 72. K–R4 K–N7 73. R–N8ch K–R7 74. R–KB8 R–R5ch 75. K–R5 K–N7 76. R–N8ch K–R6 77. R–KB8 R–R4ch (note how Black forces White's King forward) 78. K–R6 K–N6 79. R–N8ch K–R5 80. R–KB8 R–R6ch 81. K–R7 RxPch (this can now be played with check—the whole point of Lasker's maneuver) 82. K–N6 K–N6. Black has won White's passed pawn and will queen his own.

69. . . .   R–R3
70. K–R2   R–R8!
71. R–QN8

71. KxP K–N8 loses as in the above note, whereas 71. K–R1?! allows 71. . . . K–K7ch.

71. . . .   RxP
72. R–N1ch   K–K7
73. R–N2ch   K–K6
74. R–N3ch   K–K5
75. R–N4ch   K–K4
76. R–N5ch   K–K3
77. R–N6ch   K–K2
78. R–N1   R–R6

The difference between this position and those shown earlier as draws is that the Black pawns are so far advanced that White has no defensive flexibility; e.g., White's King does not have access to either his KN2 or KN1. If now 79. R–KB1 R–KB6, and since White can't move his Rook, Black's King will march in with decisive effect. As played White gives a few spite checks and then resigns.

79. R–N7ch   K–K3
80. R–N6ch   K–K4
81. R–N5ch   K–K5
82. R–N4ch   K–B6
      White resigns

After 83. R–N1 a simple win is 83. . . . R–K6 followed by 84. . . . R–K8.

GAME 63

White: E. Torre
   (Philippines)

Black: V. Tukmakov
   (U.S.S.R.)

Played at Leningrad (U.S.-S.R.) Interzonal Tournament, June 22, 1973, Round 14.

Sicilian Defense

A difficult and somewhat frustrating game for the annotator. By now Eugenio Torre is a fine grandmaster, but Leningrad was his first big international tournament and his unsteady play showed this. And Tukmakov was in simply atrocious form. The net results were many, many incomprehensible moves. First White was better, then Black, then White again; finally Black's blunders ensured his loss.

1. P–K4   P–QB4
2. N–KB3   P–K3
3. P–Q3

A fairly popular approach against the Sicilian, which no one less than Bobby Fischer uses periodically if Black has played 2. . . . P–K3. The idea is that now that Black has weakened his KB3-square, his KB fianchetto, the usual method of meeting White's buildup, may have certain disadvantages. The positions which result are like those of the King's Indian Reversed and can also arise by transposition from the French Defense.

3. . . .   N–QB3
4. P–KN3   P–Q4

This straightforward central approach is preferred by Anatoly Karpov, among others. Playable too is 4. . . . P–KN3.

5. Q–K2?!

Why put the Queen here? Normal variations continue 5. QN–Q2 B–Q3 6. B–N2 KN–K2 7. O–O O–O 8. N–R4! with perhaps a slight edge for White.

5. . . .   KN–K2
6. B–N2   P–KN3
7. P–KR4

The threat of 8. P–R5 forces a weakening in Black's Kingside pawn formation, though at the cost of some weakening in White's Kingside, too.

| 7. . . . | P–KR3 |
| 8. P–K5 | N–Q5?! |

Why accept an unwieldy doubled pawn? 8. . . . N–B4 is normal, and after 9. P–B3 Black can start Queenside play with 9. . . . P–QN4!.

9. NxN	PxN
10. N–Q2	N–B3
11. O–O	B–Q2
12. N–B3	B–N2

If Black's plan is to castle Queenside, then this move has no point and can be replaced with the immediate 12. . . . Q–B2.

| 13. P–N3 | Q–B2 |
| 14. R–K1 | O–O–O |

Black has some difficulty knowing where to put his King. The Kingside seems dangerous because Black is short on defenders there, and the center is clearly inappropriate. Therefore the Queenside looks to be the best there is.

| 15. B–B4 | K–N1 |
| 16. P–R3 | R–QB1?! |

What's Black planning to do on the QB-file? More logical is 16. . . . K–R1, getting the King out of a possible pin, and then . . . QR–K1 aiming for an eventual . . . P–B3.

| 17. Q–Q2 | P–R3?! |

Why voluntarily create an attacking object for White's QNP?

| 18. P–QN4 | B–B1 |

Black has no concrete plan and many weaknesses. The paradoxical text, though, meets with instantaneous success.

| 19. KR– |
| QB1?? |

White plans to open the QB-file with a P–QB3 or P–QB4. He wants to leave the QR on QR1 so that it can be used to advance the QRP and/or QNP.

The overall idea is fine, but the correct execution is 19. QR–QB1! with a clear advantage to White. The careless, naive, acentral text move allows Black to grab the initiative.

| 19. . . . | P–B3!! |

With the primary threat of 20. . . . P–KN4 trapping White's QB. Thanks to Black's 18th and White's 19th moves, the obvious 20. PxP is answered by 20. . . . P–K4, when White again will lose a piece. Therefore White has to try something desperate.

| 20. P–B4!? | PxP e.p. |

This is not bad, but considerably stronger is 20. . . . QPxP!. Then 21. RxP?! loses to 21. . . . P–KN4. Therefore White must play 21. QPxP, but after 21. . . . PxP he has no satisfactory continuation. For instance, 22. P–N5 PxB 23. PxN BxBP gives Black an excellent, pawn-plus middlegame, and after 22. NxKP NxN 23. R–K1 B–N2 24. Q–K2 P–Q6! 25. Q–K3 P–Q7! Black keeps a significant material advantage.

21.	RxP	P–KN4
22.	RPxP	RPxP
23.	B–K3	PxP
24.	BxP	B–N2

Even though Black has not gained any material, his positional advantage here is considerable. He has a marvelously strong center and some attacking chances along the KR-file.

25. R–K1   KR–B1?

But what does this have to do with the game? Why leave the QR on QB1? What can it hope to do there? Correct is the fairly obvious 25. . . . QR–B1!, thereby retaining the advantage and even looking forward to some play along the KB-file. Inadvisable, however, is 25. . . . P–K5?! since after 26. PxP White has ample compensation for the Exchange.

26. B–R6!

Exchanging the dark-square Bishops severely undermines the pride of Black's center, the advanced KP. The chances are now roughly in balance.

26.	. . .	BxB
27.	QxB	Q–Q3
28.	R–B5	R–B4?

In time pressure Black overlooks a simple tactical possibility. Required is 28. . . . R–R1 29. Q–K3 R–R4, and winning the KP with 30. P–N4 R–R2 31. NxP entails certain dangers for White after 31. . . . R–N1.

| 29. | N–R4 | R/4–B1 |
| 30. | RxQP! | Q–K2? |

True, Black has lost an important pawn for nothing, but is that reason voluntarily and immediately to lose a lot more? There is nothing but 30. . . . Q–B2.

31. N–N6   Q–B3

Or 31. . . . Q–B2 32. RxB QxR 33. NxR. In severe time pressure Black tries a desperate attack. Since his position remains miserable, the attack must fail.

32.	RxB	QxPch
33.	K–R2	R–B6
34.	Q–R3	Q–Q7
35.	NxP	NxN
36.	RxN	R–KB7

After 36. . . . R–QB7 the simplest is 37. R–QB5 R–R7 38. R/5–B7.

37.	RxPch	K–R1
38.	R–	
	QR7ch!	**Black resigns**

White has no shortage of wins, but the text is the most elegant. After 38. . . . KxR White mates with 39. Q–R7ch K–N3 40. Q–QN7.

GAME 64

White: V. Tukmakov (U.S.S.R.)

Black: W. Browne (U.S.A.)

Played at Madrid (Spain) International Tournament, November 27, 1973, Round 2.

Sicilian Defense (Najdorf Variation)

A fascinating fight. A creative, sharp opening leads to an unbalanced middlegame, with White generally always a bit better. The real excitement starts around move 25, when, with both sides in severe time trouble, Black starts to really complicate things. First both sides match blows, but then a serious blunder by White on move 31. allows Black to mop up in a walk. A game in which bravery is rewarded.

1.	P–K4	P–QB4
2.	N–KB3	P–Q3
3.	P–Q4	PxP
4.	NxP	N–KB3
5.	N–QB3	P–QR3
6.	B–N5	P–K3
7.	P–B4	QN–Q2
8.	Q–K2	Q–B2
9.	O–O–O	

This has followed Game 37, in which White played the less flexible 9. P–KN4. The logical text gets the King to relative safety and allows the QR to start taking part in the battle. With his next typical move, Black also shows off his aggressive notions.

| 9. . . . | P–N4 |
| 10. P–B5!? | |

The most popular moves for White have been the precautionary 10. P–QR3 and the attacking and developmental 10. P–KN4 with the plan of meeting 10. . . . P–N5?! with the sharp 11. N–Q5!. The text is a specialty of Tukmakov's, which, for reasons unclear to me, has had no followers. It looks like a good idea since White immediately attacks the most vulnerable point in Black's center, the KP.

10. . . .   P–K4

Black decides to keep the center closed, at the cost of weakening his important Q4-square. The only alternative worth discussing is 10. . . . P–N5, after which White plays 11. PxP PxN 12. PxNch. Black has two reasonable ways of capturing:

(1) 12. . . . BxP?! 13. BxN PxB 14. Q–B4! QxQ 15. BxQ B–R3ch 16. K–N1 B–B5 17. P–QN3 K–K2 18. R–Q3 KR–KN1 19. P–N3 B–K4 20. KR–Q1 with a clear advantage to White, since Black has serious difficulties with his weak pawns, as in Tukmakov–Averkin, 1973 U.S.S.R. Championship; and

(2) 12. . . . NxQP 13. Q–B4! PxPch 14. K–N1 QxQ 15. BxQ N–K4 16. B–Q5 R–QN1 17. B–KB4 P–B3 18. KR–K1 B–K2 19. R–K3 B–Q1 20. P–KR3 B–Q2 21. R–QN3 with a slight advantage to White who'll recover his pawn and keep the freer position, as in Tukmakov–Polugaevsky, 1973 U.S.S.R. Championship.

11. N–Q5   NxN
12. PxN

Intriguing but unsatisfactory is 12. N–K6?! PxN 13. Q–R5ch P–N3 14. PxNP N/2–B3! with clear advantage to Black.

12. . . .   N–B4
13. Q–R5!   B–K2

As Tukmakov points out, Black must try to consolidate his King position quickly. Immediately losing is 13. . . . PxN? because of 14. R–K1ch, and little better is 13. . . . P–N3?! because of 14. Q–B3! PxN? 15. R–K1ch K–Q2 16. PxP with White again winning.

14. N–B6   BxBch
15. QxB   P–B3
16. Q–R5ch   Q–B2
17. Q–B3

The opening phase has led to a middlegame position somewhat favorable to White. White's Knight plays an inhibiting role on QB6, and Black can hardly ever afford to exchange it since that will open the way for White's QR and KB. White also has good chances of opening either the Kingside or the Queenside for play against Black's somewhat cramped position. Black's only pride is the protected, passed KP, but this can be of importance only in a far-off endgame.

17. ...	B–N2
18. K–N1	O–O
19. P–KN4	QR–B1
20. B–N2	N–R5?!

White's reply stamps this as a waste of time. Correct is to activate the Queen immediately with 20. . . . Q–B2. If White does nothing, Black can try to carry out the plan . . . N–R5, . . . N–N3, . . . K–R1 followed by . . . NxP, as given by Browne.

21. Q–QR3   N–B4

The QP must be protected, and 21. . . . Q–B2 allows White to get his Queenside play going at no risk: 22. P–B4! N–N3 23. P–B5 N–N5 24. Q–N4!.

22. KR–K1	KR–K1
23. R–K3	Q–B2
24. R–QB1	Q–N3
25. P–N4!?	

White has been preparing to open up the Queenside and does so now. Objectively the plan is fine, though in the existing mutual time shortage the practical risk is considerable. Of course not 25. P–B4?? first since White's Queen is trapped after 25. . . . BxN 26. PxB?! P–N5.

25. ...	N–R5
26. P–B4	PxP

Black has no interest in allowing the smothering 27. P–B5. At the moment his Knight is safe since 27. QxN? allows 27. . . . QxR.

27. RxBP   P–QR4!?

Starting here Black shows great creativity and courage by complicating the position as much as possible. In time pressure this gives good practical winning chances while not really significantly increasing one's losing chances. It's true that 27. . . . Q–N4 28. Q–N3 N–N3 is safer, but after 29. R–B1 White is better in a no-risk situation.

28. Q–N3!

With the simple threat 29. PxP. Wrong is 28. NxRP? Q–N4! 29. RxR RxR 30. NxB Q–B5!, and Black's attack is decisive.

28. ...	B–R3!
29. P–N5!	BxP
30. RxN	R–N1!!

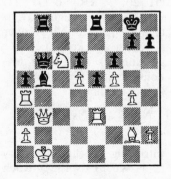

Both sides have been trading blow for blow. Now correct and necessary is the obvious 31. NxR RxN. The play thereafter can become very complicated, and lengthy analysis *after* the game showed best play to be 32. R/4–K4 P–R5 33. Q–N4 Q–B2 34. K–R1!! B–Q6! (34. . . . Q–B8ch 35. Q–N1 QxQch 36. KxQ B–B8ch 37. K–B2 BxB 38. RxRP BxP and thanks to the passed QRP White must be better) 35. QxRch QxQ 36. RxB Q–N3 37. R–K2 P–R6!. White does have a significant material advantage here, but his pieces and King are in a bind so it is not at all easy to make progress. Overall Black must be considered to have good practical drawing chances. Instead White plays . . .

31. R/4–
    K4??   P–R5
32. Q–N4   BxN

So White has not only failed to take Black's Rook but has also, in effect, left his Knight en prise. A tragedy in time pressure, but it is also Black's reward for brave practical play.

33. QxQ   RxQch
34. K–B1   BxP

And so Black is sure of a huge material advantage in a completely secure position. The only practical question remaining is whether he can reach the time control on move 40. Once he does, White immediately resigns.

35. R–Q3   R–B1ch
36. K–Q2   R–N7ch
37. K–K3   BxR
38. BxB   R–N3
39. R–Q5   R–B4
40. R–Q3   K–B1
        White resigns

Chapter 21

Vaganian, Rafael

After Petrosian, the second strongest Armenian is Rafael Vaganian. Born on October 15, 1951, in Erevan, the capital of Armenia, he has lived there all his life. At the age of twenty he became an international grandmaster. He has already taken part in six U.S.S.R. Championships.

Very talented, but erratic, his best international results are 1st at Vrnjacka Banja 1971, 1st at Kragujevac 1974, 2nd–3rd at Hastings 1974/75, 1st–4th at Costa Brava 1975, and 1st at Sao Paulo 1977. Vaganian's 1977 FIDE rating is 2545.

GAME 65

White: T. Ujtumen
(Mongolia)

Black: R. Vaganian
(U.S.S.R.)

Played at Dubna (U.S.S.R.) International Tournament, December 1973, Round 4.

Alekhine Defense
(Four Pawns Attack)

Both sides are quite willing to discuss a modern sharp variation. After the forced variations are finished, White should be able to look forward to the slight initiative of the first player. But Black can't get himself to accept this situation and continually insists on sacrificing a piece. In due course White accepts the sacrifice, consolidates his material advantage, and wins in good style. A good example of steady nerves winning over impetuousness.

1. P–K4   N–KB3

The Alekhine Defense is named for former World Champion Alexander Alekhine, who introduced it into modern tournament practice against A. Steiner at Budapest 1921. Its strategic point is to force White's center pawns forward, then challenge in the hope of annihilating them. This kind of "hypermodern" approach became quite popular in the 1920s. The debit side of the strategy is that unless Black is able to destroy White's center, this center will severely cramp Black's game. The Alekhine has never achieved broad popularity, but Fischer's two successes (one win and one draw) in his 1972 match against Spassky means, to me, that this defense must be fundamentally sound.

2. P–K5   N–Q4
3. P–QB4

In conjunction with the next two moves, this is White's sharpest approach. Also quite good and very popular in the 1970s is the modern variation 3. P–Q4 P–Q3 4. N–KB3; White keeps some central superiority and is less exposed than in the Four Pawns Attack.

3. . . .   N–N3
4. P–Q4   P–Q3
5. P–B4!

This decidedly establishes the Four Pawns Attack. Four of White's pawns are at present in essentially total control of the center. However, this means that White has been neglecting piece development. Can Black take advantage of this factor? This is the whole crux of the variation. Instead of the text, the Exchange Variation, 5. PxP, is harmless.

5. . . .   PxP
6. BPxP   N–B3

Much too sharp is 6. . . . P–QB4?! because of the simple 7. P–Q5, but a completely good (and in fact more common) alternative is 6. . . . B–B4.

7. B–K3   B–B4
8. N–QB3   P–K3
9. N–B3   B–K2

A relatively quiet move in the Four Pawns. Sharper are 9. . . . Q–Q2 and 9. . . . N–N5. The latter seems equivalent to the text in quality, but the former (with the plan . . . O–O–O) is too risky. The idea behind the text is simply to castle Kingside and then challenge White's center with . . . P–KB3. To hope for any advantage White must play sharply before Black's development is complete. The older 10. B–K2 O–O 11. O–O P–B3! allows Black eventually to achieve full equalization.

10. P–Q5!   N–N5

The obvious alternative is the interpolation of 10. . . . PxP 11. PxP and only then 11. . . . N–N5. According to the latest theory, this works out to White's benefit after 12. N–Q4 B–Q2 13. P–K6!.

11. R–B1

But here, without the center-clarifying pawn exchange, 11. N–Q4 is not quite as effective, and Black gains good counterchances after 11. . . . B–N3 12. P–QR3 P–QB4! 13. NxP PxN 14. PxN BPxP.

11. . . .   PxP

Black has nothing better. Interesting is 11. . . . P–KB3, but after 12. P–QR3 N–R3 13. P–KN4! BxP 14. R–KN1, White establishes a very strong attacking position, as in Velimirovic–Gipslis, Havana 1971, for example.

12. P–QR3   P–B4!?

Black's most active attempt to counterattack. Somewhat in White's favor are both 12. . . . N–R3 13. PxP O–O 14. BxN PxB 15. Q–Q4! and 12. . . . NxP!? 13. BxN PxB 14. PxN QxQch 15. RxQ BxP 16. O–O B–Q6 17. R–B2.

13. PxN   P–Q5
14. BxP!

White must give back part of the bounty. 14. PxP?! is unsatisfactory because after 14. . . . PxN the strength of the QBP gives White no time for 15. PxN, and after the defensive 15. PxP QxQch 16. RxQ N–R5 Black is all right.

14. . . .   PxB
15. NxP!?

An interesting psychological moment. According to analysis by Hort, White can obtain a safe, slightly superior position with 15. QxP BxP 16. P–B5 N–Q4 17. B–N5ch B–Q2 18. BxBch! QxB 19. O–O. The double-edged text shows that he's going for more.

15. . . .   B–N3?!

Black apparently has no time for this "defensive" move. The critical line is 15. . . . Q–N1!? 16. Q–K2 B–N3 17. P–B5 N–Q2, and now both 18. P–B6! and 18. N–Q5! should lead to some advantage for White. Practical tests are, however, in order.

16. P–B5

What is Black to do now? He's already a pawn down, 16. . . . N–Q2?! 17. P–K6 is miserable, and 16. . . . N–Q4?! 17.

B–N5ch K–B1 18. O–O with
the threat of 19. N–K6ch is
plain horrible. 16. . . . B–N4
is possible, however, though
after 17. R–R1! N–Q2 18. N–
B3! the best that Black can
hope to achieve is the game
continuation.

16. . . .   O–O!?

A suggestion of Timman's,
with the idea that after 17. PxN
BxP Black's active pieces have
good practical chances of
bothering White's uncastled
King. This doesn't mean that
Black's piece sacrifice is fully
sound, but he does get real practical chances.

17. N–B3!

After ten minutes of thought
the Mongolian IM decides on
the best psychological and practical course; i.e., why give
Black any chances at all?

17. . . .   N–Q2
18. B–N5!   B–N4?!

This does not work out well,
but Tal's suggestion of 18. . . .
N–N1 is hardly the kind of
course that he himself would
choose in a game. After 19.
O–O, White is better.

19. R–R1!

What now, Knight? 19. . . .
N–N1 is worse than before
since after 20. QxQ Black must
recapture with the Bishop. Ob-

jectively this is probably the
way to go, but it goes too much
against Vaganian's grain. Therefore he prefers to ditch his
Knight with . . .

19. . . .   NxKP?!
20. NxN   Q–B3
21. N–B3   QR–Q1

Black has a lovely position,
except that he's a whole piece
down.

22. Q–N3   B–R5ch?

Voluntarily exchanging one
of the attackers soon leads to a
halt of Black's attack. Considering that White's KB takes away
the important K1-square from
a Black Rook, it is logical to
put a question to the Bishop
with 22. . . . P–QR3!?.

23. NxB   QxN/5ch
24. P–N3   Q–R6
25. N–K2   Q–N7
26. R–KN1   Q–K5

This "centralization" leads to
naught, but any hope after 26.
. . . QxRP 27. Q–KB3, etc., is
also very meager.

27. K–B2   P–QR3
28. B–B4   R–Q7
29. KR–Q1!   Q–Q5ch
30. Q–K3!

This puts a definitive end to
Black's attack and hopes. The
incautious 30. K–K1? allows 30.
. . . R–K1!! with good attacking
prospects for Black because 31.

RxR?? is refuted by 31. . . .
Q–N8 mate!

30. . . .   Q–B3ch
31. Q–B4   QxQch

Forced to save the Rook but
practically chanceless.

32. PxQ   RxP
33. R–Q4   R–K1
34. R–R2!   RxP?!

Of course, 34. . . . R/1xNch?
35. BxR RxR allows 36. R–Q8
mate! With the text Black hopes
to tempt White into 35. BxPch??
BxB 36. RxR BxR with Black
better. But White has a neat
zwischenzug.

35. P–B5!   Black resigns

Additional material loss is
unavoidable since 35. . . . BxP
is met by 36. BxPch, and 35.
. . . B–R4 fails to 36. N–N3.
In the game Black apparently
did play on a few more moves,
but my Soviet source didn't
deem them worth publishing.

Chapter 22

Vasiukov, Evgeny

Evgeny Vasiukov, an international grandmaster since 1961, is another strong Soviet grandmaster who generally scores better in foreign tournaments than in national ones. Born on March 5, 1933, in Moscow, he has lived there all his life and has been champion of the city five times. Vasiukov participated in ten U.S.S.R. Championships and was on two winning teams to the World Student Championships.

Vasiukov has gained at least nine first prizes in international tournaments, including Belgrade 1961, Varna 1964, the very strong Manila 1974, and Zalaegerszeg 1977. He is coauthor of the book *Mikhail Tchigorin*, published in 1972. Vasiukov's 1977 FIDE rating is 2565.

GAME 66

White: E. Vasiukov
(U.S.S.R.)

Black: Z. Ribli
(Hungary)

Played at Wijk aan Zee (Netherlands) International Tournament, January 1973, Round 8.

Pirc/Modern Defense

A perfect game by the young Hungarian master (long since a grandmaster). With original and creative play he comes into the middlegame with some advantage. White realizes that his position is inferior and by throwing caution to the winds starts a sharp, dangerous attack against Black's Kingside. Combining defense and counterattack to an exquisite degree, Black holds White off long enough to generate his own winning combination.

1.	P–K4	P–KN3
2.	P–Q4	B–N2
3.	N–KB3	

A somewhat less active approach than the 3. N–QB3 P–Q3 4. P–B4 of Game 36.

3.	. . .	P–Q3
4.	B–QB4	

That Black has not yet developed his KN gives White a broader range of possible setups. The text followed by 5. Q–K2 is a favorite of Tal's, among others. White strives to get in an early, active P–K5.

4.	. . .	N–KB3
5.	Q–K2	N–B3!?

Rarely played, either before or after this game. Black issues an immediate challenge to White's center and is unafraid of the coming P–K5. More cautious, and common, are 5. . . . P–B3 and 5. . . . O–O.

6. P–K5!?

A logical attempt to refute Black's last move. Safe and sound is 6. P–B3, but it is questionable whether White can then achieve more than the tiniest of edges.

6.	. . .	PxP

Forced, since after 6. . . . N–Q2? Black gets hit by 7.

BxPch! KxB 8. N–N5ch, and Black is lucky to come out with only one black eye after 8. . . . K–K1 9. N–K6 NxQP! 10. NxBch K–B2 11. Q–B4ch KxN 12. QxN.

7.	PxP	N–KN5
8.	B–QN5??	

This is completely incomprehensible. White misplaces the KB and pays the price of a lost tempo for this "privilege." This can already be considered the losing move. Thematic and correct is unquestionably, 8. P–K6!, as in Kotkov–Razuvaev, Moscow 1972. Black then must prove that he can equalize.

8.	. . .	B–Q2
9.	B–KB4	O–O
10.	N–B3	

The punishment was severe in Vogt–Szymczak, Lublin 1974, after the further time-wasting 10. P–KR3?: 10. . . . KNxKP! 11. QBxN BxB 12. BxN (12. NxB loses to 12. . . . N–Q5) 12. . . . BxP 13. Q–N5 BxR 14. BxB P–QB3 15. Q–Q3 Q–B2, and Black went on to win easily. The text, by protecting the KB, prevents this tactical possibility.

10.	. . .	P–QR3
11.	B–B4	P–QN4
12.	B–QN3	P–N5
13.	N–QR4	N–R4
14.	O–O–O	Q–K1

Black has been pushing White around on the whole board and now threatens the obvious 15. . . . BxN, winning the strayed Knight. After the "normal" 15. N–B5 comes 15. . . . B–N4 16. Q–K1 NxBch 17. RPxN P–QR4 followed by 18. . . . P–R5 and a strong attack for Black. Even though White's position is in theory defensible, in practice such an approach is very often chanceless. Therefore, Vasiukov decides on a radically different course: White sacrifices material to get the attack. True, in the end this will fail, but only because the young Ribli plays as The Great Ribli.

15. P–KR3!? B–N4

The first small mine to be avoided is 15. . . . NxBP? 16. RxB!, and it is White who gains material.

16. Q–Q2 NxBP!
17. QxN BxN
18. Q–B5

There is absolutely no future in 18. Q–R4? NxBch 19. RPxN

B–QB3 20. N–N5 P–R3 21. N–B3 BxN 22. PxB P–N4, etc.

18. . . . NxBch
19. RPxN B–QB3
20. N–Q4!?

Continuing on his reckless policy, White throws two more pawns into the fray. True, 20. QxNP reestablishes material equality, but after 20. . . . P–QR4 followed by 21. . . . P–R5 Black's attack rolls on and White's prospects are bleak.

20. . . . BxNP
21. KR–N1 BxRP
22. N–B6 K–R1!
23. R–Q2 P–QR4!!

A brilliant concept: Black's QR now will be able to function both to defend the Kingside and to attack the KP. In addition, Black will be ready for a timely . . . P–QR5 advance.

24. R–R2 R–R3!
25. NxKP R–K3
26. N–Q5 B–B4
27. Q–B2!?

White again finds the best practical chance; i.e., bringing the Queen over to the Kingside. Clearly unsatisfactory is 27. NxBP?! because of 27. . . . RxP! 28. NxQ (28. BxR?! QxB 29. QxQ BxQ with a fork on the Rook and the Knight) 28. . . . RxQ 29. NxB KxN 30. B–R6ch K–N1 31. BxR KxB and Black's three connected Kingside passed pawns are a winning advantage.

27. . . .   Q–Q1!

Black must prevent White's threatened Q–KR4. Losing is 27. . . . RxP? 28. Q–R4 P–R4 29. N–B6 Q–K2 30. QxPch!! and White mates. After the text White's Knight is en prise.

28. N–B6!?

A last try, aiming at weakening the dark squares around Black's King. The sacrifice 28. RxPch is unsound after 28. . . . KxR 29. Q–R2ch K–N1 30. R–R1 P–N4!, and 28. R–Q1 is met by the simple 28. . . . BxKP! (Ribli).

28. . . .	**BxN**
29. PxB	**QxP**
30. B–N5	**Q–K4**
31. Q–R4	**P–R4**

Black is up a whole Kingside, three pawns, but his Kingside is now full of holes. White has four pieces trained along open lines against it. If left alone, White can create dangerous threats. But Black sees that White's King position is also inherently loose and combines attack and defense so adroitly that the game is over in fewer than ten moves.

32. B–B4	**Q–K5**
33. Q–N5	**KR–K1!**
34. K–N1	

34. RxPch K–N1 35. R–R2 gives Black time for the decisive 34. . . . R–QB3!. Therefore

White tries to get the King to relative safety.

34. . . .   P–QR5!

No rest for the weary! Now 35. PxP allows 35. . . . P–N6, and 35. RxPch K–N1 36. Q–R4 is met by 36. . . . Q–Q5! with White's attack stopped and Black's ready to accelerate. What White selects is no better.

35. Q–R6ch	**K–N1**
36. QxP	**Q–K8ch**
37. K–R2	

Obviously 37. RxQ? RxRch followed by 38. . . . PxQ costs White a Rook. And after 37. B–B1 Black has another tactical shot: 37. . . . BxPch! 38. KxB (or 38. K–R1 QxBch) 38. . . . R–QB3ch, etc.

37. . . .	**PxPch**
38. KxP	**R–K6ch!**
39. BxR	**QxBch**
40. P–B3	**B–K3ch**
	White resigns

It's either mate or a decisive loss of material.

GAME 67

White: K. Langeweg
(Netherlands)

Black: E. Vasiukov
(U.S.S.R.)

Played at Wijk aan Zee (Netherlands) International Tournament, January 1973, Round 13.

King's Indian Defense

White chooses an unassuming buildup against the King's Indian. By leaving the QBP back home, White renders his center less vulnerable to attack. Black is not able to come up with a coherent plan for counterplay and soon finds himself in a cramped, prospectless position. White is able to bring about a favorable two-Bishop endgame, in which he also gets an outside passed pawn. When Black plays too passively in an endgame he is ground down with zugzwang motifs. Overall a pleasant game for White all the way through. At no time is he in the slightest danger of losing but always has good winning chances. This is an excellent situation for beating the Russians.

1.	N–KB3	N–KB3
2.	P–KN3	P–KN3
3.	B–N2	B–N2
4.	O–O	O–O
5.	P–Q4	P–Q3
6.	N–B3	

Of course the "normal" 6. P–B4 leads to one of the usual variations in the King's Indian —see, for example, Game 60. The text is an unassuming approach to the coming play. White voluntarily neglects to exert fuller central influence, thereby giving Black fewer chances for central counterplay. In addition, White saves a tempo for development. White's approach is not at all harmless for practical play, and Black must defend correctly not to land in a passive, constricted situation.

| 6. . . . | QN–Q2 |

Aiming for . . . P–K4 is both good and logical. Bobby Fischer once made the claim that after 6. . . . P–Q4 *Black* was better. With all due respect, such a conclusion is rather extravagant, and after 7. R–K1, aiming for P–K4, White still has the usual first-move advantage.

| 7. | P–K4 | P–K4 |
| 8. | P–QR4 | PxP?! |

By giving up the center, Black unquestionably hands over central superiority to White. Such action should be taken only when a clear and immediate benefit can be derived, and that is not the case here. The strategically proper approach for Black is 8. . . . P–QR4! 9. B–K3 R–K1 10. R–K1 P–B3! 11. PxP PxP 12. N–Q2 N–N3 13. P–B3 B–K3 14. Q–

K2 N/B–Q2 with equality, as
in Sosonko–Dueball, Mann-
heim 1975.

9. NxP   R–K1?!

Trifunovic correctly points
out that White's next should
be prevented by 9. . . . P–QR4.
As played Black runs into the
danger of being suffocated because of a lack of room.

10. P–R5!   N–B4
11. R–K1   N–N5?!

Achieves nothing for Black
except loss of time, whereas
White gets a very strong center.
Trifunovic is again right in sug-
gesting 11. . . . B–N5!? 12. P–
B3 B–Q2 as a more workable
plan of development.

12. P–R3   N–K4
13. P–B4   N/K–Q2
14. B–K3   N–B1
15. Q–Q2   P–QR3
16. P–QN4   N/4–Q2
17. N–N3   N–B3
18. QR–Q1

A position of striking con-
trasts. White controls more
space on the Queenside, in the
center, and on the Kingside,
whereas about the only thing
that Black controls is his back
rank! White's development is
complete, his pieces in attractive, purposeful locations,
whereas Black still has much to
do to get his forces out. White
can methodically prepare for
action along several fronts;
Black has no prospects for
action—only for reaction to
hold off White. Despite his obvious advantages, White must
still work to win the position;
Black is very cramped but he
has no fundamental weaknesses.

18. . . .   B–K3
19. Q–Q3   Q–B1
20. K–R2   BxN?!

One of the general principles
of defending cramped positions
calls for exchanging pieces to
lighten the defensive task.
Black's move is in accordance
with this general approach but
suffers from the specific disadvantages of giving White the
two Bishops and weakening
Black's light squares. Creation
of the doubled QNPs is also
more in White's favor since he
can now expect to develop pressure along the QB-file. Black's
best plan is to try to keep the
status quo with 20. . . . B–Q2,
for example.

21. PxB   Q–K3
22. N–Q5   NxN
23. PxN   Q–Q2

24. B–B2   P–R4
25. RxR!

White plays the whole game in excellent practical style. The exchange of Rooks will ensure that Black gets no attacking chances whatever. This will allow White's Queen and Bishops unperturbed play against Black's Queenside.

25. . . .   RxR
26. R–K1   RxR
27. BxR   N–R2
28. Q–B4!   B–N7

Hardly a great spot for the Bishop, but Black wants to continue . . . N–B3 without blocking off the Bishop.

29. B–B1

With the plan P–QN5, and not bad. Considerably stronger, however, is 29. B–B2!, as Langeweg subsequently pointed out, logically going after the accessible QBP with B–R7 and B–N8. If Black plays similarly to the game, 29. . . . N–B3?!, his Bishop runs the risk of getting trapped after 30. Q–B2! B–R6 31. B–K1.

29. . . .   N–B3
30. B–Q3   K–N2
31. B–Q2   N–N1?!

Black ensures the loss of this endgame by playing as passively as possible. Trifunovic suggests the active 31. . . . Q–N4! 32. QxQ PxQ 33. BxQNP NxP. It is true that after 34. B–B4 N–

K2 35. P–N5 B–Q5! 36. P–R6 PxP 37. PxP P–Q4 the outside passed pawn supported by the two Bishops gives White the better chances, but Black also has a passed pawn and a generally free position; so White's win is not assured.

32. P–N5!

The creation of an outside passed pawn is still White's most promising approach.

32. . . .   PxP
33. QxNP   QxQ
34. BxQ   N–K2
35. B–B4   B–Q5
36. P–QN4   K–B1?!

Again very passive. There is still the opportunity to reach the type of position given after Black's 31st move: 36. . . . P–QB3! 37. PxP PxP to be followed by . . . P–Q4.

37. P–N5   N–B1?!

Here, too, the active move 37. . . . N–B4! has to be better.

38. P–R6

White has achieved his first objective, the outside passed pawn, whereas Black has done nothing but move backward.

38. . . .   P–N3?

Why, oh why, such passivity? 38. . . . PxP is mandatory. Black then has some chance of getting a passed pawn in the center and with it prospects for a draw. After the text, White gets a passed QRP for nothing, since White's QNP and QP easily hold back the three Black pawns. With the text Black hopes that he can keep the position sufficiently blocked to prevent any penetration by White. In practice there is invariably a winning breakthrough, and White finds it readily enough.

39. P–B5!

The start of the loosening-up process. The position is won for White; only the specific winning route is uncertain.

39. . . .	**B–B3**
40. P–R4	**K–N2**
41. PxP	**PxP**
42. K–N2	

The King should actually head for KR3—see move 46. However, since there is nothing Black can do to strengthen his position, this slight delay is immaterial.

42. . . .	**N–R2**
43. K–B3	**K–B2**
44. B–Q3	**K–N2**

45. K–N2	**K–B2**
46. K–R3	**K–N2**
47. P–N4!	**PxPch**

There is no way to prevent White's King from making progress. After 47. . . . K–B2 Langeweg gives the following winning line: 48. PxP PxP 49. B–N5! K–N2 (49. . . . B–K4? allows 50. B–Q8) 50. K–N3 B–K4ch 51. K–B3 B–B3 52. K–B4 B–K4ch 53. K–B5 followed by 54. B–Q8.

48. KxP	**K–B2**
49. B–N5!	**K–N2**
50. BxBch!	**KxB**
51. K–B4	

White now will achieve a zugzwang position, in which Black's Knight will have no move and Black's King will therefore have to give way to its colleague.

51. . . .	**N–B1**
52. B–B4	**N–R2**
53. B–B1!	**N–B1**
54. B–R3	**N–R2**
55. B–Q7	**K–K2**
56. K–N5!	

The ultimate point of the previous maneuvers. If now 56. . . . KxB 57. KxP K–K2 58. K–N7! and the KRP wins, the closest variation being 58. . . . P–B4 59. NPxP e.p. P–N4 60. P–R5 P–N5 61. P–R6 P–N6 62. P–R7 P–N7 63. P–R8=Q P–N8=Q 64. Q–KB8 mate! Black's response is equally hopeless.

56.	. . .	K–B2
57.	K–R6!	K–B3
58.	B–K8!	K–K2
59.	KxP!	P–B4
60.	NPxP e.p	KxB
61.	K–N7	**Black resigns**

Black's even a move behind the variation given after White's 56th move.

GAME 68

White: L. Espig
(East Germany)

Black: E. Vasiukov
(U.S.S.R.)

Played at Dubna (U.S.S.R.) International Tournament, December 1973, Round 2.

Reti Opening

A crush. Vasiukov allows his opponent to build up a strong, secure center, and gets smothered by it. To contain damage in the center, Black is forced to create a fundamental weakness on the Queenside. White goes so resolutely for this weakness that Black decides that his only hope is a nebulous attack on the Kingside. The net result is only that Black's collapse is accelerated. An excellent practical example to conclude the theme of "How to Beat the Russians."

1.	N–KB3	P–Q4
2.	P–B4	P–Q5
3.	P–K3	N–QB3
4.	PxP	NxP
5.	NxN	QxN
6.	N–B3	

Thus far this follows Game 32, in which White played 6. P–Q3. Usually that amounts only to a transposition of moves, but not here.

6. . . .   B–N5?!

Leads to a considerably greater misplacement of the Bishop than of White's Queen. Black's correct equalizing method was given in notes to Game 32: 6. . . . P–K4! 7. P–Q3 P–QB3 8. B–K3 Q–Q3 9. B–K2 N–K2! (on the way to KB4).

7.	Q–R4ch	P–B3
8.	P–Q3	N–B3?!

This hands the center over completely to White. Not quite satisfactory for equality but considerably better is 8. . . . P–K4 9. B–K3 Q–Q2 10. P–B3 B–K3 11. R–Q1! followed by 12. P–

Q4, with White better but not as much as in the game.

9. B–K3   Q–Q1

Or 9. . . . Q–Q2 10. P–Q4 P–K3 11. P–B3 B–KB4 12. O–O–O B–Q3 13. P–KN4 B–N3 14. P–R4 with a clear advantage for White in Keres–Euwe, Nordwijk 1938.

10. P–Q4	P–KN3
11. P–KR3	B–Q2
12. Q–N3	Q–B2
13. B–K2	B–N2
14. O–O	O–O
15. KR–Q1	

White's moves have been as simple as possible, but the net effect is overwhelming. White has a secure central superiority, and his pieces are placed in active, purposeful central direction. Even though Black has no fundamental weakness at the moment, he is in danger of slow death by asphyxiation. How did White's simple moves bring about such a commanding situation? Well, Black's moves were neither simple (witness 6. . . .

B–N5?!) nor accurate (8. . . . N–B3?! instead of 8. . . . P–K4).

15. . . .   K–R1?!

For want of a good plan, Black chooses one which is something like a cross between bad and meaningless. 15. . . . P–K3, trying to inhibit White's P–Q5 advance, has to be better.

| 16. QR–B1 | N–N1?! |
| 17. P–Q5! | P–QB4 |

With control of his Q4-square lessened, Black's best approach is to keep the position as closed as possible. However, White is able to execute a different line-opening plan.

18. Q–R3	P–N3
19. P–QN4!	PxP
20. QxNP	QR–B1
21. N–N5	Q–N1
22. P–QR4!	

White's huge space advantage is unperturbed, and with P–QR5 he threatens to force a fundamental weakness in Black's Queenside pawn formation; i.e., Black will be left with either a weak QRP or a weak QNP. Black tries to get some counterchances by offering to sacrifice his KP.

| 22. . . . | N–R3 |
| 23. N–Q4! | |

But White correctly prefers to keep Black in a total bind. After 23. QxP BxN! 24. BPxN N–B4

followed by 25. . . . NxB the
opposite-color Bishops can give
Black some drawing chances.

23. . . .	Q–Q3
24. Q–Q2!	N–B4
25. NxN	PxN?!

Objectively speaking, the
normal 25. . . . BxN has to be
better, though after 26. P–R5
White's positional advantage is
major. With the text Black
hopes (dreams is probably more
accurate) for some play along
the KN-file.

| 26. P–R5 | Q–N3 |
| 27. P–B4! | P–K3?! |

Black's position is rather
hopeless; even so it's difficult to
see what his last move has to do
with the game.

28. RPxP	RPxP
29. R–N1	R–KN1
30. RxP!	B–KB3

The KB has no effective move
to clear the KN-file, and White
can stop the routine mate threat
routinely. Black's position is
resignable.

31. B–B1	R–N2
32. B–Q4	BxB
33. QxB	P–R3
34. P–B5!	Q–R4
35. P–B6	B–K1
36. P–Q6!	

Passed pawns must be pushed!
Major material loss for Black is
unavoidable. If now 36. . . .
RxP, then 37. R–N8 is the
strongest. Black's reply is even
less satisfactory.

36. . . .	BxP
37. RxB	RxR
38. P–Q7	**Black resigns**

White has a new Queen
coming up.